Charleston Conference Proceedings 2005

Charleston Conference Proceedings 2005

Edited by Beth R. Bernhardt, Tim Daniels, and Kim Steinle

Katina Strauch, Series Editor

LIBRARIES
U N L I M I T E D
A Member of the Greenwood Publishing Group

Westport, Connecticut • London

Library of Congress Cataloging-in-Publication Data

Charleston Conference (25th : 2005 : Charleston, S.C.)
 Charleston Conference proceedings 2005 / edited by Beth R. Bernhardt, Tim Daniels, and Kim Steinle ;
 Katina Strauch, series editor.
     p. cm.
   Includes bibliographical references and index.
   ISBN 1-59158-475-2 (pbk : alk. paper)
   1. Library science—United States—Congresses. 2. Serials librarianship—United States—Congresses.
 3. Collection development (Libraries)—United States—Congresses. 4. Libraries—Information
 technology—United States—Congresses. 5. Library science—Technological innovations—Congresses.
 6. Electronic information resources—Congresses. 7. Libraries and electronic publishing—Congresses.
 8. Scholarly electronic publishing—Congresses. 9. Library cooperation—United States—Congresses.
 10. Academic libraries—Relations with faculty and curriculum—United States—Congresses. I.
 Bernhardt, Beth R. II. Daniels, Tim, 1963- III. Steinle, Kim. IV. Strauch, Katina P., 1946- V. Title.
 Z672.5.C53 2005
 020—dc22   2006023753

British Library Cataloguing in Publication Data is available.

Library of Congress Catalog Number: 2006023753
ISBN: 1-59158-475-2

First published in 2006

Libraries Unlimited, 88 Post Road West, Westport, CT 06881
A Member of the Greenwood Publishing Group, Inc.
www.lu.com

Printed in the United States of America

The paper used in this book complies with the
Permanent Paper Standard issued by the National
Information Standards Organization (Z39.48-1984).

10 9 8 7 6 5 4 3 2 1

Table of Contents

Table of Contents 1

Technology

Product Development

Collaboration

Books

Consortia Deals

Miscellaneous

The 2005 Charleston Conference, held November 2-5, 2006, was our 25th. The theme was "Things are seldom what they seem." More than 1,000 librarians, publishers, vendors, aggregators, and consultants attended.

This volume represents many of the papers, issues, and discussions that consumed us and, indeed, continue to consume us. The book is divided into eight sections encompassing journals, collection development, technology, product development, collaboration, books, consortial deals, and miscellaneous subjects. There is no question that, with the advent of the electronic revolution, the library is no longer the sole source of information. For those of us in acquisitions, collection development, serials, and electronic resources the need to justify the budget and what we do is increasingly more challenging.

Yet we all know that the library as a place is crucial. As a student said recently: "I like the silence and the scholarliness of the library. I like being surrounded by books. And I feel cultured when I am in the library."

The professionalism to which we have devoted our lives must adapt and change, and these papers represent many of the ways that we are adapting and innovating in our rapidly changing environment.

We would like to extend our thanks to Beth Bernhardt, Tim Daniels, and Kim Steinle, who have edited this volume of proceedings. It is never easy to gather, edit, and organize dozens of papers. Beth, Tim, and Kim have done an admirable job and met all of their deadlines. And our thanks as well to the entire Libraries Unlimited crew who have labored to make this volume a reality. Enjoy!

The 2006 Charleston Conference has as its theme "Unintended Consequences." Come on down to Charleston this November 8-11 and join in the discussions and debates. In the meantime, please visit our Web site at http://www.katina.info/conference.

See you there!

Cordially,

Katina Strauch
Founder, Charleston Conference
July 31, 2006

Preface and Acknowledgments

The Charleston Conference celebrated its twentieth-fifth anniversary this year! The Conference continues to be a major event for information exchange among librarians, vendors, and publishers. Almost everyone who has ever attended the Charleston Conference tells us how informative and thought-provoking the sessions continue to be. The Conference provides a collegial atmosphere in which librarians can talk freely and directly with publishers and vendors about issues facing them and their libraries. All this interaction occurs in the wonderful city of Charleston, South Carolina. This is the second year that Beth R. Bernhardt has put together the proceedings from the Conference and the first year for Tim Daniels and Kimberly Steinle. We are pleased to share some of the learning experience that we, and other attendees, had at the conference.

The theme of the 2005 Charleston Conference was "Things Are Seldom What They Seem." While not all presenters prepared written versions of their remarks, enough did so that we are able to include an overview of such subjects as journal management issues, institutional repositories, library filtering, collaborative product development, the future of books, how scientist are using books, and the growth of consortia. All of these topics are of high interest to library community and can be looked at from numerous viewpoints.

Katina Strauch, founder of the conference, is an inspiration to us. Her enthusiasm for the conference and the proceedings was motivating. We hope you, the reader, find the papers as informative as we did and that they encourage the continuation of the ongoing dialogue among librarians, vendors, and publishers that can only enhance the learning and research experience for the ultimate user.

Signed,

Co-Editors of the 24th Charleston Conference proceedings

Beth R. Bernhardt

Beth R. Bernhardt, Electronic Journals / Document Delivery Librarian, University of North Carolina at Greensboro

Tim Daniels, Learning Commons Coordinator, Georgia State University

Kimberly Steinle, Library Relations Manager, Duke University Press

Introduction

Journals continue to be a major focus of the Charleston Conference. Open access journals and their influence on the publishing industry were addressed during several key presentations. Other serials issues included serials review processes, journal articles, online access to developing countries through HINARI, and embedded digital objects

Journals

ACCOUNT MANAGEMENT WEB SITES: STREAMLINING THE ADMINISTRATION OF SUBSCRIPTIONS

Adam Chesler, Assistant Director for Sales and Library Relations, American Chemical Society, Washington, D.C.

Jill Emery, Director, Electronic Resources Program, University of Houston Libraries, Texas

Abstract

The relationship between publisher and librarian is nearly as complex as the technology that is changing the way information is published and distributed. To better organize the administrative process, some publishers are developing Web-based tools to streamline license, subscription, and account management. What can be managed through these sites (institutional branding, OpenURLs, IP updates)? What are some of the features necessary to make such a site useful for both librarians and publishers? What are the limitations? Are publishers comfortable giving subscribers a gateway into their access management systems? Will such sites enhance or degrade customer service?

This chapter explores these and other questions and addresses important issues for publishers and librarians to consider as they aim to manage more efficiently their business partnership.

Account Management

With an increasing number of libraries ordering electronic journal content directly from publishers, it is becoming incumbent upon providers to manage customer information more adroitly than in the past. Part of this entails allowing librarians access to some basic, and much account-specific, information, to ensure the smooth processing of orders and renewals. Account administration Web sites, located on publisher Web sites, are one means of managing account management process. However, there are no existing standards for what information is required. An informal meeting of nearly 50 publishers, librarians, subscription agents, and gateway hosts in Charleston spent some time discussing the key elements any such site might include, as well as some best left either in public spaces or excluded entirely.

A majority of the participants indicated that the following elements would be useful components of a "turnkey" account administration Web page:

- **IP addresses**. While it is not likely that publishers would allow direct connections to their access control systems, this would provide a place for librarians to enter updates, which would then automatically be routed to the appropriate person at the publisher and would save numerous e-mails/phone calls.

- **OpenURL server information**: Librarians want to upload this information online, rather than relay it via phone or e-mail. Similarly to IP addresses, this would not happen in real-time, but rather would reduce the time spent transmitting this information to the publisher.

- **Branding information**: Many publishers are offering institutions real estate on selected Web pages, to allow libraries to inform users that access is provided by the library by inserting their names or logo on selected pages. The administration site would be a logical place for librarians to provide this information to the publisher.

- **Contact information**: Publishers should list the people responsible for providing library support, on a resource-by-resource basis. For instance, if a publisher is providing electronic access to journal content as well as databases, the appropriate people for each product should be noted, as often customer service or support staff for one product do not manage others. This was considered important for gateway providers as well, as they manage access to content from dozens of publishers and different people or teams may provide support for specific groups of publishers.

- **Title lists**: Librarians would like to see titles for which they have paid distinguished from those made available either as promotions (trials, which should include the time period for which they'll be available) or part of a consortial agreement. Under the umbrella of the "Big Deal," libraries may have access to titles to which they do not necessarily have paid subscriptions; access may be provided for no fee or for a participation fee through a consortium. Librarians prefer some way of distinguishing between the types of access. Similarly, there may be titles that are not available to a particular institution, and an indication of which are only accessible via pay-per-view (at least, from that publisher's site) would be helpful.

- Also in the title list, the **start and end dates** of subscriptions and content access periods should be noted. Does a subscription include access to all previously published material, or to material published in the last few years? Or just the current year? When does access expire? Is it "perpetual," or is it deactivated upon cancellation?

- While many publisher licenses include similar information, there are invariably differences, sometimes in key areas. This means that any one library may have hundreds of similar, but nevertheless slightly different, rights for content from hundreds of publishers. **Specific license information** describing the rights and privileges associated with the content being offered would be helpful. While there is work being done on standardized license terms and their expression, until the time when everyone is using the same license for all content, or at least until basic terms mean the same thing to all parties, having a breakdown of basic permissions would be useful to administrators.

- A list of **journal home page URLs**, including ISSNs and the URLs for table of contents pages, would make cataloging easier.

- The account administration site would be the place to provide a link to **usage statistics** and supporting information (including descriptions/explanations).

- Librarians would like to have **payment/ordering and agent information** for each subscription noted. This would be of assistance when questions about subscription order processing arose; the basic information would be in one place and make tracking down the root of problems easier. This would include payment posting information and available grace periods per title.

One item that was universally considered inappropriate was promotional material. Librarians were comfortable with links to newsletters or other marketing pages, but did not want them cluttering an account administration site; the consensus was that this type of site should be strictly oriented toward account administration. There were other pieces of useful information that librarians felt should actually be made publicly available, not "hidden" on a password-protected site viewed only by account administrators (this did not mean that there couldn't be links to these locations from the account administrator site). These included the following:

- **Troubleshooting** and help desk information, including FAQs and instructions for use, as this information was often more immediately relevant to users than librarians.

- Scheduled **maintenance (down-time) notifications**, so users could plan their browsing activity accordingly.

- **Content posting updates**, flagging the release of new issues of each journal.

- **Publication history**, noting the start (and, if relevant, end) dates for each title, along with indications of past title and/or publisher changes.

- Details about **persistent linking structures** (e.g., DOIs) for use with electronic course pack programs (such as Blackboard). This would allow professors to set up and maintain connections to required or recommended reading.

- **Citation-download program information**. Indications of availability and set-up instructions so users could quickly download citations in their research work via packages such as RefWorks or EndNote.

While there are no doubt other elements that should (and should not) be included at an account administration Web site, the idea itself appears to be a good one for publishers to pursue if they are truly committed to handling orders in a robust and service-oriented fashion.

EMBEDDED DIGITAL OBJECTS AND THE FUTURE OF ACADEMIC PUBLISHING

Gregory A. Mitchell, Assistant Director, Resource Management, University of Texas—Pan American Library Edinburg, Texas

Tamara J. Remhof, Collection Development Librarian, South Texas College, McAllen, Texas

Introduction

Our topic concerns embedding digital objects, such as video and audio clips, in the electronic version of journal articles. We first examine how this process works, then look at the potential we see in this technology for some exciting advances in scholarly communication. Finally, we summarize the results of a survey that we conducted with journal publishers, to gain insights about their perspective on the future of embedded digital objects.

Our hypothesis is that the rapid development of video, audio, and graphics—which are digital objects—and the capability to deliver these digital objects over the Web, have enormous potential to transform communications.

Digital Publishing and Delivery Environment

The salient point is that almost all communication media today have become digital. Whether a PowerPoint presentation, a Word document, a spreadsheet, courseware such as Blackboard or WebCT, or an electronic journal article in Adobe Acrobat—all are digital objects.

Powerful new capabilities are available because of this digital format. Each digital object can contain other digital objects within it, with each of these embedded digital objects being video, audio, graphics, or text. Just as important, all of this can be delivered to users over the Web.

Even if one recognizes the technological possibility, the question may still arise: But is it all bells & whistles? We think not, because even though it could be misused in that way, it really represents an opportunity for improved communication. Using video or audio can allow you to describe things in a glance or in a few seconds of sound, rather than writing your way around and around a topic. If a picture is worth a thousand words, then imagine what a moving picture can do for you! For a virtual tour, a surgical procedure, or a dance step, it is clearly better than text alone. Plus there are the nuances that come with nonverbal communication that can be displayed—facial expressions, gestures, vocal inflections, and so on. Finally, when thinking about our digital communication capabilities in the context of learning styles, 40% of us—the largest single group—fall into the category known as visual learners. Video is a great way to teach a great many people.

Why is this coming up now? To put it briefly, we see three major factors that have come together at the right time to enable the production and dissemination of digital objects that include multimedia: technology, cost, and psychological factors.

Technology has advanced—we have ever more powerful personal computers and higher quality consumer video, more sophisticated software, and higher speed (broadband) transmission. In addition, the file sizes needed for video and audio objects have greatly decreased due to the huge amounts of compression possible for multimedia files. For example, at University of Texas–Pan American, we once shot 90 seconds of video of our provost that was 355 MB of raw video, but once compressed for delivery on a Web page, it went down to about 3.5 MB. So today's technology makes it possible for the average person to shoot content, edit and compress it on his or her own workstation, and then transmit it fast. Meanwhile, the costs for this increasing power and sophistication have decreased. The happy anomaly with technology is that we continue to get more and pay less.

Finally, there are the psychological aspects. Multimedia is the new, new thing, it is hot and attracts people's attention—and competition. As you see one company or campus start to implement this, you see competition start to jump on it, too. Video clips, animation, and music are pervasive on Web sites already; our theory is that this capability will soon infuse electronic publishing as well.

Illustrations

Currently we see two methods that can be employed to begin embedding digital objects in journal articles. The first is to simply embed a link within the article that points to a digital object—this is sort of like an embedded object, but not really quite all the way there yet. We did find some examples of publishers doing this (see *System* 32, no. 4 [December 2004], on Elsevier's *Science Direct* Web site for examples of articles with links to digital objects).

The other method, and the one that shows the real potential of this idea, is to embed objects so that they are downloaded and viewed with the document itself. For example, there is a demonstration piece from Adobe (http://www.adobe.com/products/acrobat/pdfs/a7_tryme_gb.pdf). It is not an article, but it is a PDF file, which is what publishers use for articles online.

There are some potential problems. The question arises: If this idea is both powerful and possible, why don't we see it in journals already? Briefly, some of the same areas that have made it possible to embed digital objects also remain areas of some concern.

Technology Problems

To be able to see these digital objects, they need to be encoded on the publisher's end, transmitted, and then read with some sort of viewer on the user's end. So the encoder/viewer software needs to be ubiquitous, easy to install, and free—or many people just won't bother to use it. Windows Media, Quicktime, RealPlayer, and Flash all fit in here.

Second, even when compressed, video files can get big, and if an author used lots of them, it could slow things down. It is useful to remember that a T1 line is only 1.5 mps of shared bandwidth, whereas most LANs operate on the 10/100/1000 mps standard.

Because of file sizes and data transmission concerns, a publisher would need to decide whether to deliver the files as a download in a complete package with the document, or stream the multimedia files. Downloading can be done with any server; it works best with smaller files but can slow down the document load to the desktop. Streaming will allow the use of larger files and faster loads of material to the desktop, but it necessitates a connection back to a streaming server to display the multimedia.

There will be a burden on publishers to store these multimedia files and keep them accessible in the future. Whatever standard or format the publisher uses, you can be sure that there will be new standards, new releases of software in the future. As these migrations occur, either they will need to be backward-compatible with previous versions, or publishers will need to reprocess all those files to the new standard or release. Remember the 5¼-inch floppy?

Finally, there is the problem of how to account for this rich media content in the traditional paper version of the journal. One logical way is suggested by the approach taken at *Science Direct*. A note is inserted at the end of the article, directing the reader to a Web address to view the media content that is contained in the online article. It does seem preferable to distributing a CD with the journal.

Cultural Problems

When we began thinking about this project, we were intrigued by the idea that we had seen multimedia used in other venues for years, yet not in our online journals. It seemed that the technology problems were not insurmountable, so there could be other obstacles that are more cultural or psychological in nature.

One observation has to do with the difference in culture that exists between the Web and academia. A lot of things happen very quickly on the Web in general, it's oriented to a certain extent to younger audiences, it's hip, it's fast. Many of the people who create on the Web are part of the MTV generation. But in this hip Web world we deliver journal content to a rather conservative academic market that is stodgy and slow to change.

Another observation was that this technology is better suited to some disciplines than others. It may be a great way to illustrate a dance step or surgical technique, but it would be harder to apply in history, for example, or philosophy. However, for the last two semesters at the University of Texas–Pan American, a history professor required all of his students to come into the library and learn how to edit video so that they can record presentations instead of writing the traditional history research paper.

Finally, there is the traditional problem of people simply needing to learn something new. Ever seen faculty who had a problem with that? Many campuses still have the old curmudgeon who reviles the OPAC. Even though it is relatively cheap and easy for anyone to produce multimedia files to embed in articles, some article authors will be hard-pressed to do so.

There could be potential legal problems, we thought, but as we investigated this, we found that the same rules that apply to diligent scholarship in print apply as well to the electronic environment.

First, if the author does produce the video or audio files that are used in that author's article, then there certainly isn't a problem. But what if the author samples someone else's work? For example, the author writes an article about Latin jazz, and illustrates a point with a clip from *Buena Vista Social Club*. What then? We consulted with our University of Texas system copyright attorney on this, and here is what she said: The ability to use clips of another's work is covered by fair use; the clips (like quotes) should be small, attributed, and germane to the author's point.

We decided it was time for a reality check. Even if we see embedding digital objects in journal articles as a powerful idea that is entirely plausible to implement, how do the publishers see this? We decided to ask them.

Survey and Results

We began with a list of 10 publishers that we saw as successful and that made many journals available in electronic format. We contacted each of them, told them about our idea, and asked if they would be willing to respond to a brief survey. We sent out the survey to the seven publishers that responded to our query. We got four replies, but only three completed the entire survey. One of the problems with getting responses may have been the terminology. We seemed to have confused one of the publishers because he was wondering if we meant multimedia in general or just embedding. Following is a summary of our questions and the responses we received.

1. Are you familiar with the ability to embed digital objects within other electronic objects?

   All three respondents were familiar with embedding digital objects.

2. Has your organization considered using embedded digital objects in the electronic version of your journals?

   One organization said no, it wasn't considering using embedded digital objects, one said it was, and the other said it was already doing it in the HTML versions.

3. Does your organization see the use of embedded digital objects as a viable future for publishing?

   The third question brought out some interesting points. One respondent said it had experimented with it but users weren't geared to it, so the publisher ended up going back to print to make it commercially sustainable; another was concerned with the additional cost the editing and proofing would require; and the third simply said yes.

4. Has your organization tried to publish anything with embedded digital objects in it?

   Two of the respondents indicated that they had published items with embedded digital objects and one hadn't.

5. What do you see as potential problems?

   Several problems were mentioned: one respondent was concerned about the time and costs in creating and editing digital content and supporting the additional technology. Another saw numerous difficulties, one being the long-term usability of the technical formats, another the inability of some Third World countries to have the speed needed to access the document with the embedded objects. The inability of the different platforms such as Linux to support objects that were done in MS Word or Excel was also seen as a drawback; and the size of the file was considered an obstacle.

6. What do you see as potential benefits?

   The publishers saw benefits in the ability of the user to interact with the content and the functionality of downloading with one click; one said authors would benefit from this because it might make it easier to communicate a point.

7. How do you think that readers would react to this capability?

   All felt the users would enjoy this as long as it went smoothly with no glitches.

8. How does your organization currently produce PDF files?

   All three of the publishers are producing their PDF files by scanning older files and new ones straight from the electronic text using methodology that allows them to include embedded objects.

9. If you were to implement this, would it be in all versions?

   Two of the publishers said they would implement it in the HTML versions, and one said it might add the PDF in the future. Another said it was only doing one version, PDF.

10. Would you be likely to add this capability to previously published materials?

    None would add this to previously published materials. This would have to be a "revised" version.

11. Which journals/disciplines do you see as likely adopters?

    One of the publishers wasn't sure who would adopt this, another didn't want to limit to only one discipline because he felt it depended on what the author was able to do, and the third said medical and life sciences would be the most likely adopters.

Conclusion

We have seen that multimedia can be a very powerful element as an embedded object in an electronic journal article, with the potential to improve communication. We have also seen that it is feasible and economical to do, yet some important issues remain—there is a technology gap on the part of patrons around the world, reliability of the technology needs to be very good for this to succeed, publishers need to decide whether they will embrace the new technology, and it is true that many potential users of this don't know much about it yet and may persist in just hitting the print button instead of reading articles online. So we are in the early stage of development with this technology, and it is too soon to be able to tell for sure just what direction it will go, and how fast—or slow—it will take off.

HINARI: AN INITIATIVE TO IMPROVE BIOMEDICAL INFORMATION IN THE DEVELOPING WORLD

Leo Walford, Associate Director, Journal Publishing, Sage Publications, London, England

Introduction

In this chapter I set out to describe the HINARI program, giving a brief history of its foundation, the rationale behind it, how it works, and some of the benefits it provides. I also cover some potential shortcomings and possibilities for future expansion.

What Is HINARI, and Where Did It Come From?

HINARI is the Health InterNetwork Access to Research Initiative. It is a program set up by the World Heath Organization and its partners designed initially to improve access to bio-medical journals for developing countries.

In September 2000 the Health InterNetwork was launched by UN General Secretary Kofi Annan. In December of that year Dr. Gro Harlem Brundtland, Director General of the World Health Organization, issued a press release calling for engagement in partnerships for improving health in the developing world.

Only seven months later, in July 2001, six major medical journal publishers (Blackwell, Elsevier, Harcourt, Kluwer, Springer, and Wiley) issued a statement of intent:

> The partners in the Initiative acknowledge that access to primary biomedical journals is a critical issue in developing countries—one of many obstacles to improving health—and are willing to work with committed governments, international organizations and others to find ways to open access to this information.

The initial partners included the following organizations:

HINARI Partners

World Health Organization (WHO)	Blackwell
International Association of Science, Technical & Medical Publishers (STM)	Elsevier
UNICEF/UNDP/World Bank/WHO Special Programme for Research & Training in Tropical diseases (TDR)	Harcourt
US National Library of Medicine (NLM)	Kluwer
Food & Agriculture Organization (FAO)	Springer
Yale University Library, Mann Library, Cornell University	Wiley

In January 2002 HINARI was launched by the publishers. Initially it allowed not-for-profit institutions in countries with a gross national product (GNP) per capita of less than US$1,000 per year to receive free online access to more than 1,500 biomedical journal titles.

In May 2002 a second group of publishers joined HINARI. These included American Medical Association, BMJ Group, Oxford University Press, Nature Publishing Group, Sage Publications, and Taylor & Francis.

As of January 2006 there were over 70 participating publishers, with 3,101 journals available.

Who Is Eligible, What Do They Get, and How Does It Work?

Initially HINARI was available to WHO-registered institutions in countries that have a per capita GNP of under US$1,000 per year. These institutions include universities, clinics, hospitals, and government departments.

With Phase 2, which was launched in January 2003, institutions in countries with a per capita GNP of US$1,000 to $3,000 per year can subscribe to the entire HINARI collection for $1,000 per year. Phase 2 institutions can have a free 90-day trial, and some journals are free to Phase 2 institutions. Subscribing institutions pay the WHO, not the publishers, and this money is used to train librarians and researchers in information technology so that the best use can be made of the information.

The registered institutions receive electronic access to all the journals in the HINARI collection. This includes backfile where it is available, the ability to search through Pubmed/MedLine, and the ability to make course-packs and to download articles.

The program does not provide computer equipment, but it has been reported that the availability of the HINARI materials makes it easier for institutions to get funding for their computer equipment.

Over the years the number of participating institutions has grown dramatically. There are now 1,828 institutions registered in 105 of the 113 eligible countries. Users logged in to HINARI 120,000 times in December 2005 (up from 100,000 in September 2005).

Training

Training is funded by Phase 2 institutions' subscription payments. There is a TDR (*Special Programme for Research and Training in Tropical Diseases*) HINARI training package, which is a collaboration among TDR, HINARI, the National Library of Medicine (USA), Yale University Cushing-Whitney Medical Library (USA), and Paterson Institute for Cancer Research, Manchester (UK). The individual training modules were developed through TDR-funded workshops in Africa and Asia, where librarians and information managers from 16 developing countries field-tested the material. The modules cover everything from Internet basics to how to use the journals and detailed information on how to use PubMed and manage references.

HINARI and some HINARI members also run workshops and other training around the world. There are workshops planned in Fiji, Ethiopia, Rwanda, Mozambique, Senegal, Mali, Burkina Faso, and Zambia.

What's in It for the Publishers?

Publishers have embraced the HINARI project enthusiastically. This is not surprising, as many publishers would sign up to support the UN and the WHO, and to reduce the knowledge gap between rich and poor and improve health care in the developing world. Publishers quickly recognized that this could be done without fundamentally altering or damaging their existing business models, and within existing copyright and intellectual property laws.

The way HINARI was set up also gave the publishers considerable freedom to operate their own terms/licences etc within the program, while putting some pressure on them to adopt best practice within the program. Involvement is also clearly good in PR terms.

With the added benefit that HINARI could stimulate the development of high quality research programs in the developing world, publishers clearly have much to gain through their involvement in HINARI.

What Might HINARI Achieve?

Beyond the simple aim of getting as much up-to-date biomedical journal content as possible into the hands of researchers in the developing world, there have been suggestions that HINARI might achieve other things within the countries it serves. These include

- Reducing feelings of isolation among scientists in the developing world,

- Enabling researchers in the developing world to improve the quality of their research,

- Helping to slow or stop the "brain drain" of scientists from the developing world to the developed world,

- Allowing developing world scientists to provide more accurate and informed advice to policy makers,

- Reducing the "publishing gap" between researchers in the developed world and the developing world by improving the likelihood of publication in international journals,

- Improving the quality of locally produced journals, and

- Helping to create an information culture that uses an evidence base rather than inherited knowledge.

Has HINARI Worked?

The first formal evaluation of HINARI was due to start late in 2005. However, with usage running at over 100,000 downloads a month, and with a great deal of very positive anecdotal support for the program, it is pretty clear that it has worked.

Following are three examples of feedback, taken from the HINARI Web site:

> **Romania:** "If you think you are excited about this, I can tell you that everyone here, academics, students and staff are absolutely thrilled."

> **Gambia :** "It has been a very popular initiative here. Intellectual isolation is considered one of the factors (that mean that) African Research centres cannot develop world class researchers. This can go some way to changing that."

> **Tanzania:** "Free access to scientific journals will very much enable scientist to have access to new publications hence be informed on what other scientist are doing especially in effort to fight the deadly tropical diseases which affect most of African countries southern of Sahara."

HINARI's Limitations

All programs have their limitations. For HINARI, a number have been identified, some of which may be rectifiable, some of which are trickier as they do not necessarily fit so neatly with the aims of the publishers. These limitations include that

- Not all the information that is needed is available electronically (e.g., medical textbooks),

- The $3,000 GNP threshold undoubtedly excludes some countries that would benefit,

- There is potential for information overload given the limited experience with IT of some users,

- Some especially relevant journals (e.g., tropical medicine) may not be available because their commercial viability could be damaged, and

- The focus on biomedicine (and latterly social sciences) may leave gaps.

In spite of these limitations, it is clear that HINARI has been—and continues to be—of great benefit to the institutions it serves.

Expansion and the Future

All through the first three years of the program, the partners have sought to expand it, and not just with additional publishers and their journals, but also by expanding coverage. HINARI's scope was expanded to include social science titles. In October 2003 a sister program, Access to Global Online Research in Agriculture (AGORA) was launched. This was followed in early 2006 by Online Access to Research in the Environment (OARE).

> We have had a number of discussions at WHO about whether it is possible to clone, in other areas of work, the kind of partnership that has evolved in HINARI. From my own experience, I rather doubt that this is possible. It would be difficult to replicate the imagination, generosity and sheer good will that you publishers have shown since we began working together.—Barbara Aronson, World Health Organization

The publishers have committed to the current form of HINARI and AGORA until 2006, when they were scheduled for reassessment. Given the launch of OARE and the effectiveness of the HINARI and AGORA programs, it is likely that the programs will be continued and built on in the coming years.

Further Information

HINARI: www.who.int/hinari/en/

AGORA: www.aginternetwork.org/

When you think of the Charleston Conference you think of collection development. With the growth of electronic resources, collection development librarians find themselves looking for ways to accurately evaluate these resources. Several 2005 presentations dealt with ways to evaluate electronic resources. Additional key topics essential to collection development were presented, including cooperative monographic collection development, dealing with gifts, and institutional repositories.

Collection Development

COOPERATIVE MONOGRAPHIC COLLECTION DEVELOPMENT PART II: THE COLORADO NOT-BOUGHT PROJECT—COOPERATIVE COLLECTION DEVELOPMENT WITHOUT A SHARED APPROVAL PLAN

Joan Lamborn, Head of Library Administrative Services, University of Northern Colorado, Greeley

Michael Levine-Clark, Head of Collection Development, University of Denver, Colorado

This program was the second in a series of three on cooperative collection development. The first program covered recent developments in cooperative collection development in the Ohiolink consortium. The second program presented a cooperative collection development initiative based on the Ohiolink not-bought model involving members of the Colorado Alliance of Research Libraries. The third program in the series described the development of two pilot shared approval plans by members of the Tri-College Consortium (Bryn Mawr, Haverford, and Swarthmore).

Colorado Alliance of Research Libraries

The Colorado Alliance of Research Libraries was founded in 1974 by five libraries in the state: University of Denver, University of Colorado at Boulder, Colorado State University, University of Northern Colorado, and Denver Public Library. Current membership consists of 10 institutions. The additional five libraries are Auraria Library, Colorado School of Mines, Regis University, University of Wyoming, and Colorado College. The Alliance was formed in response to political pressure from the state to purchase resources cooperatively and consequently require less state funding for collections.

Cooperative collection development began as a formal process. COLA (Colorado Organization for Library Acquisitions) started as a separate organization and became part of the Alliance in 1978, when it was renamed the Committee on Library Acquisitions. The participating libraries contributed to a special account that was used for joint purchases agreed upon by all. The committee purchased large microform sets that were housed at one institution and available to all of the participating libraries. For example, the Gray Education Collection was purchased and kept at the University of Northern Colorado. After a period of joint collecting, the committee focused on collection policy statements and became inactive in the late 1980s when collection policy decisions became politically difficult to resolve.

Cooperative collection development activity resumed informally after the implementation of Prospector in 1998. Prospector is a shared online catalog that displays the holdings of the Alliance libraries as well as other libraries in the region. With Prospector it was now possible for selectors to view the holdings of other libraries and use that information to make selection decisions. Materials could also be requested through Prospector and delivered via a statewide courier system.

Prospector was one new tool to support cooperative collection development. Vendor systems such as YBP's GOBI were another. Presented with these opportunities and continuing limited state funding, the deans of the Alliance libraries endorsed a more formal process for cooperative collection development. A Shared Collection Development Task Force was formed. Representatives from the Alliance libraries responsible for collection development were appointed to the taskforce. The taskforce was chaired by one of the deans and reported to Member Council, which consists of the deans of the Alliance libraries.

Planning the Not-Bought Project

The Shared Collection Development Task Force decided to follow the not-bought model developed by Ohiolink libraries. The purpose of the project was to enrich the monograph collection represented in Prospector by purchasing titles not already acquired on approval or firm order. One significant difference was that the Ohiolink project grew out of cooperation among bibliographers; the Alliance libraries were beginning with the tool and needed to build trust and collaboration among the selectors. Another difference was that the Alliance libraries used bibliographic records in Prospector, rather than vendor-supplied information, to identify not-bought titles.

To build support for the project, the taskforce organized a series of meetings that involved selectors and later representatives from YBP. An initial meeting in May 2004 provided an opportunity for selectors in the scientific, technical, and medical areas to become aware of areas of emphasis at other institutions and discuss the possibility of a cooperative collection development project. In August 2004 representatives from YBP gave a presentation to selectors on Ohiolink's Not-Bought Project that could serve as a model for the Alliance project. After attending training sessions on the use of GOBI in October, selectors were ready to start participating in the project.

The Project

To identify books not purchased by any Prospector libraries, lists of ISBNs are generated from the holdings in Prospector. YBP then matches those lists against the contents of GOBI2, their approval database. The titles identified by YBP as "not bought" are those that were treated on approval six months ago or longer, so as not to interfere with approval plans and other existing acquisitions mechanisms. The project was initially identified as a scientific-technical-medical (STM) project, but since all ISBNs from Prospector were being sent to YBP, it seemed a shame to then exclude non-STM disciplines. The project thus shifted naturally to include all disciplines.

The initial ISBN list was sent in September 2004, and consisted of books with a publication date of 2002 or later. This date was chosen rather arbitrarily as a good starting point allowing some retrospective coverage, but not overwhelming selectors with too many titles. As a future project, it might be worthwhile to consider an earlier starting date as a way of doing a broad retrospective analysis of gaps in the collections. A second list was sent in February 2005, and a third in April 2005. There were problems with ISBN matching in the April list, leading to many of the supposedly "not-bought" titles already being in Prospector. YBP and Alliance personnel are working together to resolve the problems.

Once YBP has generated a list of titles in GOBI2 that are not in Prospector, the titles are organized into folders in GOBI2 for selectors to examine. The folders are arranged by LC call number and are accessible to all selectors through a consortial account. Selectors can choose to order these books and can make comments for other selectors to take into account as they look through the lists.

Many of the books were not bought in the first place for a reason: they are low level, reprints, or undesirable. But selectors have identified some titles that they have considered worthwhile. In fiscal year 2005, around 300 titles were purchased across the disciplines. Since the April list was not usable, the bulk of these titles came from the first two lists.

When we started this project, we were concerned about buy-in from selectors, who already are being counted on to do too much with too little money. There was concern that the participation in the project would take a lot of time and would take money away from core materials that had to be bought. The lists, however, are relatively short, with only about 100 titles per folder. The small size, combined with the fact that the lists are only generated quarterly, means that participation does not take much time. Some of the libraries involved set up separate funds so that selectors would not need to use money from existing funds. Since this meant extra funds for those willing to take the time, this solved the concerns about availability of funds.

An added benefit of the special funds was an easy method of tracking purchases. From the beginning we wanted to be sure we could keep track of the books we had purchased so we could assess the success of the project over time. Some libraries have used notes in the order records for tracking. Others are using a vendor code.

The "not-bought" project is a way to begin collaborative monographic collection development. It works in a consortium without a shared approval plan or even a common book vendor, because it relies on Prospector to identify the books that the group has bought. Prospector also has allowed selectors to get used to the idea of counting on another institution to purchase a book.

There are some obvious benefits to this project. Clearly, the most obvious is that it has allowed us to improve the overall collection. Less obviously, as we have identified books that have been missed, we have been able to use that information to improve our existing approval plans. Perhaps most significantly, the process has helped us to get more comfortable with the idea of cooperation. As we move forward with cooperative monographic collection development, this is very important.

What are our next steps? We have talked about bringing in another vendor or vendors, certainly Blackwell's, which would allow us to compare service and coverage. We have not discussed this, but it might make sense to bring in non-Alliance Prospector libraries. Prospector is an Alliance endeavor, but Prospector includes holdings from non-Alliance libraries in the region. Since we are using Prospector to identify "not-bought" titles, it makes sense to consider expanding the group to all academic Prospector libraries. Finally, we are beginning to talk seriously about some sort of shared approval plan(s), which would allow us to coordinate selection into the future. The "not-bought" project could continue as a way of identifying things missed in the past and through whatever sort of shared approval plan(s) we implement.

5TH ANNUAL LIVELY LUNCH ON ISSUES IN HEALTH SCIENCES COLLECTION DEVELOPMENT

Convener/Moderator: Ramune K. Kubilius, Collection Development/Special Projects Librarian, Galter Health Sciences Library, Northwestern University, Chicago, Illinois

Speakers: Lynn M. Fortney, Vice President, Director, Biomedical Division, EBSCO Information Services; Jeffrey G. Coghill, Collection Development & Electronic Resources Librarian, East Carolina U. William E. Laupus Health Sciences Library, Greenville, North Carolina

The theme of the 25th annual Charleston Conference (CC) in 2005 was "Things are seldom what they seem," and in the fifth annual Lively Lunch on health sciences collection development issues, the session moderator and presenters tried to make some predictions about what "things" will be like in the future as well. About four dozen attendees gathered in the spacious conference room allotted for the session in the Embassy Suites. Future conveners of the session may want to keep in mind the comments of some veteran attendees who remarked that the more formally arranged room and the more formal styles of the presentations were not as conducive to casual discussion and boxed lunch eating as experienced in previous CC Lively Lunches on health sciences collection development.

Moderator Ramune K. Kubilius (Northwestern University, Galter Health Sciences Library) highlighted some events and news items impacting collection development that took place since last year's Charleston Conference and a few that were announced as forthcoming in 2006. (The handout from the session, which was compiled with assistance from colleague Elizabeth Lorbeer of Rush University Medical Center in Chicago, was distributed to attendees and submitted for posting on the Charleston Conference Web site, http://www.katina.info/conference/2005%20Presentations.htm, where it will remain for about one year post-conference.) Developments listed on the handout included publisher/vendor mergers and acquisitions, journal title issues (mergers, e-archiving policies), open access; various other issues, and anniversaries in the scholarly publishing world. A cautionary tale about full text online through third-party vendors was illustrated by "Case Study: The Future of Full-text Access" from the medical library discussion list, MEDLIB-L (http://www.mlanet.org/discussion/medlibl.html), posted Tuesday, October 25, 2005 by Theresa S Arndt, Taubman Medical Library, University of Michigan (reprinted in the handout with the posting librarian's permission).

Jeffrey G. Coghill (East Carolina University William E. Laupus Health Sciences Library) shared his insights and experience being a subject selector for *Doody Core Titles in the Health Sciences* (*DCT*) (http://www.doody.com/dct/) now in its second year (editor Dan Doody introduced the undertaking at CC's 2004 Lively Lunch). J. Coghill used PowerPoint slides to illustrate his description of the *DCT* title selection/review that has automated the core title selection process, improved methodologies, and included faculty and librarian reviewers. *DCT* seeks to enhance the biomedical collection tool concept exemplified by the now ceased Brandon/Hill core titles lists. Challenges to working librarians who are *DCT* selectors include short turnaround time (initial scoring to follow-up is one month) and timing (during summer months). The number of subjects selectors cover varies; the presenter covers six subjects! One enhancement that J. Coghill would recommend is that *DCT* developers explore a better/different scoring system. During the question and answer period, participants asked if in the future *DCT* may grow to include a journals component, and J. Coghill indicated that the matter has been raised, to his knowledge. Other participants presented arguments, pro and con, about the utility of core lists for experienced collection development librarians. (A show of hands indicated that most of the attendees had not attended Angela D'Agostino's CC 2004 presentation, "Hard Core Selection Made Easier") . An article on *DCT*, listed on the session handout as "accepted for publication" at the time of CC, later became available in PubMed Central (http://www.pubmedcentral.nih.gov/articlerender.fcgi?artid=1324773).[1]

Lynn M. Fortney (EBSCO Information Services) shared her insights from the perspective of being a long-time health sciences librarian, who in recent years has worked "on the other side," the vendor world, and how that world is adapting to survive and to meet today's customer needs. She reviewed the biomedical information landscape, jokingly referring to the need for publisher/vendor representatives' histories/"genealogy charts." It is hard for librarians and providers to keep track of where colleagues work(ed), what parent company owns what, and so on. She looked at the past, using presentation themes and vendors of past conferences of the Medical Library Association and others as a launching point. "Hot issues" of past conferences may seem humorous now, but some themes still resonate. Projecting the future (2015), she described a scenario of how the information needs of patients and health professionals will be met, sketching out "descriptions" of what information products will have been developed to assist them. The patient? Mike at "WalSoftRx." The physical medical library of 2015? Food, "teaching center" spaces, etc. Journals? A series of articles published after peer review and copy editing. Clinical journals? More expensive, as personal subscriptions drop, with more hospitals licensing consortial packages. Databases? Integrated into clinical decision support systems and EMRs (electronic medical records). Discussion between presenter and attendees was time-restricted, but mention was made of clinical information tool costs. Librarians will have to learn outcome- as well as case-based budget request preparation for a variety of scenarios and budget ranges.

Following are recent publications of the speakers included in the session handout:

> Susan Nash Simpson, Jeffrey G. Coghill, Patricia C. Greenstein. "The Electronic Resources Librarian in the Health Sciences Library: An Emerging Role." *JERML (Journal of Electronic Resources in Medical Librarie*s) 2, no. 1 (2005): 27–39.

> Lynn Fortney, "From the 'Other' Side: Working for a Vendor." *Reference Services Review* 32, no. 1 (2004): 89–92.

> *Reference Services Review,* special Issues: Emerging roles of health sciences librarians (Parts 1 and 2, 2004–2005).

> Ramune Kubilius, "E-books in the Health Sciences." *Against the Grain* 17, no. 1 (February 2005): 36, 38–40 (special electronic books issue).

Notes

1. James Shedlock and Linda J. Walton, "Developing a Virtual Community for Health Sciences Library Book Selection: Doody's Core Titles," *Journal of the Medical Library Association* 94, no. 1 (January 1006): 61–66.

GIFTS-IN-KIND: MAKING THEM WORK FOR YOU

Dustin Holland, Director, Better World Books, Mishawaka, Indiana

Patrick Kindregan, Associate Director, Better World Books, Mishawaka, Indiana

Under the watchful eye of the community, libraries face the challenge of "responsibly" managing surplus material. For the past several decades, libraries have employed various strategies to handle surplus material, particularly gift books. Strategies include doing nothing, trashing or recycling the books, storing or selling the books, refusing or limiting community book donations, and finally, donating the books to other organizations.

Many librarians ask: What do I do with the gift book donations that I do not want to add to my library's collection? Better World Books has a no-cost, environmentally friendly solution. Our company acquires discarded and donated material from libraries across the United States and sells the material online, generating funding for both libraries and non-profit literacy initiatives.

From a warehouse in Mishawaka, Indiana, Better World Books employs unique proprietary software to inventory, price, and sell books collected from libraries on over 14 online marketplaces, including Amazon.com, Abebooks.com, Alibris.com, Biblio.com, and eBay. Many different types of books can be sold in the third-party online marketplace, including new books, ex-library copies, and gift book donations. Ex-library books are sold with traditional library markings, including, stickers, labels, due date cards, and stamp plates. In addition to former library books, online sellers have great success with hardcover fiction/nonfiction, textbooks (2000 and newer), travel books (2000 and newer), dictionaries, trade paperbacks, and rare/collectible books.

Better World Books' no cost Library Discards & Donations program works well with small rural libraries as well as large metropolitan libraries. Shipping supplies are provided to the library to collect surplus books destined for sale via the Internet. Better World Books also pays for all shipping costs (no deductions) for the books to be transported to a central warehouse. Upon arrival, the books are scanned, priced, uploaded, and sold on each online marketplace. At the end of each calendar year quarter, 20 to 25% of net proceeds are returned to the library; furthermore, Better World Books donates 15% of net proceeds to a non-profit literacy partner chosen by the library. Net proceeds are defined as the sale price minus any marketplace commission. To maintain program transparency, libraries have the ability to log into an online sales report to view sales, commissions, and payments on a daily basis.

As of January 2006, over 325 libraries across the United States had discovered the benefits of partnering with Better World Books. By partnering with various service providers, libraries can reasonably utilize technology to manage their surplus materials—all at no cost to the library. This ultimately allows library staff and volunteers to focus on what they do best—promoting library advocacy, raising library awareness within the community, developing literacy programs, and ensuring that patrons have enjoyable and productive visits to their library.

GOT DATABASES—NOW WHAT?

Audrey Powers, Research Librarian for the Science and Technology, University of South Florida, Tampa

Database Evaluations: A Collaborative Process with Objective Results

When I started this project five years ago I worked in a small, academic library. At mid-year we were faced with a serious budget cut in which we had to give money back to the state. As a result, the decision was made to review the database collection to be sure that there were no extraneous databases that cost too much and were underutilized.

The problems we were facing were

> Cuts in funding,
>
> Rising costs,
>
> Duplication,
>
> Librarians having "favorites," and
>
> Some databases not being used

The solution we arrived at follows. An evaluation process was developed to guide evaluators through a collaborative process with objective results. The advantages of this process include that pertinent data are gathered, it is adaptable for a variety of user populations, it can be electronically administered, and it is customizable. This three-step process—prepare, gather data, and results—will enable a collaborative process with objective results.

Phase I: Prepare

The *known data* include

> Cost (actual cost per year),
>
> Use (annual use statistics),
>
> Cost per use,
>
> Duplication (duplication of journal titles), and
>
> Peer comparisons (availability at peer institutions)

The *evaluation* part of the process includes the following criteria:

> Content,
>
> Unique content,
>
> Ease of use,
>
> Instruction,
>
> Overall quality, and
>
> Need.

The electronic evaluation form (see Figure 1) can be put on a library Web site and/or sent out via e-mail. This process can be used to evaluate an existing database collection, a discipline specific group of databases, a trial database, or a comparison of a trial database to an existing database. The database name at the top of the form is hyperlinked to the database. When you click on the hyperlink the database opens in a pop-up window for searching, but the evaluation form remains open. The evaluative part of the form is based on a Likert scale of 0 to 4, with 0 being the lowest score and 4 being the highest score. There is a place for comments as well.

As a customizable, electronic form, you can create several standard templates, copy the template you want to use, and then customize it to suit your needs. I have three standard templates: for faculty, librarians, and students. Depending on the type of evaluation project being conducted, and who the evaluators are, you can include as much or as little of the known data as appropriate. For instance, you may not want to include the cost of a database on a student or faculty evaluation form. Use statistics will be nonexistent if a trial database is being evaluated. On a student evaluation form the criterion "Instruction" should be changed to "Assignment use."

Phase II: Gather Data

During this phase, a team leader will obtain the *known data*, distribute the evaluation forms, and conduct the *evaluations*. When you create the form and database in FrontPage, the respondents' results are automatically dumped into an Access database.

Phases III: Results

Once the evaluation period is over, the results phase allows for collation and presentation of the results, which could include a recommendation or action plan.

When the form is posted on a Web site or e-mailed to potential evaluators, the evaluators access the database, conduct searches, and complete the evaluation forms. In this case, a trial for xreferplus was conducted. The evaluation form was posted on the library Web site; therefore students, faculty, and librarians were the evaluators. Known data were not presented on the evaluation form, and there were 27 evaluators.

When the forms were submitted the results were dumped into an Access database (see Figure 2). Then the results were exported from Access to Excel (see Figure 3). The averages for each criterion (content, unique content, ease of use, instructional value, and overall quality) were determined as well as the composite score or total (see Figure 4). Then the final results were put into a clear and legible format for presentation (see Figure 5). In addition, information can be gleaned from the comments (see Figure 6).

Database

<u>Known Data</u>

Cost:

Use:

Cost/use:

Duplication:

Peer comparisons:

<u>Evaluations</u>

Content: 0   1   2   3   4

Unique content: 0   1   2   3   4

Ease of use: 0   1   2   3   4

Instruction: 0   1   2   3   4

Overall quality: 0   1   2   3   4

0 = Inappropriate 1 = Very Unsatisfactory 2 = Unsatisfactory 3 = Satisfactory 4 = Very Satisfactory

Need: _____Inappropriate   _____Useful   _____Essential

Comments:

Figure 1. Database Evaluation Form.

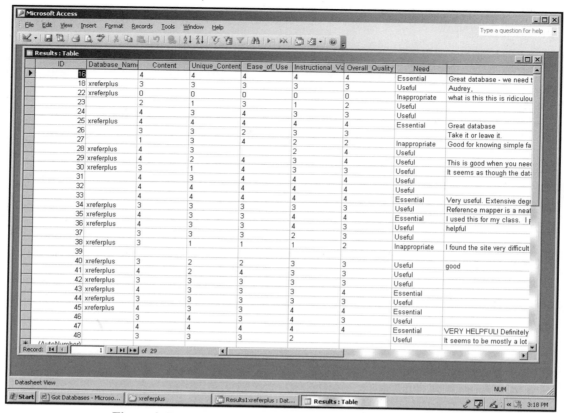

Figure 2. Results of Evaluation Survey in Access Database.

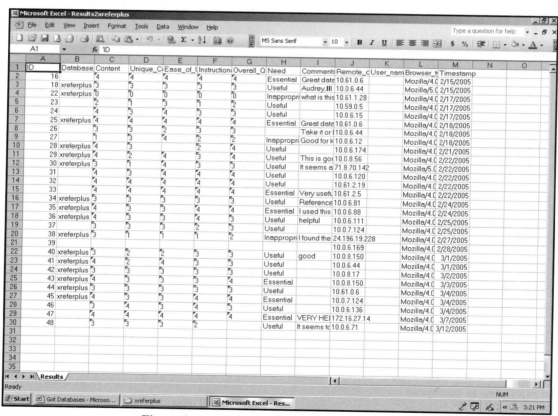

Figure 3. Results of Evaluation Survey in Excel.

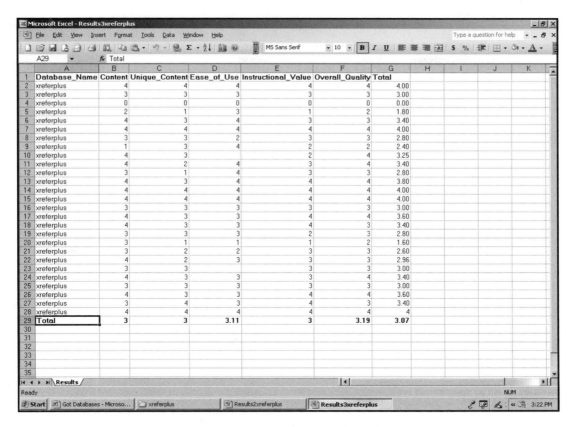

Figure 4. Averages for Each Criterion.

Content	3
Unique content	3
Ease of use	3.11
Instructional value	3
Overall quality	3.19
Composite score	3.06

Figure 5. Final Results.

Comments

- Great database. We need this for our collection.

- What is this? This is ridiculous. Are you serious?

- Great database.

- Take it or leave it.

- Good for knowing simple facts, but gives little background information.

- It seems as though the database may duplicate some of the other literature database we already have, but it seems useful that reference materials are collected in the same place.

- Very useful. Extensive degree of information. Also very fun!@

- Reference mapper is a neat feature.

- I used this for my class. I plan to use it from home in the future.

- I found this site very difficult to use and very limited in what it gave in return.

- Good.

- VERY HELPFUL! Definitely needed!

- It seems to be mostly a lot of dictionaries, some of the dictionaries go in depth on a topic, which is nice.

Figure 6. Evaluation Survey Comments.

WHAT CAN THE ROLE OF TECHNICAL SERVICES BE IN MANAGING INSTITUTIONAL REPOSITORIES?

Tim Daniels, Digital Technologies Librarian, Georgia State University, Atlanta

Elizabeth Winter, Electronic Resources Librarian, Georgia State University, Atlanta

Introduction

Collecting and managing the digital scholarly output of a campus is a task that many libraries have begun to take on, and identifying and collecting these materials is the first step. How are libraries identifying and collecting these materials, and how successful have their efforts been?

Once you have some of these materials in hand, what does your workflow look like? How do you acquire, process, catalog, and make digital objects available? Because of their experience in obtaining and organizing materials, technical services staff would seem a natural fit for the role of managing repositories, but is this the case in practice? Are academic libraries examining opportunities to redeploy existing technical services staff to support growing institutional repositories?

Our program covered strategies for populating institutional repositories and the role technical services staff can play in managing them. We introduced three possible workflow strategies and discussed the impact that establishing an institutional repository may have on staffing in technical services.

Overview of Institutional Repositories

Over the past several years, institutional repositories have begun to grow in popularity as a way in which libraries can work with campus faculty and information technology departments to house and preserve the intellectual output of universities, departments, and campus organizations. Institutional repositories are also being used to increase access to digital materials and expand the visibility of a university's "born-digital" scholarly output (materials that begin their existence in electronic formats, as opposed to printed materials that are digitized retroactively). Institutional repositories allow faculty members to self-archive their scholarly materials, which may include pre-prints, post-prints, working papers, datasets, supplementary materials, and learning objects.

How do these materials become part of institutional repositories? Generally, they are either submitted by the authors themselves or are obtained and added to the repository by librarians or other library staff members. Collecting and managing the digital scholarly output of a campus is a task that many libraries have begun to take on, but identifying and collecting these materials is only the first step. What does the workflow for creating and maintaining a repository look like? Who in an organization is responsible for acquiring, processing, cataloging, and making available these digital objects? As we are in the process of working through some of these issues at Georgia State, we determined that it might be fruitful to think about the ways institutions are—or could be—working with institutional repositories. We are interested in investigating ways in which libraries are involving—or could involve—acquisitions and cataloging personnel in the management and maintenance of institutional repositories.

Role of Technical Services Staff

Because of their experience in obtaining and organizing materials, technical services staff would seem a natural fit for the role of managing repositories. Often, however, technical services staff play little or no role in the operations of institutional repositories. Those who most frequently work with repository materials are cataloging personnel, who sometimes assist in the creation of metadata for submitted items, though acquisitions personnel are not typically involved in IR work at all. Are institutions missing out on opportunities by not including acquisitions staff?

Receiving library materials, verifying items and bibliographic information, and creating basic metadata are tasks that acquisitions staff are already trained to do. Further, due to the increase in numbers of electronic resources over traditional formats in many libraries, there may be a decrease in the amount of work that acquisitions personnel have traditionally done. In addition, acquisitions and cataloging staff already work closely in many ways, so for institutions that want to have successful IRs but are not having the success they would like in getting their IR off to a solid start, it seems natural to employ cataloging and acquisitions staff together in the management and maintenance of IRs. What can this involvement look like?

Work Flows

As we examined the existing workflows in our library and the possible processes for working with our institutional repository, we constructed the following workflows (see Figures 1 through 3). Each is designed to be used with a particular means of populating a repository. Batch processing is used when a collection of materials is obtained such as a group of white papers from a college or a single professor. Regularly submitted materials can be materials that are collected on a schedule. And last, self-submission is when a faculty member or contributor submits material to the repository directly. These workflows can be adapted for use in a variety of IR settings.

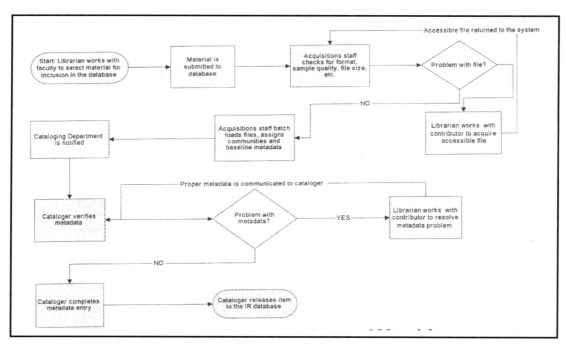

Figure 1. Batch Processed Materials.

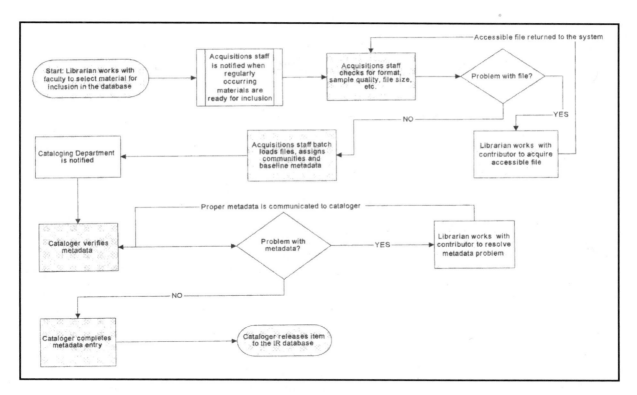

Figure 2. Regularly Occurring Materials.

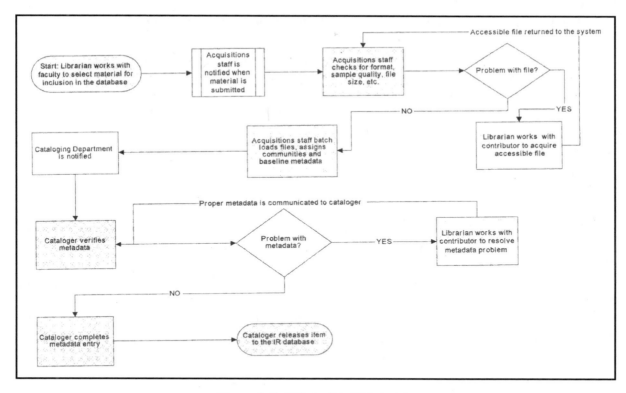

Figure 3. Self-Submitted Materials.

Discussion

After presenting these ideas and possible workflows, we asked session attendees to engage in a discussion of the role of technical services staff in working with IRs, as well as a few of the broader questions related to institutional repositories. This generated some thoughtful discussion.

We asked attendees at institutions with repositories what their biggest IR challenge was. Perhaps not surprisingly, nearly everyone agreed that content recruitment was the most difficult aspect of starting and maintaining a repository. It is often quite difficult to achieve faculty "buy-in" for depositing their scholarly output and digital objects into an institutional repository. Involving multiple library personnel in working with an institution's repository may be especially helpful for solving this problem. Employing library staff to seek out content proactively and provide the practical efforts necessary to identify, acquire, process, and make available digital objects should remove many of the practical barriers to the willingness of faculty to deposit their scholarly output. Greater efforts on the part of library staff—necessitating lesser efforts on the part of faculty—should lead to an increase in the percentage of faculty who make their content available in institutional repositories.

Another challenge raised by attendees was a lack of administrative or institutional support for institutional repositories. Some said they were having difficulty convincing their institutions to devote resources to starting a repository—that this was not a priority. We mentioned the marketing function of IRs as a potential counter to this lack of administrative interest. If an institution is able to make its scholarly output freely available through an IR that allows its metadata to be harvested via Open Archives Initiative harvesting protocol and to be displayed publicly, the institution's scholarship will benefit from increased external visibility.

Attendees seemed genuinely interested in the possibility of involving technical services staff in IR management, though there was some question as to how to implement the ideas and workflows we proposed. Internal political considerations and departmental reporting lines were two hurdles mentioned that would need to be overcome in order to involve technical services staff (particularly acquisitions staff) more readily at some institutions. Our primary idea for overcoming these hurdles is to consider the parallels between the skills needed for traditional acquisitions work and IR work and to attempt to communicate these clearly and thoughtfully to the appropriate parties at one's institution.

A final interesting point for discussion was the future of institutional repositories. We asked attendees their thoughts on discipline-specific repositories versus institutional repositories and shared some of our own thoughts on this topic. Because of the mobility of faculty members from institution to institution, are faculty more likely to identify with—and deposit their materials in—discipline-specific repositories than institutional repositories? While some of our attendees agreed that this might be the case, the thought didn't seem to discourage others from considering how to continue to develop and grow their institutional repositories. This question seems to be worth investigating further.

Technology is changing the way libraries do business. These changes are approaching quickly without ample time for research and analysis. The 2005 Charleston Conference provided librarians the opportunity to discuss technology issues such as library filtering, peer to peer file sharing, user behavior, and how to plan for the future.

Technology

ANYTHING GOES, OR DOES IT? LIBRARIES AND FILTERING

Lisa Richmond, College Librarian, Assistant Profession of Library Science, Wheaton College, Illinois

I would like to begin by stressing all that I think we on the panel have in common. We need to be reminded of this if we are not going to magnify our differences out of proportion or forget what we in fact do share and can build on together. I think we must all be grateful that we live in a liberal democracy; we are convinced of the good of having an informed and intelligent citizenry for the purpose of self-government; we acknowledge the repressions of the past; and we would consider unjust any law such as the one Milton fulminated against in his *Areopagitica*, of censorship of all materials before publication. We believe that libraries and reading change lives; that learning is good; that we ought not to be afraid of knowledge; and that the library, especially the public library, plays an indispensable part in all of this. There is a wonderful book by Jonathan Rose, *The Intellectual Life of the British Working Classes*, which has brought home to me poignantly the fundamental rightness of the thirst for knowledge and the real barriers that existed in the past to keep people "in their place" through ignorance. If you are not familiar with this book, I recommend it to you.

I was asked to be on this panel particularly because I work at Wheaton College, which, as Mr. McKinzie has said, currently uses an Internet filtering program, called Web Sense, on the entire campus network. Thus, the decision to filter was not a library decision but was decided by the senior administration to be applied on every computer. According to the Web Sense documents I have, this software works by blocking sites that have been selected into one of 90 categories by Web Sense staff. Wheaton selected six of these categories to block; they fall mainly into the categories of pornography sites (my rough definition of this might be "those sites that exist to gratify the sexual appetite") and gambling sites. The concern here is with sites that lead to activities that can develop an unusually powerful hold on a person and which, we believe, are not neutral but harmful to the person who does them and possibly to others also. The concern is not with sites that describe or promote wrongdoing in general; Web Sense has not been set to filter out plagiarism sites, for example, or hate sites. The concern is not with knowledge, either; for example, sites that Web Sense considers to be "sex education" sites are not filtered out. The problem our community sees is not one of knowledge, but of will. This is what I'd like briefly to try to explain.

In passing, I should also mention that the great majority of students support the filtering. The college also acknowledges that it isn't a perfect system by any means. Some things are filtered out that shouldn't be, and there are ways to get around the blocks. We have a process for getting sites released when errors are found, although that comes with the inevitable hassles and delays.

Most people at Wheaton believe that pornography is harmful to the person who engages in it, harmful spiritually, emotionally, and socially. It is not a right expression or fulfillment of our sexual natures. If we consider it to be harmful to us, why are we drawn to it? Socrates, in the Platonic dialogues, taught that the human soul—and by "soul" he meant something like the inner, animating center of oneself, not particularly a religious concept—the human soul is composed of three parts: the rational, the appetitive, and the "spirited element." The rational and appetitive are fairly straightforward to understand, but the spirited element perhaps requires some explanation. In the *Republic*, Socrates tells the story of a man walking past Athens' place of public execution, where corpses lay. Socrates say that the man "desired to look, but at the same time he was disgusted and made himself turn away; and for a while he struggled and covered his face. But finally, overpowered by the desire, he opened his eyes wide, ran toward the corpses, and said, 'Look, you damned wretches [speaking to his eyes], take your fill of the fair sight' " (*Republic* IV:440a). This anger toward his overpowering desire was an expression of the spirited element. Perhaps St. Paul meant something similar when he said, "I do not understand my own actions. For I do not do what I want, but I do the very thing I hate. . . . Wretched man that I am!" One of the four cardinal virtues of the ancient world was "moderation"—*sophrosune*—the unslavish, and therefore freely chosen and freely experienced, harmony of reason and appetite. This distinction between what is done slavishly (such as addictive behavior) and what is done freely (with reason and appetite in harmony) was a very important one in ancient Greek philosophy. (Among other things, the Greek form of education known as "liberal education" was grounded in this thought.)

If we consider the foregoing as one way of understanding a truer and deeper freedom, a kind of freedom of the individual person that is not commonly reflected upon in our society, we can also consider freedom in relation to human communities. Wheaton is a Christian community, and thus some of its convictions will not apply to other types of communities. But here is how Wheaton understands freedom in its community:

One of the most important teachings of the New Testament is that we as fellow believers are members of one body, metaphorically the "body of Christ." This is one of the meanings of the Eucharist (or Mass or Lord's Supper)—it expresses a participation in that body. It is interesting to note that in many places the idea of freedom and of community coincide in biblical teaching. St. Paul, for example, says, "For you were called to freedom, brethren; only do not use your freedom as an opportunity for the flesh [I suggest that "flesh" here means something like "selfish inclination"], but through love be servants of one another. For the whole law is fulfilled in one word, 'You shall love your neighbor as yourself.' " "All things are lawful, but not all things are helpful. All things are lawful, but not all things build up. Let no one seek [merely] his own good, but [also] the good of his neighbor." "It is not right to do anything that makes your brother stumble." None of us *needs* to view pornography. If we don't struggle with its powerful draw, we should be very grateful. Then in consideration of our brothers and sisters we would do well to choose to set aside this unnecessary stumbling block. This is another kind of freedom: the freedom to choose the good for ourselves and for each other.

The entry on "censorship" in the *Encyclopaedia Britannica* concludes in this way: "It is tempting to . . . insist that no one should try to tell anyone else what kind of human being he should be. Yet, cannot it be said that only they are truly free who know what they are doing and who choose what is right? All others are, in varying degrees, prisoners of illusions and appetites, however much they may believe themselves to be freely expressing themselves."

HOLLYWOOD MOGULS AND THE TERROR OF P2P

Bruce Strauch, Professor, The Citadel, Charleston, South Carolina

It's truly strange to think that this all begins with the humble VCR. How quaint those long ago days of the 1980s when the exciting prospect of in-home movies was confounded by the difficulty of attaching the dratted thing to your television. And after all the subsequent turmoil, how passing strange to think that Hollywood got so bent out of shape about it all.

Network TV, in its desperate bid to compete prime time with cable, began broadcasting old movies. And out there in America's living rooms, couch potatoes were taping them. Otherwise law-abiding, tax-paying Americans were sitting there patiently shutting the VCR off during the interminable ads and then starting it back up again. And building a—gasp—library of movies.

How many times would anyone watch the same movie? And was there really a market for those movies anyhow? And how long before the tape wore out?

But Hollywood couldn't see this. It was in high dudgeon. Something was being filched from its control, and by golly the moguls were going to sue. And sue they did.

Sony-Betamax became a much talked about case. Even though Betamax went busted. But the Supreme Court was forced to face the problem of laying secondary liability on "technologies capable of substantial noninfringing uses."[1]

As has become now so familiar, it got all balled up in applying the copyright law of print media to the evolving age of new copying technology. The Court held that "The sale of copying equipment, like the sale of other articles of commerce, does not constitute contributory infringement if the product is widely used for legitimate, unobjectionable purposes. Indeed, it need merely be capable of substantial noninfringing uses."[2]

To arrive at this conclusion, the Court had to find that "time-shifting" was "fair use" under copyright law and that this was a significant part of America's activity.[3]

Ironically, this was an appeal from California, where the Ninth Circuit had found that the primary purpose of VCRs was piracy and had held against Betamax.

And likewise ironically, the Supreme Court clearly stated that Congress was the body to adjust copyright law in response to changing technology. Indeed it says right there in Article I of the Constitution that Congress has the power to promote arts and science: "When, as here, the Constitution is permissive, the sign of how far Congress has chosen to go can come only from Congress."[4]

New Technology: Dum-Da-Dum-Dum

The year 1998 saw a patent granted for MP3 compression allowing songs to be squeezed onto small files and opening the door to downloading and sharing copyrighted music. Then in 1999, Napster exploded file-sharing on the American scene, mystifying adults but becoming an all-consuming passion of the young and making "ripping" a household word. And peer-to-peer technology made all this possible. Under this paradigm, each network node is an equal "peer" able to serve or consume data from any other node.

In order for Napster to make money through streaming advertising, however, it used a "hub and spoke" technology whereby users had to register and consult a central file index before ripping. The client would send a search request and Napster would locate the desired song and transmit it.

The centralized file index was the killer. The Ninth Circuit found Napster liable due to actual knowledge of the infringements and the material contribution it made to the process. In doing this, the court simply dodged the Sony standard of "substantial noninfringing use" and focused on Napster's conduct instead.[5]

Since litigation takes close to forever, there was time for Grokster and StreamCast to get organized and try to seize the Napster market. Naturally, a class of 27,000 companies, conglomerates, combines, and song writers that own nearly every single movie and piece of music in the US of A went after them.[6]

Tweaking the P2P System

P2P had gone beyond the Napster model and eliminated the central server. Each computer connects with others that use similar software and is both server and client. Grokster and StreamCast not only decentralized indexing but collected no user registration information. Yes, it was a see-no-evil approach.

StreamCast uses Gnutella open source software. Our outlaw teenager sends a search request to all computers in the network for that desired song. Open source means the software is in the public domain. Yes, he or she even gets that for free.

A Dutch company, KaZaa BV, developed "supernode" architecture whereby numerous computers operate as indexing servers and our teen accesses the nearest one. This was marketed as "FastTrack" and was initially used by both Grokster and StreamCast. Following a spat with KaZaa, StreamCast developed its own variety of Gnutella called "Morpheus."

The only importance of burdening you with this is that Grokster and StreamCast folks couldn't communicate with one another. They were each in their own virtual worlds. Which limited the theft in some minimal way.

Now, along with all the music stealing, our users can share heavy partying photos, recycled term papers, or public domain works. Stealing of course is the biggest part of the traffic, estimated at around 90%.

After being chastised by the Supremes in *Sony*, the Ninth Circuit decided to let technology roll and held for Grokster/StreamCast. The lead sentence of the opinion approaches the sublime. At least for legal writing: "From the advent of the player piano, every new means of reproducing sound has struck a dissonant chord with musical copyright owners."[7]

Contributory Copyright Infringement

To show this, you need (1) direct infringement by a primary infringer—the outlaw teen, (2) knowledge of the infringement by Grokster, and (3) material contribution to the infringement by Grokster. (1) is a given, so the issue is (2), knowledge.

And How Is It That You Know Stuff?

Once more, we must refer back to *Sony Corp. of America v. Universal City Studios, Inc.* The Supreme Court said there is no constructive knowledge of infringement if you could show the product was "capable of substantial" or "commercially significant noninfringing uses." This was derived from the "staple article of commerce" doctrine found in patent law.[8]

The Ninth Circuit had already applied this in *A&M Records v. Napster.*[9] As there were substantial legit uses of Napster, constructive knowledge was out, and the music owners had to show that the defendant had reasonable knowledge of specific infringing files.[10]

On remand of *Napster I* the district court required the plaintiffs to inform Napster of specific files, which Napster would then block. This was appealed, and the Ninth Circuit upheld the district court, leaving the burden on the plaintiffs to provide names of particular files before Napster was bound to act.[11]

What Did Grokster Know, and When Did It Know It?

There is no issue of fact whatsoever that Grokster has substantial noninfringing uses. The Court cited the band Wilco, who were jacked around by their record company, so they put out an album for free downloading and got so much buzz going that the record company offered them a new contract.

The Court noted that thousands of other bands have debuted their work through free downloads, as well as noting Project Gutenberg with its public domain literary works and the Prelinger Archive with movies.

The only response to this by the bloated big boys was that Grokster was mostly used for theft. But that's not the standard for constructive knowledge. Your heart and presumably your brain is pure if you produce a product with virtuous uses.

And on to Material Contribution

Remember we're not dealing with a central server with an index of available files. Napster provided the site for big-time infringement; Grokster et al. didn't do this. It's the users who provided file storage and index maintenance. With both the Gnutella and KaZaa networks, the software owners could keep exchanging files even with Grokster and StreamCast shutting up shop entirely.

Okay, Then How About Vicarious Copyright Infringement?

And once again there are three elements: (1) direct infringement by a primary party, (2) direct financial benefit to Grokster, and (3) the right and ability to supervise the infringers.[12] This theory grew out of agency law's *respondeat superior*. The idea is that if you have the right to control someone's bad behavior, you should be liable if you don't.

Right and Ability to Supervise

There is a historic split here between the "dance hall operator" who can control what music is played and the "landlord" who has no control over what his tenants are doing behind closed doors.[13] With Grokster and StreamCast, there is no registration or log-in procedure.

There is no ability to block what the users are doing. They are landlords and not dance hall operators.

Turning a "Blind Eye" to Infringement

As a last gasp, the music companies argued that Grokster should not be permitted to turn a blind eye to all that theft going on out there. The Ninth Circuit said there was no separate "blind eye" theory of vicarious liability. And anyhow, what was Grokster supposed to do if it had no ability to supervise?

But Public Policy Oughta Do Something About This

The Ninth Circuit said we live in a "quicksilver technological environment" and courts are not capable of fixing the direction of innovation.[14] Old markets will always be roiled by new technology—tape recorders, copiers, video recorders, PCs, karaoke machines, and MP3 players. And speaking of quicksilver, things are moving right along. BitTorrent is a jim-dandy bit of software allowing you to copy a full-length movie in two hours rather than the twelve required by KaZaa.

Going to the Supreme Court

Explaining the earlier ironic comments, those famous activists of the Ninth Circuit declined to make new law, leaving it up to Congress as the Supreme Court had said in *Sony*. But of course there was the appeal to the Supreme Court, which now reversed the Ninth Circuit holding that the promotion of infringement along with distributing a piracy-capable device creates liability.[15]

The Supreme Court focused on how Grokster and StreamCast set out to promote infringement in capturing the Napster market. Grokster/StreamCast got into business as Napster was sued, anticipating the big shut-down. StreamCast sent out an ad kit boasting of their potential to capture Napster users: "We have put this network in place so that when Napster pulls the plug on their free service . . . or if the Court orders them shut down prior to that . . . we will be positioned to capture the flood of their 32 million users that will be actively looking for an alternative."

And lo and behold, many of these pirates would e-mail Grokster asking questions about copyrighted works. And Grokster would helpfully send guidance. And Grokster advertised itself as a Napster alternative since Napster had been nailed.

StreamCast's Morpheus software was designed to search for "Top 40" songs, which of course were always under copyright. A Grokster newsletter touted their ability to provide copyrighted material.

The Court actually referenced the few folks who desire a free Decameron or Shakespeare but said it's small potatoes next to those who want a free latest release by Modest Mouse, whoever that might be.

Tension Between Two Values

And what would those values be?: supporting creative pursuits thru copyright versus promoting communication technology innovation by limiting liability for copyright violation. The Court reasoned that the vast number of infringing downloads made it impossible for Music Titans to effectively go after the pirates. So practicality pushes the Court to allow a suit for secondary liability on a theory of contributory or vicarious infringement.[16]

To recap, you infringe contributorily by inducing direct infringement.[17] You do it vicariously when you profit from it and do nothing to stop it.[18]

Let's go back to *Sony*. Videocassette recorders were sold primarily for "time shifting," which is taping a show and watching it later. Sony showed no intent to promote infringing uses, and the VCR had significant noninfringing uses. This approach left "breathing room for innovation."[19]

The Ninth Circuit read *Sony* to say that a product capable of noninfringing use can never have secondary liability if it is misused. But Sony does not require courts to ignore evidence of intent to promote piracy. "If vicarious liability is to be imposed on Sony in this case, it must rest on the fact that it has sold equipment with constructive knowledge of the potential for infringement."[20]

Going beyond the characteristics of a product, it's important whether evidence shows a producer meant to promote infringement. Inducing or enticing the commission of an infringement would be a classic case of unlawful purpose.[21] So if you don't just expect infringement, but invoke it through advertising, then you're liable.[22] Advertising an infringing use or giving how-to-do instructions are nice evidence of encouraging direct infringement.[23]

So there's liability if you distribute a device and by clear expression or other affirmative steps foster infringement. Mere knowledge that the device can be used for infringement is not enough. Neither are standard stuff like offering technical support or product updates. There has to be culpable expression and conduct.

And Some More Facts on Point

Grokster had an electronic newsletter promoting its software capability to access popular and extremely copyrighted music. Anyone could see it was offering the alternative to Napster downloads of music. It even named its software "Swaptor."

StreamCast advertised to Napster users its "OpenNap" software. A "fact-finder" could easily see it was likewise offering an alternative to Napster's massive infringement. And it had those cute ads like "When the lights went off at Napster . . . where did the users go?"

Neither company attempted to develop any sort of filter to cut down on the piracy. And since both companies earned money through advertising, high-volume use—which really means high-volume piracy—upped their revenue.

Kicking the Can

Yes, the Supreme Court has merely kicked the can down the road. The software still works even without Grokster and StreamCast in business. And America's youth has been totally trained to steal music. Which means that when the next Grokster comes along, it will not have to foster infringement. Everyone will know exactly what to do without being told.

Indeed, a whole "philosophy" of P2P has arisen. Lawrence Lessig called it "the art through which free culture is built."[24] Musicians chafing under the control of music moguls view P2P as an opportunity rather than a threat.[25]

And consumers are eating it up. Neil Netanel wrote in the *Harvard Law Review* that P2P file sharing is "a vehicle for finding works that are otherwise not available, discovering new genres, making personalized compilations, and posting creative remixes, sequels, and modifications of popular works. By engaging in such activities, people who might previously have been passive consumers now assert a more active, self-defining role in the enjoyment, use and creation of cultural expression. They also share their interests, creativity, and active enjoyment with others."[26]

Roiling Markets

And the roiling market technology always has a new nightmare out there for Hollywood. Jon Lech Johansen, a 15-year-old Norwegian geek, wrote a computer program that permitted the copying of DVDs and posted it on the Internet for all to use. Now as a 21-year-old, still-living-at-home geek he has hacked Apple's software for its Internet -based iTunes, removing the barriers to unlimited copying.

And he is particularly peeved that he is forced to watch commercials on a DVD and has to drag DVDs around with him when he travels rather than being able to download them to his laptop. So he easily wrote a program to circumvent the encryption and began ripping DVDs. He has been prosecuted twice in Norway, and as befitting the much lionized national hero that he is, has twice been acquitted. His legal defense costs were paid for by the Electronic Frontier Foundation, which promotes reduced restrictions on digital technology.[27]

Notes

1. Sony Corp. of Am. v. Universal Studios, Inc., 464 U.S. 417, 442 (1984).
2. *Id.* at 442.
3. *Id.* at 456.
4. *Id.* (quoting Deepsouth Packing Co. v. Laitram Corp., 406 U.S. 518, 530 (1972)).
5. A&M Records, Inc. v. Napster, Inc., 114 F. Supp. 2d 896, 1023 (N.D. Cal. 2000).
6. MGM Studios, Inc. v. Grokster, 380 F.3d 1154 (9th Cir. 2004).
7. *Id.* at 1154
8. *Sony,* 464 U.S. at 440–42.
9. A&M Records v. Napster, 239 F.3d 1004 (9th Cir. 2001) ("*Napster I*") .
10. *Id.* at 1027.
11. A&M Records v. Napster, 284 F.3d 1091 (9th Cir. 2002) ("*Napster II*") .
12. *Napster I,* 239 F.3d at 1022.
13. Fonovisa, Inc. v. Cherry Auction, Inc., 76 F.3d 261, 262–63 (9th Cir. 1996).
14. AT&T v. City of Portland, 216 F.3d 871, 876 (9th Cir. 1999).
15. Metro-Goldwyn-Mayer Inc., et al., Petitioners v. Grokster, Ltd., et al., 125 S. Ct. 2764, 2005 U.S. LEXIS 5212 (2005).
16. See *In re* Aimster Copyright Litig., 334 F.3d 643, 645–46 (CA7 2003).
17. See Gershwin Publ'g Corp. v. Columbia Artists Mgmt., Inc., 443 F.2d 1159, 1162 (CA7 1971).
18. Shapiro, Bernstein & Co. v. H.L. Green Co., 316 F.2d 304, 307 (CA2 1963).
19. See *Sony,* 464 U.S. at 442.
20. *Id.* at 439.
21. *Black's Law Dictionary* (8th ed. 2004), 790.
22. Kalem Co. v. Harper Bros., 222 U.S. at 62-63.
23. Oak Indus., Inc. v. Zenith Elecs. Corp., 697 F. Supp. 988, 992 (ND Ill. 1988); Fromberg, Inc. v. Thornhill, 315 F.2d 407, 412–13 (CA5 1963) (demonstrations by sales staff of infringing uses supported liability for inducement).

24. Lawrence Lessig, *The Future of Ideas: The Fate of the Commons in a Connected World* (2001), 9.

25. See *Artists, Musicians and the Internet,* Pew Internet & Am. Life Project, Dec. 5, 2004, at ii.

26. Neil Weinstock Netanel, "Impose a Noncommercial Use Levy to Allow Free Peer-to-Peer File Sharing," *Harvard Journal of Law & Technology* 17 (2003): 1, 3.

27. Steve Stecklow, "Repro Man," *The Wall Street Journal,* October 15–16, 2005, A1 and A8.

SEARCHING FOR GODOT: IS THE SEARCH FOR ONLINE RESOURCES EVER COMPLETE?

With apologies to Samuel Beckett

Ashlee Clevenger, Psychology Major, College of Charleston, South Carolina

Carol Toris, Associate Professor, Psychology Department, College of Charleston, South Carolina

Research suggests that, both in Internet searching[1] and in life at-large,[2] people often are more confident in their behaviors and decisions than is warranted. A survey of patrons at the College of Charleston Addlestone Library explored factors related to their confidence in the adequacy of their Internet searches. In addition, both college students' strategies for completing an online search when the desired outcome is predetermined and faculty instruction to students regarding adequate search strategies were explored.

The Demographics of Search Engine Use

A nationwide phone interview survey of 2,200 adults conducted by the Pew Internet and American Life Project on Search Engine Users reported some interesting findings regarding Internet and, more specifically, search engine use:[3]

- 84% of internet users have used a search engine.

- 47% of searchers will use a search engine no more than once or twice a week; 30% of searchers will use a search engine at least once a day.

- 44% of searchers say they regularly use a single search engine, 48% will use just two or three, 7% will use more than three.

- 87% of searchers say that they have successful search experiences.

- 68% of Internet users claim that search engines are a fair and unbiased source of information; 19% say they don't place trust in search engines.

- 92% of search engines users say that they are confident in their search abilities; of those 92%, 52% say they are very confident.

- Those most confident in their searching are young, better educated, and found in a higher income bracket.

- Of people aged 30 and under, 94% expressed confidence in their search abilities.

Since this survey was conducted, the Pew Internet and American Life Project has continued, and the latest data, from September 2005, indicate that the daily use of search engines continues to increase dramatically, from 30% of the Internet using population in June 2004 (as cited above) to 41% in September 2005. These numbers represent a daily increase in users of Internet searching from 38 to 59 million people in a little more than a year. Clearly, university librarians and faculty should give careful attention to this pervasive information resource.

Confidence in Internet Searches

In the psychological literature, there is growing support for a construct called the *over-confidence effect*; namely, that people place too much confidence in the insightfulness of their judgments, overestimating the chances that their decisions about the present are sound and that their predictions about the future will prove correct.[4] While this is particularly the case in research focusing on self-assessment, numerous studies also support the assertion that confidence in one's judgment of facts is unrelated to accuracy in judgment (compare Fischhoff et al.[5] and numerous studies on eyewitness testimony by Elizabeth Loftus).

All of this begs the question as to whether or not the reported confidence of people in their search abilities is warranted. The answer to such a question would entail a precise measure of the accuracy and completeness of a search, something beyond the scope of our inquiry here. However, we thought we might be able to shed some light on this topic and to learn something about the use of search engines and, more generally, online instructional resources, on our own campus. Toward this end, three studies were pursued: (1) a survey of our library patrons, (2) an examination of student success in searching the literature for a class writing assignment, and (3) an inquiry into faculty instruction on online searching.

Library Users Survey

A survey was conducted at the College of Charleston Addlestone Library on students' online search habits. The uses of search engines, databases, and online library catalogs were examined through the responses of a randomly selected group of patrons. Here are some of our findings:

- Who were our respondents?
    - Student library users at the College of Charleston (N = 101)
    - 18 to 33 years of age, with a mean age of 20.6
    - 33% male, 67% female
    - 12% freshmen, 23% sophomores, 21% juniors, 36% seniors, 8% 5+years

- What is their reported exposure to available educational technology and other resources?
    - 92% reported they had a home computer to which they had access.
    - 38% reported they had taken a college-level computer class.
    - 72% reported they had used e-reserves for at least one class.
    - 88% reported they had used WebCT for at least one class.
    - 61% reported they had taken a course involving in-class computer use.
    - 59% reported that they had either taken a library tour or had a guest librarian lecture in at least one of their classes.
    - 99% reported that they had used an online search engine.
    - 78% reported that they had used an online database.
    - 87% reported that they had used the online library catalog.

○ 55.1% reported that they use the computers on campus at least once a day; only 4% reported that they do not use the computers on campus.

○ 70% reported that they perform an online search at least once a day.

• How do these students conduct online researching?

○ Approximately 48% of the students surveyed said that they were moderately likely to extremely likely to begin their research from the library home page.

○ On average, 65 to 75% of students evaluated the three information media studied here (search engines, databases, and library catalogs) as useful sources (i.e., a "4" or "5" on a scale where 5 = extremely useful).

○ Students report that they are more likely to use a search engine than a database or online library catalog when doing research for a class. ($F(2,71) = 38.04$, $p<.001$).

○ When asked about research habits in finding sources:

- 9% stop searching as soon as they've found one good source.

- 63% sample 10 or fewer sources and use the best of those.

- 16% sample more than 10 sources and use the best of those.

- 12% claim to examine all available resources to find the best sources.

○ A series of correlations reveals that students' reported likelihood of using a search engine or library catalog is statistically significantly related to reports of finding the information one is looking for, having confidence that one has found all the information one needs, and being confident that the information one has found is factually correct. With databases, however, although likelihood of use is related to reports of finding the information one is looking for and having confidence that one has found all the information one needs, it is not related to confidence that the information one has found is correct.

○ Regarding the three resources studied, search engines, databases, and the library catalog, confidence that one has found all the information one needs in the use of one resource is unrelated to confidence in the use of the others, with the exception of databases and the library catalog, where confidence in one resource is positively correlated ($r(71) = .42$, $p<.001$) with confidence in the other. The same holds true regarding confidence in the correctness of the information found. Only database and library catalog confidence are related ($r(71) = .594$, $p<.001$).

○ Use of the library catalog for research is statistically significantly related to use of a database; $r(71) = .609$, $p<.001$. Neither of the other relationships concerning use among the three resources studied (library catalog and search engines or databases and search engines) was significant.

○ On a scale of 1 to 5, where 1= not at all confident and 5 = completely confident, the average response to confidence that one has found all the information one needs with search engines was 3.3 (SD = .88, n=100), with databases was 3.5 (SD = .93, n=79), and with the library catalog was 3.3 (SD = .93, n = 88).

- What do they know about search engines?

  - There is some confusion among students as to what constitutes a search engine. Incorrect responses included Infotrac (a database); Geocities (a Web community); WebMD (a health Web page); and Mozilla (an Internet browser).

  - On average, students could name three actual search engines when asked on a free-recall question.

  - The search engines most likely to be identified were: (1) Google, (2) Yahoo, and (3) Ask Jeeves.

  - When given a definition of a search engine, 92% reported that they had a preferred search engine. Of those with preferred engines, 65.2% preferred Google and 21.7% Yahoo. 13.1 percent preferred other engines or multiple engines.

  - Our respondents believe that, on average, 39.87% (SD= 20.3, n=100) of the information on the Internet is factually incorrect.

- What difference did it make to take a library tour given by a librarian or to have had a librarian give a guest lecture in one of their classes?

  - If respondents had had a tour of the library or a librarian as a guest lecturer, they were more likely to evaluate the library catalog as a useful source of information ($t = 3.95$, df = 92, $p < .015$) and to begin the search for online resources to complete a class assignment from the library home page ($t = 3.45$, df = 92, $p < .037$) than was someone who had NOT had a library tour or librarian guest lecturer.

  - Having had a library tour or lecture by a librarian or not did not distinguish their reported likelihood of using the library catalog, finding the information they needed there, or their confidence in the factual correctness of any information they found there. Neither did participation in a tour or lecture affect their evaluation of the usefulness of search engines or databases as sources of information.

Discussion of Survey Findings

Not surprisingly, our participants, who were students queried while in the library, were even more likely than the general population to report having used search engines (99% vs. 87%) and to report using them on a daily basis (70% vs. 55%). Our respondents were much more likely than the general population to have a preferred search engine (92% vs. 44%).

Unlike the Pew survey, we did not ask our respondents directly about their confidence in their search abilities, but rather focused on their confidence in the resource's capability to allow them to find all the information they need and in their perception of the correctness of that information. While the average confidence in these tools was only in the midpoint of our rating scales, if one was likely to use a resource, one was also likely to be confident in the capability of the resource to help him or her find the needed information, and to trust in the correctness of that information.

In the future, it would be instructive to repeat this survey with a larger sample that is more representative of all our student body. (For example, the largest class on campus, freshmen, were proportionately underrepresented here.) If students are already in the library, they are perhaps more likely to be technologically savvy and academically focused than their peers who do not frequent the library.

Student Completion of a Literature Search Assignment

A pilot study was conducted wherein 19 students enrolled in an upper-level psychology research writing course were examined for their ability to correctly conduct a literature search. Although the students were working on different topics, all were pursuing tasks with a known "correct" outcome: namely, to find supportive literature for the claim that certain psychological constructs were related to certain nonverbal behaviors. An assessment of the students' library resource experiences before completing the assignment revealed that 17 of the 19 students reported having used PsycInfo before, and 9 of 19 had had formal library instruction (a tour or lecture by a librarian) at some point in their college career. Fifteen of the students (78.9%) were able to correctly conduct their literature searches and find appropriate sources. Of the four students who did not successfully complete the assignment, all reported having been exposed to PsycInfo before and all but one had had a formal library tour.

From this small sample one might tentatively conclude that, while formal library instruction may be helpful, is not necessary to predicting students' successful searching of the empirical literature in psychology. This may be because students have received assistance in other places in the psychology curriculum. Neither does exposure to appropriate databases and library instruction guarantee success in correctly employing such resources, although the number of students who do not appear to benefit is in line with what one might expect if ability and motivation to perform a task are normally distributed. It is important to note, however, that success on this assignment was defined as finding ANY, not ALL, appropriate resources. It would be interesting to discover if library instruction is related to more successful comprehensive searches.

Faculty Instruction in the Use of Online Resources

An attempt was made to systematically identify faculty who gave written assignments that required searching the literature and to explore whether or not these faculty provided instruction in the use of online resources. The original plan was to examine the syllabi of all faculty in the School of Humanities and Social Sciences (N = 301). It quickly became apparent, however, that the syllabi supposedly kept on file in each department as public information were often not available. Consequently, the sample was redefined to include only those faculty in the four largest departments that did have such records. Of this new sample of 117 faculty, it was determined by a perusal of their syllabi that 92 had given major writing assignments requiring a search of the literature. These faculty were contacted and asked if they had distributed any written (and therefore verifiable) instruction on the use of online resources. Of these, only 81 faculty members were still available on campus. A written request sent to these faculty resulted in 19 responses, of which 3 reported having given such instruction. One handout consisted of a two-sentence description of InfoTrac and a two-sentence description of JSTOR; a second handout was an excerpt from a library handout description of PsycARTICLES, PsycINFO, and Science Direct, and the third handout was a list of Web sites that are used by journalists (e.g., the U.S. census Web site, the link for the local newspaper, etc.)

It's hard to conclude much from this meager response, although there are three possible interpretations: (1) we had few respondents because few faculty provide online resource instruction, (2) more faculty may provide online resource instruction but they do so verbally, so it is difficult to verify and not assessed by this endeavor, or (3) more faculty may provide such instruction, but they did not report this to us.

We recommend that more formal assessments of exposure to search strategies be conducted by the college's administration, which might be better able to invoke compliance with requests for curricular information than we were. Each department should ensure that students are being exposed to the research tools in their field, especially with regard to the ever-changing development of online resources.

Conclusion

So is the search for online resources ever complete? We can't say for sure, perhaps no one can, but we know that our search for an understanding of the prevalence and influence of these resources on our campus and in our lives should continue. Clearly, as students, faculty, and librarians, there is much we still need to learn about how we do and should conduct our searches of the information world around us.

Notes

1. Pew Internet & American Life Project, *Search Engine Users*, 2005 [Online], available: http://www.pewinternet.org.
2. D. Dunning, C. Heath, and J. M. Suls, "Flawed Self-Assessment: Implications for Health, Education, and the Workplace." *Psychological Science* 5 (2004): 69–106.
3. Pew, *Search Engine Users*.
4. Dunning et al., "Flawed Self-Assessment."
5. B. Fischhoff, P. Slovic, and S. Lichtenstein. (1977). "Knowing with Certainty: The Appropriateness of Extreme Confidence." *Journal of Experimental Psychology: Human Perception and Performance* 3 (1977): 552–564.

Acknowledgments

We would like to thank Katina Strauch, Head, Collection Development Department of the Addlestone Library, for her inspiration and support of this project; Sheila Seaman, Assistant Dean, Public Services of the Addlestone Library, for sharing with us some important background research in the area, and David Cohen, Dean of Libraries of the College of Charleston, for allowing us to survey patrons in the library. Thanks also to the department chairs and faculty members who helped us in our efforts to assess faculty instruction in using online resources.

S everal sessions at the 2005 Charleston Conference focused on product development. These presentations explored how librarians and vendors can work cooperatively to create a useful product. This type of collaboration is extremely helpful for all parties involved.

Product Development

ANATOMY OF DIGITAL PRODUCT DEVELOPMENT: A PATHOLOGICAL LOOK AT PRODUCT DEVELOPMENT IN THE LIBRARY MARKET

Nathan Norris, Medical Librarian, Beth Israel Deaconess Medical Center, Boston, Massachusetts

Meg White, Executive Director, Digital Business Development, Rittenhouse, King of Prussia, Pennsylvania

Stephen Decroes, Director of Sales, Marketing and Right for McGraw-Hill Digital, New York, New York

Mike Simmons, Library Manager, Sparrow Health System, Lansing, Michigan

This presentation and discussion over lunch provided insight from three different stakeholders in a shared product development experience. The shared product experience is a Web-based content platform called the R2 Library, which was designed to deliver content intended for the medical library market. This experience served as a framework for a more general discussion on product development for libraries and stakeholder involvement in this process. Topics discussed include the product development cycle from conception to delivery. One of the conclusions from this session is that effective communication and execution based on feedback among each of the stakeholders is extremely important in determining if a product will ultimately be a success.

This program consisted of a moderator and three speakers followed by a question and answer session; the complete program lasted approximately 1.5 hours.

The first speaker was Meg White, Executive Director of Business Development for Rittenhouse and R2 Library Project Manager. Meg discussed the software development lifecycle, as well as how the R2 Library product was conceived, created, and presented. The company's experience factored in much more collaboration and iterative development than most established models include. Meg also emphasized that while many projects do ask for customer or user feedback, it is critical to listen and act on this feedback appropriately. She acknowledged that this process can be slow and sometimes painful, but pays significant long-term dividends.

The second speaker was Stephen Decroes, Director of Sales, Marketing and Rights for McGraw-Hill Digital. McGraw-Hill Digital was one of the publishers that provided some content for R2. Stephen discussed how his company evaluates such a partnership opportunity, how it fits into his company's business goals and overall strategy, content selection, and communication with partners.

The third speaker was Michael Simmons, Director of the Sparrow Health System Library in Michigan. Michael discussed his participation in piloting R2 and other products, communication tools, product feedback, and participation outcomes. One of his conclusions is that librarians should formalize partnership arrangements, recognizing time and resource commitments. In addition, collaboration should span all elements of the vendor/librarian relationship, communication should be specific, and gathering feedback from end-user trials is important.

The moderator was Nathan Norris, Medical Librarian at the Beth Israel Deaconess Medical Center library in Boston.

Discussions with the audience following the presentations focused on five areas:

Librarian involvement in company advisory boards and product development.

Discussion regarding corporate strategy vis-à-vis publishers' relationship with vendors.

Vendor strategy for successful product creation.

Differences between publishing and distribution.

Pricing strategy.

COLLABORATIVE ROLE OF LIBRARY ACQUISITIONS IN DEVELOPMENT AND TESTING OF VENDOR SYSTEMS

Sha Li Zhang, Assistant Director for Collections and Technical Services, University of North Carolina at Greensboro

Glen Worley, Manager, Monograph Acquisitions and Approval Plans, University of Texas, Austin

John Williams, Public Service Administrator and Manager of Acquisitions, Wichita State University, Kansas

Dan Miller, Electronic Services Consultant, Blackwell's Book Service, Lake Oswego, Oregon

Abstract

Intensive competition for library markets constrains book vendors to offer technologically enhanced services that streamline acquisitions workflows and improve efficiency of transactions. These technological endeavors not only benefit both sides but also require collaborative efforts from both sides. In this program, the presenters from three university libraries and a book vendor offered their experience and observations: first on the part technological interdependence makes in forging the traditional business/client model of library/vendor relationships into a true collaboration that benefits the end user; and second in developing with the vendor Web-based selection and ordering modalities in Collection Manager and Blackwell's new order management and distribution system. The issues, benefits, and recommendations of these collaborative activities are discussed.

Introduction

Beta testing of monographs vendor information and processing systems is focused on creating utilities that are cost effective for the vendor to maintain and efficient for the client libraries to use. Of all the facets of the library/vendor relationship, this testing of prototype systems and new systems is the most collaborative and, perhaps, the most far reaching within the library community. This chapter focuses on testing of Blackwell's Book Service's Collection Manager system in the late 1990s by the University of Texas and testing of Blackwell's CMS order processing system by Wichita State University in 2004 as examples of this sort of collaborative effort. Further comments on lessons learned through these tests and comments on beta testing generally are also offered out of the experiences of these two projects.

Advantages that accrue to libraries that commit to the performance of beta tests are

- better-prepared library acquisitions staff,
- team efforts between the vendor's system developer and library staff,
- well-informed vendor design decisions,
- flexible workflows, and
- smoother implementation of new systems.

Some notable recent examples of such testing are the following:

- Kansas State University Libraries as a beta testing site for Endeavor's Voyager ILS in the mid-1990s,[1]

- The Library of Congress as a beta testing site for Endeavor's Unicode OPAC module in 2003,[2] and

- Innovative Interfaces beta testing in 40 libraries of its Millennium Silver Module in 2004.[3]

The most recent major beta test, of course, was Blackwell's Book Service's test of its CMS order processing system, during which the company partnered with 12 of its approximately 5,000 active academic library clients in 2004. Blackwell's Book Service specializes in the supply of books (printed and, increasingly, electronic) and bibliographic support products to academic, research, and leading public libraries throughout the world. It is the market leader in combining traditional bookselling expertise with the latest developments in library technology. Blackwell's supports firm orders (purchasing titles one by one), standing orders (purchasing all volumes in series), and approval plans (based on profiling libraries and books and matching the profiles on a weekly basis to send books and new title announcements to libraries automatically). Blackwell's also offers added value technical services such as a Web-based selection and order system called Collection Manager, MARC records with books, book processing, table of contents (TOCs) in machine readable form, etc. The discussion here, however, focuses on the role of technology in bookselling, customer beta testing of Blackwell's CMS ordering and distribution system, and customer involvement in collection manager development.

The Role of Technology in Bookselling

Prefatory to discussing cooperative systems development, it is appropriate to discuss the role technology plays in bookselling to libraries. As a distributor, any bookseller must distinguish and differentiate itself through value-added services since a book is a commodity that can be received in its identical form through a variety of sources. Technology's role in contributing to these value-added services is derived from the nature of bookselling, where identification (or discovery), evaluation, selection, and ordering must be supported in an environment in which there are numerous "products" (say, over 50,000 new scholarly titles per year) that must be described in minute detail to distinguish between different titles, different editions of the same title, different formats of the same editions, etc. Given the large number of items for sale, technology is particularly suited to addressing this, in Blackwell's case in the form of our Web-based Collection Manager system, which is described later. And the same concerns pertain to value-added services like MARC cataloging, shelf-ready services, and TOC enrichment, which help libraries successfully support identification, evaluation, and selection for their users. And finally, these concerns apply to internal operations, since they are needed to accurately and efficiently identify, select, and order titles from suppliers to support accurate and timely supply to customers. Again, given the large number of items for sale, technology is particularly suited to addressing this issue, in this case in the form of our CMS distribution and order management system described below. Blackwell's views customers' involvement in developing, testing, and implementing these technology-based systems as essential, since customers are the primary beneficiaries and stand to gain or lose the most from efforts and accomplishments in these areas.

Collaborative Development of Blackwell's Collection Manager

Collection Manager (CM), Blackwell's Web-based selection and ordering system, was developed in 1995–1996. Originally envisioned as a tool for providing access to user-friendly displays of libraries' approval profiles, Collection Manager has undergone extensive enhancement over the years to integrate selection and order functionality. Blackwell's abided by two development principles:

- Support the fundamental elements of collection development: identification, evaluation, selection, and ordering of titles; and

- Create a system that adapts to the way librarians work, rather than requiring librarians to adapt to Blackwell's internal procedures.

From its inception as an idea presented to Blackwell's senior management to the present day, the prototype process has relied extensively on HTML and JavaScript to display "front end" functionality. This relatively easy and low-cost method for demonstrating enhancements to client libraries provides Blackwell's with the ability to present the proposed enhancements at library conferences, in libraries, and to focus groups. It also offers the flexibility to integrate libraries' suggestions into the design before implementation. Finally, Blackwell's has found that prototyping in this manner provides an unambiguous method for conveying specifications to programmers.

Once programming is complete, enhancements are beta tested with up to 10 customers before implementation. Initially, Blackwell's undertook beta testing on test servers; more recently, a method has been found to screen enhancements from all but beta test libraries on Blackwell's production server, allowing the test libraries to use enhancements in a production environment. Once beta testing is complete, enhancements are implemented for all Collection Manager users by lifting filters on the enhancements. Through these processes, Blackwell's has found a reliable test bed for designing, vetting, and implementing enhancements to its Collection Manager system. Historically, prototyping and beta testing of CM has involved the following:

- The original prototype focus group included 18 librarians.

- The biannual focus group includes 45 librarians.

- Enhancements are routinely beta tested with 10 library partners.

- Mega-enhancement that added acquisitions functionality in 1998 was beta tested with 59 libraries.

- The current survey includes 85 libraries contributing to prioritization of enhancements.

University of Texas Beta Test of Collection Manager

The University of Texas Libraries has used Blackwell's Book Service as its major approval plan vendor since 1984. The contract for our approval plan comes up for competitive bid every three years. As far as library system technology goes, Texas is one of a few Association of Research Libraries (ARL) members that do not have an integrated library system. Currently it uses the text-based Innovative Interfaces INNOPAC Acquisitions and Serials systems. Because of this state of technological affairs, Texas cannot avail itself of all the enhancements offered by vendors, but it can collaborate with Blackwell's in the development of its Collection Manager product because of its size (fifth largest ARL library system), and this collaboration does benefit both parties.

Before Collection Manager existed, University of Texas selectors were intimidated by the approval plan. The "greenbar" paper printouts of the approval plan profile were visually and intellectually daunting. Equally intimidating was the individual title profiling information provided by microfiche and, later, by New Titles Online (NTO). Most selectors avoided using NTO because of log-in difficulties inherent with Telnet clients used by the library. UT Libraries went so far as to pay Blackwell's to provide a marked copy of its subject code thesaurus so that the approval plan manager could know which subjects were assigned to a given sub-profile.

In spite of periodic training sessions, the approval plan manager became the de facto "oracle" for the approval plan. Selectors routinely asked for interpretations of the display from NTO or, worse, asked that the approval manager look it up for them. Much time was devoted to the same sorts of questions: "Will the book be sent on approval?" Acquisitions personnel became the interface between the vendor and the user despite all the best intentions of Blackwell's and its programmers.

It was obvious that the Texas approval plan was not being used efficiently in its collection development strategy. Since selectors chose to avoid using NTO and the paper copies of sub-profiles, they constantly duplicated on firm orders the same titles that would arrive on the approval plan. The policy, to return approval titles that are also on firm order, frustrated selectors as the book on the approval review shelf was returned when the copy that was on firm order had not yet arrived. This situation was disadvantageous to all parties. The selectors and acquisitions personnel spent much time needlessly ordering titles that would have been supplied on approval. Blackwell's had to accept returns and lose sales. Selectors spent time waiting for questions to be answered by others because the learning curve for understanding NTO and the approval plan profile was steep.

The Collection Manager prototype was demonstrated in 1995 to UT Libraries' personnel. Shortly afterward Texas was asked to help beta test the product. At this time, the UT Libraries approval plan was one of the largest administered by Blackwell's and, as mentioned previously, the manager had acquired years of experience in answering selectors' questions concerning the plan. Collection Manager promised to allow selectors to integrate the approval plan into their selection strategy, making more efficient use of their time.

The beta test at Texas was approached from the viewpoint of three different interest groups:

Acquisitions

- Compliance issues

- Will it improve efficiency?

- Improvement over NTO and paper profile

Bibliographers/Selectors:

- Ease of access and use

- Display understandable/intuitive navigation

○ Worth the time to learn the system

Patrons/End users:

○ Does it get the book on shelf faster?

During beta testing of Collection Manager it was very important for both Blackwell's and the beta testers to keep in mind what was a necessary feature and what might be an "interesting" feature. In other words, both parties must collaborate to ascertain the elements of the product that would be used regularly and the parts that were superfluous.

As the primary tester at UT, the manager approached testing from the viewpoint of his position not only as approval plan manager, but also as a selector with limited knowledge of the workings of the approval plan. The latter was the most important, as the workflow situation would not improve if Collection Manager was not used by the selectors. Selectors base their use of various systems on first impressions. If their first experience with a vendor's system is negative, it is very difficult to convince them to try again. Also, one person's experience will influence his or her colleagues. The operation of the product had to be intuitive enough that users would be willing to put in the time to learn the basics of operation. An overly complicated system would not improve upon the NTO model.

Phase 1 of Collection Manager was designed to support the approval plan, and beta testing at UT was conducted to make sure that Collection Manager would improve workflow for selectors. It became obvious quickly that selectors could get the information they needed provided that they were willing to use the system. In order to determine whether or not this would happen, selectors were asked to use the product under the supervision of the manager and give their impressions. Collection Manager was also incorporated into the daily aspects of the job of approval manager to ascertain whether its features would improve workflow.

Use of the product indicated the features where improvements might be needed. Since the basic structure of Collection Manager was set, testing of the available features was more important than suggesting extensive redesign. Accordingly, extreme tests of Collection Manager were made by running ridiculous searches and compiling lists of titles that would push the system to its limits. Confusing terminology was also noted; for example, the original text for the "book action icon" was "book sent." UT suggested the change to "book selected" since selectors would assume that the book had actually been shipped if the original text was used. This was important because it represented a particularly important and persistent question from our selectors.

Phase 2 of Collection Manager allowed selectors to use CM to place orders for titles as well as check the approval status of titles. This offered the potential for real improvements in the ordering process by eliminating the need to rekey data present in Collection Manager. However, the ordering model as envisioned by Blackwell's personnel was not the model used by UT Libraries. This illustrates the need for collaboration between vendor and customers early on in the design phase of new systems, as customers using the same library systems may have different requirements and/or workflows dictated by other constraints such as local compliance regulations or other systems that interact with the library system. In this case, vendor-customer collaboration during the beta test provided the happy result of Blackwell's learning a new way that Collection Manager could be used in the ordering process, and Texas benefited from adding Collection Manager to our ordering process.

The beta test of Enotes, or electronic forms, provides a good example of how a product can be enthusiastically received by some portion of the desired market, but not all. Enotes was widely appreciated by UT's science and technology selectors, but viewed askance by some of our selectors, who have been reluctant to abandon their old system of sorting paper forms.

The beta test of the Sales and Returns reports illustrates the difference in perception of features by different user groups. The manager found the ability to run his own sales and returns reports very valuable and uses this feature on a regular basis. However, selectors found this feature more intimidating and tend to request that reports be generated for them rather than do it themselves. This does not necessarily mean that this is an unnecessary enhancement, but shows that not all users will embrace every feature of a vendor's product.

Over the last eight years both Blackwell's Book Service and the UT Libraries have seen benefits due to the collaboration in development of the various stages of Collection Manager. All three interest groups—Acquisitions, Selectors, and Patrons—have benefited from this collaboration. Over half of the English-language monographs purchased by the UT Libraries are received via our Blackwell's approval plan. Last year this amounted to just under 17,000 titles. One full-time employee (FTE) in Acquisitions handles all aspects of processing the approval plan materials, from unpacking boxes to paying invoices. Quite simply, it is the most efficient procurement method that UT Libraries employs to purchase books. Our entire technical services processes are built around the weekly shipment of approval books. With the exception of RUSH titles, all other titles have a lower priority than the approval books.

Since the inception of Collection Manager's capability to export records with order information to our INNOPAC system, firm orders to Blackwell's have doubled. Over the last three fiscal years firm orders to Blackwell's have accounted for 31% of all UT firm orders. At the same time, the number of approval titles returned to Blackwell's because they were already firm ordered has dropped dramatically.

Selectors appreciate that beta testing of Collection Manger features by UT Libraries has resulted in a product that caters to their concerns and needs. Selectors now send suggestions to pass along to Blackwell's for future enhancements and are now much more familiar with their portions of the approval plan. Most selectors now use Collection Manager as the first source to check before placing an order request. Older selectors now educate their younger peers on how best to use the approval plan and Collection Manager. This interaction did not occur prior to the rollout of Collection Manager. The number of "will this book come on approval" questions to the approval plan manager has dropped considerably, and such questions now are usually from new selectors. This year selectors were required to use Collection Manager to review all their approval plan sub-profiles for subject and publisher coverage, and also non-subject parameters. In the past this would have been possible only by the on-site presence of a Blackwell's representative and the manager working with all 33 selectors on an individual basis.

Getting selectors to use Enotes, rather than the traditional paper form, is a continuing process. As one might expect, selectors in the science and technology areas have adopted the use of Enotes, and their positive experience is encouraging their more cautious colleagues to try using electronic forms. However, the old model of compiling forms and waiting until the end of the fiscal year to make selections is no longer effective. As print runs grow smaller, selectors will need to submit order requests quickly before the book goes out of print. Enotes are delivered about three weeks before the paper form arrives, and this amount of time can make a difference between getting the book or not.

Because of the ability to load order requests from Collection Manager directly into our INNOPAC system instead of rekeying data, UT Libraries' firm order unit has been able to re-allocate staff to help in other areas. Since the order requests from Collection Manager are visible to all selectors in the CM display, duplicate orders for the same title have dropped. Also, the loading of order requests directly into the ordering system allows for the use of the ordering systems' searching and reporting features on these order requests. This is not possible for order requests sent via paper forms or e-mail. There is also a translation program that updates the locally developed OPAC on a daily basis in order to display titles that are newly ordered in the catalog. Order requests from Collection Manager are usually processed very quickly, so library patrons get the benefit of this efficiency by seeing the on order display for titles, reducing patron purchase requests and inter-library loan requests.

The CMS Project

CMS was the moniker given to the project replacing Blackwell's order management and distribution system. The project was undertaken because Blackwell's Book Service's technological infrastructure did not allow adequate adaptation to changing business needs and opportunities. There existed excessive duplication of data; code that was increasingly difficult to support; and systems developed around once adequate, but later outdated, concepts. The objective of CMS was to remove these impediments from the practice of our business, allowing Blackwell's to reinvent processes and in some cases products themselves, while providing better support for customer needs. The vision was to implement a vendor package to upgrade the processes in the Blackwell's distribution centers. The objectives were to speed order fulfillment and increase overall efficiency to allow an increase in volume.

Blackwell's decided to purchase an off-the-shelf system because it would be less expensive than developing a system in house, and because the expertise of the supplier would provide broader insight than was in house into the requirements and features of a robust order management and distribution system. The choice of an off-the-shelf system posed two challenges: interfaces with existing Blackwell's systems and functional gaps (i.e., it became obvious that with the combination of Blackwell's business practices and its visionary requirements, several functional gaps existed in the off-the-shelf software requiring some customization of the software).

Beta Test Principles, Goals, Structure, and Process

The purposes behind Blackwell's CMS beta test were to validate as many business processes and flows as possible, to increase the comfort level with thorough testing of functionality and reliability, to do a minimum amount of "throwaway" work, and to minimize disruption to customers. Beta test goals included testing by a cross section of Blackwell's U.S. and UK customers, verifying processes around orders, verifying that system and network connections operate, verifying that legacy systems could send data to the new system, verifying that financial systems could process data from the new system, verifying that other Blackwell's systems (e.g., financial, bibliographic) interface properly with the new system, and developing an internal/external communications plan.

The test structure involved inclusion of 12 beta customers chosen based on mix of service and location attributes; processing of approvals and firm orders from EDI, manual order entry, and Collection Manager; loading of open orders for beta customers into the new system; receiving firm orders in the new system that were originally purchased through the old system, not converting publisher purchase orders created in the old system into the new system; updating supplier for Purchased Part record in new system with the correct list price, discount, and supplier; added invoice number and supplier name received in old system to the Purchased Part record (for Blackwell's finance department); and entering new firm orders for beta customers directly into the new system.

The beta test process took place from April 26, 2004, through August 30, 2004 (i.e., four full months). Blackwell's held weekly conference calls with beta customers, and daily briefings were held with each distribution location, focusing on new problems found and progress on previously identified issues. Successes and failures were noted and remedial actions taken on failures. The decision to go live was based on beta customer input, along with input from internal managers. It was in this beta test process that collaboration with Blackwell's library partners was critical. The weekly conference call between all beta customers and key Blackwell's staff helped reveal critical issues that had to be addressed.

Wichita State's Beta Test of CMS

The Blackwell's beta test of its CMS materials control software occurred over a four-month period in the middle of which was fiscal year rollover. Blackwell's last major software implementation was in 1997 with Collection Manager. Participation in the CMS beta test was by invitation and based on recommendation of Blackwell's regional sales managers. In the Mountain Plains region, only the University of Texas and Wichita State were recommended and were both selected. The recommendation was based on their approach to managing acquisitions, commitment to highly automated procedures, EDI invoicing, and MARC record supply. In the case of Wichita State, the relationship with Blackwell's extends even further as they have a competitive sole source arrangement with them dating to November 1996. This arrangement was just renegotiated with Blackwell's after application by two other major vendors and a competitive process.

Beta testing is a noticeable subdivision of intellectual property law. It has legal ramifications. Wichita State did not enter into the test lightly and subjected the vendor's software to the harshest criticisms. A formal agreement was also signed by the Libraries' dean before the test took place.

The complex of interfaces that must necessarily harmonize to produce increased efficiencies of library acquisitions and vendor supply of materials is now daunting. Merely conceptualizing a proposed increase in efficiency is challenging. Just on the library side of acquisitions transactions, inputs from a vendor in the form of EDI invoices and MARC record supply must comply with multiple protocols of platform, operating system, ILS software, etc., before bibliographic, encumbrance, and expenditure data can be verified by an operator.

Adding to this is the proper interfaces among selector, Blackwell's Collection Manager, the acquisitions assistant charged with ordering and encumbrance, warehouse shipment of materials, the freight hauler, and the accounting assistant charged with verifying the audit trail. None of the separate elements is simple, and the combination of tasks is highly complex even without the addition of hardware and software protocols. The pending interface between this already complex system and universitywide ERP software, with its own requirements of best practice, brings this complexity to an even higher level (see Table 1).

Table 1

Year of Implementation	Relational Database: Oracle	Server & programming lang.: Sun/Unix/Java	Client O/S: Microsoft	LMS: Endeavor	LMS: Innovative*
1977	ver.1				
1979	ver.2				OCLC Interface
1981			MS DOS		Acquisitions Module
1983	ver.3 (in C)				
1984	ver.4 (VAX & IBM)				
1985	ver.5 (C/S & MS DOS)				Serials Control
1987					OPAC
1988	ver.6				
1989		SPARCstation 1			Circulation Module
1991	ver.6.1	Solaris 2			
1992	ver.7	SPARCstation 10	Windows 3.1		
1993		Unified UNIX		rel. 1	
1995		JAVA	Windows 95 (end of DOS)		Web OPAC
1996					Millenium
1997	ver.8, 8i & rel.2 (XML)	SUN Enterprise 10000 (hi end)			
1998		Solaris 7	Windows 98	rel. 2	
1999					Millenium w/ Oracle
2000		Solaris 8/SPARCcenter 2000	Windows 2000 & NT		
2002	ver.9i	Solaris 9	Windows XP	rel.2.1	
2003					Elec. Res. Mgt.
2004	ver.10g			ENCOMPASS	
2005		Solaris 10		ver. 5	
					*Note:
					UNIX-based in C/C++
					& JAVA. May be
					implemented under
					ORACLE w/ SUN
					server

Both the University of Texas and Wichita State have made substantial staff reallocations based on the efficiencies of Blackwell's operations since the implementation of Collection Manager. In the case of WSU, MARC record supply via bulk loads of bibliographic records overnight and EDI invoicing were developed alongside the shift to using Collection Manager for selection and ordering. These changes have allowed for transfer of personnel/positions out of acquisitions. In Wichita's case, those positions went to the Libraries' systems unit.

As an agency of the State of Kansas, Wichita State has made notable progress in rapidly recording encumbrances through creation of purchase orders (POs) attached to bibliographic records and rapidly converting those encumbrances to expenditures upon receipt of materials with EDI invoices correctly attached to the appropriate POs. The objective of any acquisitions transaction, however, is twofold: to ensure that materials ordered and paid for are received (the fiscal part of the mission) and to facilitate rapidly placing those materials in the hands of patrons (the operational goal of the mission). The second objective sometimes gets lost. At Wichita State, supervisors and managers are firmly versed in operations research and, because of repeated partnerships with graduate students in other colleges and faculties of the university (particularly engineering), we have refined materials handling techniques in order to supply new materials to patrons rapidly. A chart has been developed by Acquisitions, confirmation of an application of Pareto's 80/20 rule that indicates that approximately 80% of circulation charges occur in the 20% of most recent imprint years available to patrons (see Figure 1).[4] The chart stops in 2000, as acquiring imprints of 2001–2005 is still being actively accomplished. Making new materials available rapidly underwrites increased utilization of materials and the chart is used to support that assertion.

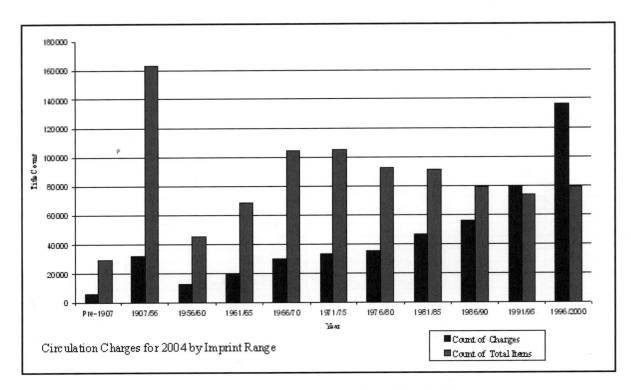

Figure 1. Circulation Charges for 2004 by Imprint Range.

Keeping this second, service-to-the-patron objective in mind, WSU monitored data concerning issues of fulfillment in its Voyager system before, during, and after the beta test with Blackwell's to determine the internal impacts of being involved in the project. The beta test was uniformly successful in improving the time-to-fill with regard to book supply. Average time improved by 59%. For both libraries and State of Kansas agencies, this is an important attribute. Materials are on-site rapidly and encumbrances are converted to expenditures more quickly. In terms of the overall number of transactions processed pre- and post-beta test, the project represented a 13% decline in volume with Blackwell's in terms of discrete transactions. In other words, an internal assessment of the likelihood of an order being filled was rapidly made and least eligible firm orders became deal directs. Blackwell's soon became aware of its growing problems with throughput and added a second shift to process materials. Data collected through September 1, 2005, indicate that Blackwell's now is at least on par with the volume of materials it was able to process prior to the beta test.

The beta test and the subsequent implementation was the second major change in interface with Blackwell's since 1997. The first was Collection Manager. Collection Manager concurrently produced bulk MARC record supply and EDI invoicing: WSU slip-streamed multiple operation changes out of one utility. Those effects, however, were years in the making and, even though WSU customized its NOTIS system to make some things possible prior to 2000, it really was not until it implemented Endeavor's Voyager in January 2000 that it was able to exploit Blackwell's technical services as fully as possible.

In the case of the beta test, the changes in its conduct of business came within nine months. One reason that the change has been so swift is the closeness WSU developed with Blackwell's staff through the beta testing process. There is a much more frank relationship.

Some firm orders, as opposed to NTAS orders, were switched to deal direct temporarily simply because firms have always caused problems as an agent for the State of Kansas. Agencies must convert encumbrances to expenditures by the end of the fiscal year. Agencies cannot carry forward an encumbrance. It must be spent on a desired title or a title that is available must be bought and paid for. What has continued to happen since the end of the beta test is a trip-wire "fill or kill" disposition toward aging orders. This is facilitated because of the convenience and reliability of other online vendors who can inform on the Web at the time of order whether the book will appear in a stipulated period of time. Those vendors also take money immediately with a credit card. Because of the beta test, there arose a tendency to purchase more high-dollar, special promotional material, which is probably good for the collection. And Blackwell's MARC record purchase has been shifted into the materials budget on savings that have accrued because of a renegotiated, long-term arrangement with Blackwell's. All of these impacts on the conduct of business have been good for WSU Libraries, and they have been good (if painful in the getting) for Blackwell's. WSU is back to business as usual, and Blackwell's has a completely modernized system that will underwrite its competitiveness for decades.

What Did Blackwell's Learn (Was Beta Testing Successful?)

Beta testing was successful because Blackwell's learned of several issues and defects during beta testing that were addressed through implementation of 11 upgrades to the system in the course of beta testing. However, beta testing was not successful due to a key issue not revealed until system go-live in September 2004. This issue was whether the system could handle the full volume of processing. At go-live Blackwell's encountered difficulty with the high volume of transactions associated with normal processing, for example, threshold limits, keystrokes entered, and queries. These were not network or telecom problems, but, rather, high volume against the database. One particularly nettlesome issue was queries against the database. Initially, there was little ability to limit queries, and it was too easy for a user to inadvertently ask the database to return every bit of information it contains. Obviously, this slowed processing. Blackwell's didn't see this in beta, because we had experienced "core team" members (a.k.a. "super users") performing the functions. Still, there were some things we could have done to educate the users before go-live about good querying practice.

Was Full-Volume Beta Testing Possible?

Blackwell's believed that a full-volume beta test was prohibitive for a few reasons, the most important being that replication of all databases would have been a very costly undertaking. In addition, running parallel systems would have stretched staff and hardware capacity.

Non-parallel full-volume testing would have required a shut down of Blackwell's operations for weeks to put everyone onto the task of pretend actions on the new system. This would have been a monstrous task to plan, as Blackwell's would have had to fully migrate data from the old system to the new, process new orders of all types into the system, while hanging onto them for entry into the legacy system in the event that beta testing failed.

The result was that implementation was problematic, particularly with respect to maintaining a level of throughput to which Blackwell's customers were accustomed. However, as statistics show, Blackwell's is now back to (or has exceeded) pre-implementation levels of throughput and turnaround times. Moreover, Blackwell's now has an order management and distribution system in place that supports superior customer service, more nimble systems enhancements, and easier adaptation to changing business needs and opportunities.

Survey of CMS Beta Test Participants

The following libraries participated in the CMS beta test:

Vanderbilt University

University of Texas at Austin

University of Hawaii

University of Manitoba (Canada)

Oregon State University

Firenze Euro (Italy)

Kent University (UK)

KOC University (Republic of Turkey)

Demontfort University (UK)

Dartmouth University

Notre Dame University

Wichita State University

An online survey asked respondents to reply concerning the nature of their planning, support, and perception of the beta test of CMS and whether they thought a positive contribution had been made because of the project. In only two areas (vendor support/feedback during the project and an understanding of the purpose of the project) was there any disagreement with project goals and conduct. That disagreement also amounted to only 20% of responses in both cases. (See Figure 2.)

Do you agree with the following statements?	Strongly disagree	Disagree	Agree	Strongly agree	Total
The vendor was well prepared for the beta test			100%		100%
My library had a comprehensive plan for the beta test		20%	80%		100%
My library administration supported the beta test		20%	60%	20%	100%
The vendor representatives provided needed consultation during the beta test		20%	20%	60%	100%
My library had a full level of commitment to the beta test			40%	60%	100%
Designated staff were assigned to participate in the beta test			80%	20%	100%
The productivity and contribution of my library was acknowledged by the vendor during the beta test			60%	40%	100%
I understood the advantages of the project both for Blackwell's and its clients		20%	40%	40%	100%

Figure 2. Results of a Brief Survey of Participating Libraries.

Conclusion

From the beta testing by the University of Texas and Wichita State University of Blackwell's Collection Manager and CMS systems, two conclusions are apparent:

- Integration of disparate systems requires careful planning and design.

- It is all about conservation of fiscal resources to provide patrons with more materials, at lower cost, and more quickly.

Patrons, library technical staff, and vendors are irrevocably locked into technological codependence upon one another, and it is the libraries' ethical obligation to be certain that an increasing supply of a commodity becoming increasingly difficult to acquire and process in a timely manner is available. Testing of improvements in vendors' supply and support systems is crucial to the success of that endeavor.

Notes

1. Douglas Bates, cited in e-mail from Charlene Simser, Head, Cataloging and Serials, Kansas State University.
2. Anne Della Porta, "Implementing Unicode at the Library of Congress," in *Endeavor User Group Meeting 2004* [Online], available: http://support.endinfosys.com/cust/community/vgroup/eu2004/74.pdf.
3. "Innovative Announces Millennium Silver." *Advanced Technology Libraries* 33, no. 4 (2004): 7–8.
4. Gwen Alexander and John H. Williams, "The Impact of an Accelerated Improvement Workshop on Ordering and Receiving," *Library Collections, Acquisitions and Technical Services,* 29, no. 3 (September 2005): 283–294.

Different types of collaborative projects were presented this year at the Charleston Conference. Librarians are now finding themselves in more collaborative relationships than they have been in before. Several topics were addressed, including the role of librarians in academic integrity, developing liaison programs, academic and public libraries working together, and how to create dialogue for collaboration.

Collaboration

"ACADEMIC INTEGRITY": THE ROLE OF LIBRARIES IN ADDRESSING PLAGIARISM ON CAMPUS

Chris Matz, Collection Development Librarian, University of Memphis Libraries, Tennessee

What is the role of the library in the "academic integrity" movement? While faculty members, university administrators, and information technology specialists work to discourage plagiarism in its electronic forms, librarians cannot afford to be content with merely following their directives. Using existing strategies, such as information literacy and copyright/fair use guidelines, librarians can help develop critical thinking about academic ethics in students and faculty alike.

This Table Talk was marked by a lively exchange of track records from librarians who were already managing the details of anti-plagiarism technology on their respective campuses, often with little or no support from units outside of the library. Turnitin remains the leading brand name for online prevention tools, though iThenticate and other products were also mentioned. The spectrum of librarian responsibility is broad, ranging from orienting faculty and students to the prevention tool to outright technical administration. One of the many "duties as assigned" we were warned about in library school, it seems.

Much of the current energy seems to be directed toward detection and enforcement rather than education. No doubt some students are indeed plagiarizing by buying products from paper mills or simply copy-and-pasting right off Internet sites, and many of them do so knowingly. Many others, though, "cheat" from lack of awareness of academic ethics, not having been exposed to concepts such as citation styles, copyright, or fair use prior to entering college. It is here that authors such as C. Brian Smith and Gail Wood believe librarians can make headway, incorporating the information literacy process (often already in use) to impart methods of locating information and then critically evaluating it.[1] Bringing teaching faculty into this process is vital. Assignments should optimally be developed that emphasize research methods and make expectations of "integrity" a shared partnership of faculty, students, and librarians.

One concrete example of this support is the Creating Copyright Friendly E-Reading Lists that we use at the University of Memphis Libraries. It guides the scholar through stable URL options for the various databases to which the library hosts access. It also includes guides regarding the subject and content level featured in each database. With so many students and faculty eschewing an in-person visit to the library in favor of remote access to online materials, this is an especially valuable resource for meeting "best practice" goals for academic integrity. The near future will undoubtedly bring many others.

Notes

1. C. Brian Smith, "Fighting Cyberplagiarism," *Library Journal: Net Connect* (Summer 2003): 22–23; Gail Wood, "Academic Original Sin: Plagiarism, the Internet, and Librarians," *Journal of Academic Librarianship* 30, no. 3 (May 2004): 237–242.

A BAKER'S DOZEN OF COLLABORATION TIPS FOR SMOOTH-SAILING PARTNERSHIPS

Jack Montgomery, Coordinator of Collection Services, Western Kentucky University, Bowling Green

Roxanne Spencer, Western Kentucky University Libraries, Bowling Green

Lisa Rice, Assistant Director, Bowling Green Public Library, Kentucky

Author's Note

This chapter is an expansion of a handout provided for the session "Bookmarks, Bookfests, Book Sales, Songfests and SKYMAPP: Creative Ideas for Building Community Involvement and Marketing Your Library Programs" presented by Jack Montgomery and Roxanne Spencer, Western Kentucky University Libraries, and Lisa Rice, Bowling Green Public Library, at the Kentucky Library Association/Kentucky School Media Association Annual Conference in Fall 2005. A revised version of this talk was also presented by Jack Montgomery and Roxanne Spencer at the 25th Annual Charleston Conference in November 2005.

In a guest editorial in the *Journal of Academic Librarianship*, Roger Guard noted that, "Collaboration is a topic that has been in vogue for at least the last three decades in librarianship."[1] So, collaboration is nothing new to veterans among us who have attempted it in school library media centers and public, academic, and special libraries. For new school library media specialists and librarians, however, learning the ins and outs of successful collaboration takes time and additional effort. To initiate collaboration, we must first promote our library's services, collections, and talent. In a school or small library, the "talent" may be the solo librarian. How much time and effort can the lone librarian devote to building partnerships for outreach to the community outside the school or library's walls? That is, perhaps, the catch-22 of collaboration and partnerships: Without the outreach effort, without promoting and marketing ideas for joint projects, there is no collaboration, there are no partnerships.

Many of us have seen the fruits of collaboration and partnerships: More patrons, greater community awareness and support, satisfied school administrators, more involved parents, more engaged students. So, despite the additional time and effort required to develop ideas and build partnerships for collaboration, the results are usually worthwhile. Here, then, are a few ideas for making collaborations more likely, hopefully more successful, and easier for library staff pressed for time and energy.

Finding Partners for Collaboration

Partnerships can be long-term or short-term, and single or annual events. Some ideas for simple, ongoing collaborations that make a mark in the community and at your library follow.

Say you are a small public library in a small town. Your local businesses and fraternal organizations are tapped to support the local high school football team, charitable fundraisers, the local hospital, humane society, senior group . . . the list goes on. In a small town, the donation dollars can only stretch so far. By shifting the angle a bit, you can look at local business support slightly differently, which can make or break a partnership. Not all support has to be in cold, hard cash.

Seeking to promote a family literacy program at your school? Tap the local coffee shop or fraternal organization for early evening "breakfasts," where school administrators, early grade teachers, parents, and kids are invited to family storytime and scrambled eggs at an agreed-upon price. Parents and pupils are happy—fed, with an outing and a story event, supported locally. Teachers and administrators become more visible in the community, translating to good publicity for the school. The business owner is content—more customers, more cash in the till, and for fraternal organizations, more visible support for the school and community.

Don't know what to do with the boxes of weeded materials from your public library? Library staff cannot sell them if they were bought with state funds, but the Friends of the Library can. But why stop at the local level for the used book sale? Why not donate part of the proceeds to the senior or community center or to disaster victims in another state? The Friends of the Library can alert used book dealers across the state of the book sale, and you may find a handful of these resellers at the library doorstep, complete with handtruck and delivery truck.

There are dozens of ways to develop simple or more formal partnerships and collaborations that benefit the library and the community. What may not always be clear is to how to go about forming the collaborations successfully, so each partner's roles and responsibilities are carefully spelled out.

Tips for Developing Successful Partnerships and Collaborations

Any time one organization seeks the assistance of another in a promotional or marketing endeavor, questions will undoubtedly arise about the various duties and obligations of each partner. As the library representative approaching a local business owner or local institution, be prepared to handle the partnership as a business partner, not just as a local nonprofit community service organization. Here are some ideas to bring to preliminary meetings:

1. **Put It in Writing:** Plan to have a formal, written agreement for collaborations and partnerships—a handshake isn't enough. Even in a small community where everyone knows everyone else, a written agreement will help avoid the pitfalls of misunderstanding or mistakes, or will provide an out for either side if unexpected emergencies arise. Each partner must contract to certain financial obligations, personnel requirements, and outcomes. These should be clearly laid out in a formal, written agreement, signed by both parties.

2. **Define the Mission and Goals:** Create a mission statement and define goals and objectives for the collaborative project. The two (or sometimes more) partners involved may come to the table with different ideas about the need for and outcome of the collaborative project. Discuss each partner's vision of the event, and refine the discussions into a simple, clear mission statement with well-defined goals and objectives, so everyone is working from the same set of plans.

3. **Lead and Delegate:** Elect officers and delegate tasks. It is a good idea to select cochairs from the different partners to represent balanced leadership for the collaboration. Define individuals' roles and be sure duties are divided fairly and are clearly understood to avoid duplication of efforts. Prepare for the inevitable 80/20, whereby 80% of the work is done by a core 20% of the committee members.

4. **Who Pays for What:** Define sources of funding and support early. If the library seeks support from local businesses rather than exchange of services, a detailed bud-

get with a short but definitive description of the plan and its financial needs will give the potential funder more concrete numbers to crunch than simply asking for support to fly in and lodge a guest author.

5. **Location, Location, Location:** Schedule regular meetings in a neutral location or rotate meetings at each participating facility. Library as place still makes a powerful statement in most communities. Friends of the Library can help partnership meetings go more smoothly by providing refreshments for the businesspeople whose support the library seeks. A neutral place, such as a local restaurant special occasion room, community center, or the business partner's conference room, could be scheduled for alternate meetings.

6. **Brainstorm, Then Distill:** Sometimes we can pick and choose committee members from a large personnel pool; at other times the same small group of people are available to participate. Brainstorm freely, then distill, *everyone's* ideas. Listen to everyone's ideas and suggestions, and give each speaker equal time to voice ideas and concerns. There will often be a pie-in-the-sky idealist seated right next to the doomsday naysayer. You can glean useful information from both extremes. Have a designated note-taker—the flip chart, easel, and colored marker method for distilling broad ideas is still a handy way to keep track of input from various sides. Be willing to share the spotlight—it's never just "your" idea.

7. **Be Diplomatic:** Remind participating library staff of their service orientation; good communication and people skills are crucial to successful partnerships and collaborations. Diplomacy can be more important than other skills in group planning activities.

8. **When to Call It Quits:** Know when to bid and when to fold. Sometimes the best intentions take us down a very slippery slope . . . . Some partnerships seem good on paper but not in practice. Despite the 80/20 rule noted above, the library cannot do the work of both partners. If either the library or the partner is not fulfilling its stated and agreed-upon obligations, the better course might be to bow out early, before there has been an investment of too much time, effort, publicity, and expense.

9. **Short Meetings Get More Accomplished:** Keep meetings short and sweet—no longer than an hour. Everyone, no matter how enthusiastic about the partnership or the even, has too much to do outside of this collaboration. Assign someone to distribute minutes to committee members via e-mail.

10. **Marketing and Promotion:** Identify publicity sources and share promotional ideas, materials, and costs. Unless the local business partner is a newspaper, advertising agency, or publisher, the library may have to rely on its own talent to provide promotional materials such as posters, direct mail, ads, or flyers. Perhaps a library staff member or frequent patron has some graphic design talent. Be sure both parties sign off on all promotional materials before distributing, to avoid misunderstandings about sponsorship of the event.

11. **Review and Restrategize:** Reconvene the committee after the partnership event to recap and reassess strategies for future collaborations. Remember to avoid pointing the finger at individuals to assign blame for bloopers. Mistakes will be made; the point of reconvening after the event is to identify mistakes and seek constructive solutions for next time. Blaming the other guys only breeds distrust and enmity. You

can use this opportunity to seek feedback from the local community on the pros and cons of the event and to seek ideas for future collaborations.

12. **Building on Success:** If the partnership has proved fruitful, this opens the door for future projects between these partners. But do not be afraid to seek support for other projects from other sources. Success breeds success. To avoid spreading personnel and other resources too thin, have a long-range plan for collaborative events, and as much as possible, rotate committee membership among library staff and supporters.

13. **Be Proactive:** Never underestimate the value of a good cup of coffee and a healthy heaping of praise in smoothing troubled waters! This is another way of saying be proactive rather than reactive. Ask questions at meetings and "back at the ranch," in case library staff on the committee are uncertain about voicing concerns in a partnership meeting. Proactive communication leads to successful collaboration. You can use this opportunity to seek feedback on the event from the local community as well.

There are many opportunities to collaborate, for small and large libraries and in small and large communities. What is needed is the incentive, inspiration, leadership, and determination to develop productive partnerships to benefit both parties and the community. With some foresight and planning, a willingness to work together for the good of the whole, library collaborations are win-win situations for all involved.

Ideas for Library Partnerships or Collaborations

- You can seek partners and sponsors from other nonprofit organizations and local businesses to support your library's efforts at community outreach.

- Family literacy projects

- Regional culture presentations, such as Kentucky Live!

- Local or regional musical guests/performance artists

- Dramatic readings

- ESL or language classes to meet community needs

- Attic Treasures Appraisal: Invite the community to bring their family heirlooms for appraisal by regional jewelry, art, and crafts experts.

- International festival: Celebrate your community's diversity

- Young artists and performers: Partner with schools to showcase talent

- Demonstrations: From baton twirling to stamp crafts to quilting to model-making to woodworking, showcase local craftspeople in your community.

- Young writers: Encourage budding authors with a contest

- Celebrate local authors and performers with readings or performances

- Partner with local dance or martial arts studios for demonstrations

- Book fairs and book sales: the tried and true are still good community fundraisers!

Notes

1. Roger Guard, "Guest Editorial: Musings on Collaboration and Vested Interest," *Journal of Academic Librarianship* 31, no. 2 (March 2005): 89–91.

Bibliography

Archer, Michael Scott. "Bookselling: Broward Library's Literary Feast." *Publishers Weekly* 248, no. 11 (March 12, 2001): 21–22.

Brown, Carol. "America's Most Wanted: Teachers Who Collaborate." *Teacher Librarian* 32, no. 1 (October 2004): 13–18.

Bush, Gail. "Walking the Collaborative Talk." *Knowledge Quest* 32, no. 1 (September/October 2003): 52.

Buzzeo, Toni. "Tips and Tactics: Using Communication to Solve Roadblocks to Collaboration." *Teacher Librarian* 31, no. 5 (June 2004): 28.

Coatney, Sharon. "Primary Voices: Building a Collaborative Culture." *Teacher Librarian* 32, no. 4 (April 2005): 59.

Donham, Jean, and Corey Williams Green. "Perspectives On . . . Developing a Culture of Collaboration: Librarian as Consultant." *Journal of Academic Librarianship* 30, no. 4 (July 2004): 314–21.

Gregory, Gwen H. "Cover Notes: Don't Hesitate to Collaborate." *Information Today* 22, no. 4 (April 2005): 40.

Stefl-Mabry, Joette, and Jennifer Goodall Powers. "Collaborative, Problem-Based Learning: University and K-12 Partnerships." *Knowledge Quest* 33, no. 4 (March/April 2005): 14–16.

Topper, Elisa F. "Making Meetings Work." *American Libraries* 35, no. 9 (October 2004): 70.

BOOKMARKS, BOOKFESTS, BOOK SALES, SONGFESTS, AND SKYMAPP: CREATIVE IDEAS FOR BUILDING COMMUNITY INVOLVEMENT AND MARKETING YOUR LIBRARY PROGRAMS

Presented by Jack Montgomery, Associate Professor & Coordinator, Collection Services, Western Kentucky University Libraries, Bowling Green

Roxanne Myers Spencer, Assistant Professor & Coordinator, Educational Resources Center, Western Kentucky University Libraries, Bowling Green

Our presentation is offered here for the *Proceedings* in the way we delivered it at the Charleston Conference, as a loosely scripted talk.

Jack (*introduces himself and Roxanne*): Good afternoon! My name is Jack Montgomery. I'm the Collection Services Coordinator at Western Kentucky University. My colleague, Roxanne Spencer, Educational Resources Center Coordinator, and I are here to talk about programming, planning, and engagement of the libraries with each other and the community.

> A. This is an area we academic librarians have not always considered our turf, but now it has become an essential part of our overall marketing strategy. We are in and are about service and human interaction. Public libraries have long recognized this and, in terms of marketing, are way ahead of us.
>
> B. This program is about how two libraries with different agendas can and have worked together to our mutual benefit.
>
> C. This program is about ideas. What we hope to offer you today are ideas that have worked for us. We will present them to you in a realistic manner, the good and bad, aspects and outcomes. We won't sugarcoat our experiences to make ourselves look successful. That would be disingenuous. These ideas and programs all take a lot of work and dedication, but if you're willing to invest, can bring very solid and positive results to your institution.

Roxanne: Recent library literature is full of articles about collaboration and partnerships, particularly to encourage school librarians to collaborate with classroom teachers. Public libraries have had to rely on the support of local businesses to provide special events for the communities they serve. It is only more recently that academic libraries have joined the collaboration craze, and the community outreach efforts in most cases pay off for all involved.

Developing and producing successful collaborative events requires a lot of effort, patience, and luck. Sometimes funding is readily available from local or national businesses who want to contribute to the community, and sometimes, these collaborations make it on a wing and a prayer!

WKU Libraries, the Bowling Green Public Library, and Barnes & Noble Booksellers have formed several successful partnerships in the past several years. There have been, and will probably continue to be, ups and downs in the negotiating and implementation process. But so far, for the past half-dozen years or more, WKUL, BGPL, and B&N have successfully built partnerships and collaborations that have produced meaningful and fun events for the Bowling Green community and win-win situations for the partners. Here are some examples.

Roxanne

One Campus-One Community-One Book 2004–Ongoing

The Southern Kentucky Book Fest partners are pleased to sponsor our third One Campus-One Community-One Book. This project is intended to cultivate reading and discussion by bringing the entire Western Kentucky University campus and the Bowling Green community together around one book—for 2006, the title chosen is *In Country*, by Kentucky native Bobbie Ann Mason. We encourage many to read the book and attend the public discussions as well as give us comments via our website bulletin board. Several events are planned, including author visits, discussions, and a viewing of the movie version of *In Country* (1989), starring Bruce Willis.

> 2004: *A Parchment of Leaves* by Kentucky Literary Award Winner, Silas House.
>
> 2005: *Coiled in the Heart*, by Scott Elliott
>
> 2006: *In Country*, by Bobbie Ann Mason

There were discussions, author visits, and other special events in conjunction with WKUL, BGPL, and B&N.

Following the success of our first On the Same Page project in 2004, Mike Thaler, author of *Teacher from the Black Lagoon*, the Southern Kentucky Book Fest partners will once again sponsor a communitywide reading project for children. Beginning October 17 and ending during Children's Book Week in November, children will be asked to read a book and discuss it among their friends, classmates, and family.

The book chosen is *Horrible Harry and the Locked Closet*. This book was written by popular children's author Suzy Kline. Ms. Kline will be here November 16–18 to meet and discuss her book with those children who participated in the project.

Southern Kentucky Book Fest

Now the largest book festival held in Kentucky, from 1999 to 2005 the Book Fest grew in attendance from 3,400 to about 8,000; and the number of authors participating has grown from 85 to nearly 200.

> 1999: 90 authors, R. L. Stine, <u>Goosebumps</u>
>
> 2000: 103 authors, LeVar Burton, NextGen, Reading Rainbow
>
> 2001: 150 authors, Sports Editor Dick Schaap, Lynn Hightower, Bobbie Ann Mason
>
> 2002: 200+ authors, Homer Hickam, Karen Robard
>
> 2003: 150+ authors, David Baldacci, Robert Morgan
>
> 2004: Teresa Medeiros, Charlaine Harris, Rosemary Wells, Mike Thaler
>
> 2005: Sue Grafton, Sharon Creech
>
> 2006: Pat Conroy, Jack Gantos, Elizabeth Berg

Kentucky Literary Awards, Presented by the Southern Kentucky Book Fest

Eligibility: Books eligible for the Kentucky Literary Awards must have been written by a Kentucky author or have a Kentucky-related theme. A Kentucky author is defined as a writer meeting one or more of the following qualifications: a native-born Kentuckian; an author living in Kentucky; an author whose permanent home address is Kentucky but who does not at present live in Kentucky.

Any individual, organization, or company may nominate books to be considered for these awards. The book must have been published and distributed between January 1 and December 31, 2004. No self-published, publish-on-demand, non-English, or re-printed book will be considered. Textbooks, children's books, edited collections and anthologies will not be considered.

Categories: Entries may be submitted for either of the following categories: Fiction, Non-fiction, and Poetry.

Kentucky Writers Conference, 2004–Ongoing

This conference will feature Kentucky writers and their work. Some of the Kentucky Literary Award nominees will participate in writing workshops, readings, and special presentations. These sessions will take place on the campus of Bowling Green Community College (WKU South Campus) and will be open to high school students, WKU students and the general public.

The sessions will begin on Thursday, April 6 at the Bowling Green Community College and continue through Friday, April 7, 2006. On Friday, April 7, we will also announce the winners of the Kentucky Literary Awards at a luncheon held in their honor.

Jack

Lecture Series

It is difficult to find an evening free with the demands of work, family, and faith, but on Thursday evenings twice a month, WKUL and Barnes & Noble Booksellers present two lecture series:

Faraway Places . . . with Strange Sounding Names: 2000–Ongoing

Exciting, international travel talks by Western Kentucky University faculty. Not just dry scholarly research, but bringing vibrant international culture and customs to the BG community. Previous talks include: Digging in the Holy Land, archaeology; Norway, Cuba, New Zealand, Belgium and the Netherlands, culture. Upcoming, Belize, Portugal, and Life and Death in Ancient Egypt (forensic anthropology) (http:www.wku.edulibraryfaraway).

Kentucky Live! Southern Culture at Its Best! 2002–Ongoing

From dramatizations to readings to food-tastings to discussion, KY Live! Presents contemporary and historical talks on the events that shaped the Commonwealth in the past and those that sustain it now and into the future. Recent programs include Jackson's Orchard, Thomas Merton, The Bosnians Come to BG, Hill Billy: A Cultural History, Moonlight BBQ Inn, Jesse James as Confederate Outlaw, and Alice Gatewood Waddell, BG resident, African American artist. (http:www.wku.edulibraryeventskylive).

SKYMAPP: Southern Kentucky Musical Archives Preservation Project (SKYMAPP)

Let me tell you about a work in progress. As we are all aware, none of us are getting any younger. Most of us have memories of popular musical events embedded in our memories. Ever wondered what became of all that music and those people? These are the sort of questions that gave birth to SKYMAPP. We want to collect and preserve the rich cultural history of popular music in South Central Kentucky before it slips from memory and is forgotten. I am now a "local" musician in the Bowling Green scene. About two years ago, during a tour of the archives at the Kentucky Museum, I realized that no one was trying actively or systematically to collect the popular form of music or reach out to those who play or listen to popular local music or could help us with this idea. Soon I met Graham Hudspeth when he came to hear my former band "Lost River" play at various events. It was there that we got to know each other and I shared my vision with him and his wife Dory. True to the exceptional type of persons they are, they jumped right into the project. Those of us who make up the popular musical community feel an urgent need to record and preserve our shared memories of the events, the talent and the music from this wonderful musical era in South central Kentucky. There were many who were part of the music in the 60s, 70s and 80's who have left this world and their story all but lost to future generations.

The local music scene is an important part of any communities' musical and cultural heritage but one often overlooked until too much time has passed to build an adequate record of its presence. I also know from my own hometown,(Columbia, SC) how quickly that history can vanish only to be inadequately recovered later in bits and pieces, if at all. I've had, as a result, a vision of building a collection of music and memorabilia that would reflect the last 30 years(at least) of BG's popular local and regional music scene. I would be very interested in working with you to secure, conserve and protect these materials for future generations.

SKYMAPP's Mission: The Southern Kentucky Musical Archives Preservation Project (SKYMAPP) is dedicated to selectively collecting, organizing and preserving the popular musical history of the Bowling Green and South Western Kentucky region for the study, research and enjoyment of everyone.

Goals and Objectives: To that end, those involved in SKYMAPP will:

1. Create an online archive of information about people, places, and events in the history of popular musical culture. Popular musical culture is defined as musical culture performed in public for the entertainment and/or edification of the community at large.

2. Collect selective memorabilia and other physical objects that support the mission of SKYMAPP

3. Create exhibits, programs and publications in a variety of formats to publicize, promote and chronicle the popular musical history of the Bowling Green and South Western Kentucky region.

    We also envision this as a growing collection to which each new generation of musicians could contribute and support both physically and financially. The Kentucky Library and Museum has an exceptionally talented and dedicated group of professionals who are also committed to preserving the many aspects of Bowling Green's rich cultural heritage.

As I've said in my responses to the potential donors: "They would give any donated materials the best care and organization possible anywhere in Kentucky today." This project could also provide a way to engage the community in a manner we may not have previously. We recently had an exhibit on the "The Hilltoppers," a 1950s vocal group that became famous and even landed a spot on Ed Sullivan and released several records. It was a masterful piece of museum work and community relations.

Because we had so little of the Hilltoppers memorabilia, we had to go hunting for memorabilia on eBay and the like. It was at that moment when it came to me: "What if we could collect this material before we have to pay for it!" A future exhibit on the popular music scene in a Bowling Green would tap into the hearts, minds and memories of the people of this city and region and properly promoted would say to the community that Western cares about the daily life of the community in a new way. Musicians would hear of this collection and want their memories preserved as well. Many of these people, like famous country songwriter Bill Lloyd, are now prosperous and well connected could be approached to perhaps support the development and conservation of this and other parts of our wonderful collections.

I can also see local historians using the collections to write popular histories, articles, and the like. In this way, WKU Libraries could become a model for this approach to community engagement. We could all take credit for reaching out and opening doors

The first step in this process is our survey which we developed and have sent out to over 70 local musicians. We decided to keep it short to encourage participation. We have heard from around 50 folks so far and have received many suggestions of possible contacts.

Community involvement so far:

Interviews

Publications

Exhibits, concerts, etc

Designed as an ongoing project SKYMAPP (Southern Kentucky Musical Archives Preservation Project)

4.   Secure appropriate funding for the maintenance of SKYMAPP.

Scope: Our geographic area of focus for SKYMAPP will include the Bowling Green–Warren county area as well as the area from Hopkinsville to Burkesville and from Cave City to the Tennessee state line

Date range: 1950–date

Java City and Music at the Library Programs: An Update

Many of you may remember that about two years ago, I did a poster session here at KLA on our new venture into operating a coffeehouse inside the Library and the programming of entertainment. I suppose this part of my presentation is an update on that project.

In case you do not remember, Java City as a coffeehouse within the confines of the WKU Library in an old lobby to the original library in August 2002. In 2003, we decided to begin to try to become a center for campus activity by using the space for events and to present entertainment. To that end, the University Libraries Java City Live Entertainment Committee was founded with the mission: "To provide adequate and appropriate planning, networking and implementation required for the establishment of a regular schedule of live entertainment programs and other events in the 'Java City' coffee shop in the Helm-Cravens Library Complex." The committee was and still is composed of librarians, library staff, and interested members of the faculty and staff of the university, who would sponsor and encourage the participation of their students in these programs as well as interested members of the community. The WKU dean of libraries, the director of marketing for WKU dining services, and the Java City manager shall serve as ex officio members. All committee appointments are the responsibility of the dean of libraries. I serve as chair of the committee.

I am here to say that Java City has been an unqualified success at many levels, including:

1. Increased traffic in the library

    Java City opened around August 18, 2002

    Gate Counts for August through November 2002 as compared with 2001 and 2000: To date our gate counts have averaged over 20,000 additional people coming into the library per month as compared with gate counts before Java City was inaugurated.

August–September	
8/18/02–9/18/02	65,265
8/18/01–9/18/01	41220
8/18/00–9/18/00	37,264
September–October	
9/18/02–10/18/02	56,730
9/18/01–10/18/01	38,845
9/18/00–10/18/00	39,117
October–November	
10/1/802–11/18/02	66,732
10/18/01–11/18/01	44,398
10/1/800–11/18/00	37,856

2. Use of reference services has more than doubled. One advantage is that the reference desk is located directly inside the library side door to Java City.

    2002–2003 2000–2001 1999–2000

    August 1,514 500 563

    September 2,528 988 1,158

    October 2,259 1,231 1,430

    November 1,994 1,331 1,472

3. Entertainment: Since we began our scheduling of entertainment in September of 2003, we have booked 42 separate events with an additional 9 event on schedule so far for fall of 2005. We have had a variety of events from Poetry Slams, Receptions, Art Sales, Speaker's Corners, Book Signings as well as musical performances in jazz, folk, choral groups, open mikes, classical big band, alternative rock, and even an old time dulcimer band. We have had singer songwriters from Bowling Green, Nashville, Louisville and Stamping Ground, Kentucky.

The momentum has kept growing and we average five events per month when school is in session or not on holiday. In spring of 2005, we decided to begin to offer a small stipend of $50.00 per performance or $100.00 for those that travel over an hour to play. Our dean, Michael Binder, who has supported Java City since its inception has found the funds in donated monies. We are currently seeking sponsorships for future programming. Most of the musical performances are scheduled as part of what we call our "Noontime Concert Series." Once a week, on a Tuesday or Wednesday at noon

We have invested in a stage and public address system adequate for performances both inside and outside the actual facility. If the weather is good, the performance are held outside on the patio by the library and has drawn crowds of as large as 200 people as this area sits on a major traffic area for the university. People stop, have lunch, and listen.

The public perception of the library as a campus center by the students, faculty and university community has grown each year and as I announced the beginning of our fall season in August as our first performer readied himself, I was greeted to a round of cheers and applause. That felt good.

Is there a downside? Well, not a downside but I must say it takes a lot of time and effort to do something like this. You have to have a *committed group* of folks who set up, monitor, and take down the equipment. You need folks to canvas the university and local community for talent. Sometimes you need to meet the talent and audition them. We are not a karaoke bar where just anyone can get up and play. That would be a waste of money and ruin the reputation we've worked so hard to build. You need people who are willing to go around and post flyers to advertise the events as well securing people to create the signs. We have partnered with WKUs IMAGEWEST, a student-run public relations firm, which supplies us with our table cards and posters. We advertise for performers in the student, and sometimes the local, papers. Sounds like a bit of work, and it is, but the payback, I believe, is worth it in terms of the Library's overall outreach and engagement program to both the students and community. This is a venture that needs to be carefully planned and systematically implemented. We have over the past two years "gotten our act together" so to speak. We learned that the commitment in terms of labor was the libraries' alone, and it just works better that way. Each member of the library team knows his or her role and is committed to delivering the goods. We do have some limitations, which we make clear to all who would use our facility, such as:

1. Amplified musical or vocal presentations that will interfere with studying in the library or interfere with other schedules.

2. Presentations that contain questionable lyrics or language. The committee reserves the right to request transcripts of presentations in advance of the performance and reserves the right to refuse or terminate a performance that violates the above-mentioned standard or violates established community standards for public behavior. Part of the standard for appropriate language includes the guidelines of the F.C.C. for words, which may not be said on broadcast radio or television.

The events scheduled for "Java City" are for entertainment purposes only and hence the committee does not approve presentations that include partisan political rhetoric or speeches espousing political, racial, or religious agendas. This does not include the presentation of religiously oriented music but refers to polemical or evangelizing oratory. We originally said that the "Java City" events are also not a forum for public debate, but we have allowed "Speaker's Corners" under tightly controlled situations sponsored by the university. Knock on wood, no trouble so far.

To avoid any problematic issues associated with public performance and ASCAP regulations, material presented at "open mike" events should be original compositions or material in the public domain. The committee can assist performers in making these determinations.

The committee reserves the right to prohibit from performing any person judged to be intoxicated or bringing in or using any intoxicating substance in the "Java City" facility. No trouble so far.

Roxanne

Bowling Green Public Library Programs

The Bowling Green Public Library provides several of its own unique programs in conjunction with WKU Libraries, Barnes & Noble, and various sponsors. Among these community outreach programs are the following:

- Prime Time Family Reading Time is a family literacy project developed by the Louisiana Endowment for the Humanities, to help at-risk children and families become interested in reading. Carefully selected children's picture books form the nucleus of weekly family storytime and discussions at the local public library. There is a storyteller and a children's literature scholar, who work together to present the story and encourage discussion about the themes of the various stories. These broad themes touch everyone's lives: friendship, fairness, trickster tales, determination, courage, fear . . . everyone can relate to the characters and events in children's tales, which is what makes this program so successful. From 11 libraries less than 15 years ago to more than 37 libraries nationwide, the Prime Time Family Reading Time provides an excellent opportunity for public and academic library collaboration, which in turn engages underserved populations in meaningful stories and dialogue—along with healthy snacks before storytime, too.

- National Family Literacy Month, which includes

  ○ Books and Baskets,

  ○ Children's Book Week,

  ○ Proclamation Signing, and

  ○ Author visits and book signing events

- Famous Barr Used Book Sale, which helps to fund the SOKY Book Fest

- Black History Month @ Your Library, featuring a Celebration of Kentucky African American Writers

- Sigma Phi Epsilon Book Drive

- "Meet the Authors" Reception

- "Never Judge a Book by Its Movie" Writing Contest

- WKU Scholarship

- FLEX: Foreign Language Exploration, which taps the skills of multilingual faculty and staff from WKU, who teach basic foreign language skills in four-week sessions

- Supporting ALA Public Programs, such as The Sixties: A Film History of America's Decade of Crisis and Change, and Frankenstein Art Exhibit: Penetrating the Secrets of Nature

Roxanne: There are many ways to make outreach and library collaborations work. Seek out your colleagues and counterparts in your community and brainstorm ways to make libraries more prominent and valued in your community! Share your successes and failures with us today.

COLLABORATIVE ELECTRONIC RESOURCE LEADERSHIP: CREATE DIALOG IN TIMES OF TECH-STRESS

Joan E. Conger, MLIS, MA.OD.

Abstract

Joan Conger presents for discussion principles of collaborative leadership found in her book *Collaborative Electronic Resource Management*. Join colleagues at all levels of leadership as we learn to bridge divides, create cohesion, and tap the wisdom of your organization and your customer base. Lower tech-stress, larger budgets, and more loyal patrons are never a guarantee, but collaborative leadership starts you in the right direction.

Introduction

An effective library serves its customers well within the resources available, all the while improving its services and strengthening its share of resources. An effective library is aware of changes in its environment and relies on a constant flow of information into and throughout its organization. This information is rich and diverse, ranging from understanding customer needs, awareness of the technological advancements to meet these needs, deciding the realities of who gets what resources to implement these advancements, and sharing creative insight between colleagues. An effective library does not just keep up, it innovates.

An effective library maintains a balanced flow of information into and within the library. If information flow is restricted, change becomes surprise and ratchets up the stress of never being in control, of always being on the defensive. If information flow is turbulent, change becomes constant and churns up the stress of always responding, of never stopping to reflect or plan or innovate. Even with a perfect level of information flow, change will inevitably unsettle established knowledge and habits.

An effective library, therefore, also nurtures a culture of collaborative learning to tap the collective strengths of awareness and creativity. This collaborative learning shifts the view of organizational management from solely a command structure into a more collaborative structure within which everyone makes decisions by learning from each other. Collaborative learning regulates the flow of information to optimum levels and promotes effectiveness.

An effective library leader* finds a balance between command and collaboration. Under effective command management, library leaders refer to a central organizational purpose to order the chaos of new information. Library services cohere around a reputation for quality and consistency. Through the balancing of collaborative leadership, library leaders rely on organizationwide collaborative learning, the learning from each other during decision making, to loosen restrictions on information flow. Because library services delight the customer through quality and innovation, a library's response to change needs to flow through the paths of both management purpose and collaborative learning.

Command Management: The Core Purpose

The management structure most familiar and most established in our organizations looks to a hierarchy of managers to tell others what to do. Information is filtered through a manager's firm grip. A well-conceived management plan takes its strength from the manager(s) knowing the future well enough to direct others' actions in the right direction.

Relying only on a command management structure contains a twofold weakness. The command structure puts a lot of pressure on the manager to get the plan (and the future) right. This structure also takes decisions out of the hands of professionals at the front line and places them in the hands of a supervisor at one remove from the actual work and often at one remove from the customer who benefits from the work.

If a good manager has a well-developed plan and can read the future well enough to tell everyone else what to do, then this management structure works well. Indeed, to some extent planning is crucial for successful service delivery in any organization; good planning infuses a consistent organizational purpose into decisions made across the organization. Good management creates and consistently applies a core purpose for the organization that becomes the pivot point of all actions taken in response to change.

But as the sole source of forward motion, command management unbalances organizational actions. Command management responds to change but only through the understanding of one or a few individuals. Decisions follow a prescribed direction, use a trickle-down information flow, and "innovate" within a given set of rules. Because of the needs of complex organizations in environments of constant change, command management presents an ever-present danger of overload of the narrow decision-making "circuitry," or information flow, within a command hierarchy. Command management does not collaboratively learn from, innovate, and act in response to the forces found within the rich network of professional and customer relationships. Command management may accept feedback, but it does not invite co-creation.

Assume for the moment that members of an organization are all imperfect, that managers will, therefore, never develop a perfect plan ahead of time, and that, consequently, managers will never know the future well enough to command exactly the right action. How do organizations create a management system that allows for imperfect knowledge and mistakes?

Planning is most effective when it creates a container of organizational purpose within which continuous learning among colleagues can flourish. Management is most effective when command authority is leavened by collaborative learning.

Collaborative Leadership: Decisions through Learning

A strong organization is aware of changes in its environment. Environmental change, however, creates discomfort in established plans, knowledge, and habits, and these changes bring chaos, large or small, to established systems. Collaborative learning, learning from each other during decision making, is the safe way to break old habits and assumptions. When collaborative learning occurs within the framework of an organization's purpose, the organization's responses will not founder on chaos. Instead, environmental change presents the opportunity for the organization to regenerate into a stronger entity that is adaptive, innovative, and respected. (See Figure 1.)

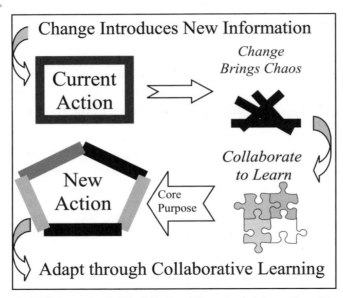

Figure 1. Collaboratively Find Better Ways to Achieve Core Purpose.

This is not to suggest a false dichotomy: "Learning is good, therefore planning must be bad." However, without collaborative learning, the manager-enforced plan narrows information flow to one person and restricts action around each new challenge to reactive action. Reactive action disintegrates into crisis-mode interactions among members of the organization. The spiral of firefighting expends great amounts of energy that dissipate quickly and leaves professionals at all levels of an organization with a feeling of always being surprised and of always hitting the pessimistic brick wall of assumptions and habit.

Collaborative leadership responds to the chaos of change by expecting all professionals to collaboratively learn their way out of habit and assumption. If allowed to flourish, collaborative learning builds up within an organization's network of professionals sources of adaptive decision making untapped by command authority. An effective organization weaves into a command hierarchy strong threads of collaborative leadership, allowing all professionals to collaboratively learn their way into effective decisions.

Adaptive decision making takes direction from command management's expressed core purpose, then distributes innovation into information-rich collaborative learning relationships throughout the organization. When management expects and supports these relationships, members of the organization build and tap their network of learning relationships to create innovative solutions. Change becomes a chance to take action, to learn, and to strengthen the networks with which to respond to the next change in the environment. As collaborative leadership takes hold, those in the organization respond to each new challenge through existing relationships built around previous learning experiences. Trust develops between people, trust grows in the process itself, and adaptive learning becomes easier for the organization over time.

From Collaborative Learning to Action

The structure of command management designates a few managers to manage other managers or the work of the front line. The benefit of this structure lies in the consistency with which the organization adheres to its core purpose. Collaborative leadership treats all members of the organization as leaders, both as knowledgeable in their own jobs (otherwise why are they employed in that job?) and as colleagues contributing to others' successes at their jobs. The benefit of collaborative leadership is that all sources of information, both external and internal to the organization, are immediately available to decision making and innovation through each of these professionals. A balanced flow of information, one that neither starves nor overwhelms decision making, takes advantage of both these structures of management to move from collaborative learning through decision to action.**

Command managers who prefer expediency usually

- follow the existing plan,

- decide from their own understanding of a situation,

- try to sell affected professionals on "buy-in" after a decision is made, and

- attempt to achieve compliance through directives and accountability measures.

This path is expedient (for the managers) because it bypasses the chaotic period that collaborative learning must go through to reach good decisions.

Collaborative leaders who prefer the effective path

- choose to distribute ownership of both the issue and the solution to all involved,

- discover what exists in the collective knowledge,

- invite all effected to become co-creators in the solution, and

- by default suffuse compliance with enthusiastic contribution.

This path is effective because it taps many points of view, and the more people are involved in the decision/information, the more that compliance is almost guaranteed with little or no extra work.

The manager who is also a collaborative leader

- clearly expresses the core values and general direction of the organization;

- treats all participants as leaders, expecting and supporting collaborative learning;

- does not detail the content of innovative efforts; and

- is eager to learn as much as or more than all other participating leaders.

Collaborative learning best begins by getting the whole system (all those directly affected by the change) together in a room, from the part-time shelver to the customer to the librarian in a far-off department to the upper-level administrator. For large projects this may have an impact on many people and require an expert facilitator, and learning to facilitate is a skill developed early by any effective leader. Beginning with all the information present in the organization allows any smaller decision-making groups to infuse the entire process of innovation with high-quality information and not default to assumption or habit.

How Can I Have Any Influence?

No matter where we are in the organizational chart, we all have bosses and colleagues, people trying to get us to cooperate and people we are trying to get to cooperate. Changing other people is notoriously difficult, so how can you influence information flow, collaboration, and innovation within your own sphere of influence, whether you are a manager or on the front line or both?

Always act as a leader whatever your position in the organizational chart:

- Be aware of the relationships necessary for good flow of information. Seek to strengthen existing relationships and to create new ones.

- Be aware of where you restrict information flow in decision making to only your own understanding and seek to expand the flow by inviting others to co-create (not just give feedback).

- Pay attention to opportunities for adaptive learning by, and from, everyone.

- Always act from a position of learning. Seek information, even that which comes from lack of success. To reduce fear, welcome breakdowns or mistakes as opportunities to learn.

- Be forgiving of yourself, others, and the process. Everyone is trying to make it through; what can you do to make it easier?

- Keep it simple. Break down complex projects into smaller modules for quick-learning wins that motivate. Keep solutions elegantly simple.

- Treat everyone around you as a leader by giving them information, asking for their knowledge, inviting them to co-create with you, and helping them to act from a position of learning.

Occasionally,

- Go down the hall to talk to someone instead of sending an e-mail.

- Serve coffee, or bottled water, at a meeting that you host.

- Send thank you e-mails and publicly recognize help that you have received.

- Use the "cc:" line in e-mails to keep colleagues informed.

- Spend an entire conversation only asking questions.

- Go ask questions of someone you rarely ask, like a shelver, a supervisor in another department, or a customer. Sit down with them and have one of those question-only talks.

- Stretch yourself into learning something new by choosing the weird idea, the new task, or the different route to the same end. Treat mistakes as opportunities to learn.

- Find an article on collaborative leadership and send a link and a synopsis to your colleagues.

Conclusion

A successful, effective, innovative library serves its customers with the most powerful resource at its disposal, the collective knowledge of all members within its organization. Management by collaborative learning creates a system within which people naturally do the best thing at the time because collective knowledge is put to work within adaptive decision making. Information is no longer restricted to a manager's understanding of the external and internal environments. Within the parameters of organizational purpose set by the manager, the flow of information opens to include everyone's perspective and enriches decision making toward the highest result: delighted customers.

Notes

* I use the word *leader* in its widest possible interpretation. A leader is someone who, by making the best decision with the information available, promotes and strengthens the organization's core purpose. Ideally, an organization should give every employee the organizational support to become a leader.

** Because collaboratively learned information is the best source of good decisions, the health of an organization is not reflected in the accountability of employees as individuals but in the quality of their participation in collaborative decisions as measured through the organization's support of its learning networks.

Bibliography

Read First

Covey, Stephen. *Seven Habits of Highly Effective People.* New York: Simon Schuster, 1990.

Peck, M. Scott. *The Road Less Traveled.* New York: Touchstone, 1978, 2003. (If you only read one book on this topic, read this one.)

Wheatley, Margaret. *Leadership and the New Science: Discovering Order in a Chaotic World.* San Francisco, Berrett-Koehler, 1999.

Also Read

Block, Peter. *Stewardship.* San Francisco: Berrett-Koehler, 1993.

Conger, Joan E. *Collaborative Electronic Resource Management: From Acquisitions to Assessment.* Westport, CT: Libraries Unlimited, 2004.

Follett, Mary Parker. *Mary Parker Follett Prophet of Management: A Celebration of Writings from the 1920's.* Boston: Harvard Business School Press, 1995.

Patterson, Kerry, et al. *Crucial Conversations: Tools for Talking When Stakes Are High.* New York: McGraw-Hill, 2002.

Scholtes, Peter. *The Leader's Handbook [of Deming's Quality Management].* New York: McGraw-Hill, 1997.

Senge, Peter, et al. *The Fifth Discipline Fieldbook: Strategies and Tools for Building a Learning Organization.* New York: Currency Doubleday, 1994.

Joan Conger, MLIS, M.A.OD, is a veteran of electronic resource management in libraries. She has written *Collaborative Electronic Resources Management: From Acquisitions to Assessment* (Libraries Unlimited, 2004). She is a doctoral student in organization behavior and occasionally speaks to organizations, facilitates organizational change, and writes for professional publications.

CUSTOMIZING FACULTY'S NEEDS: DEVELOPMENT OF A LIAISON PROGRAM (A SUBJECT LIBRARIAN'S PRIORITY)

Gayle Chan, Collection Development Librarian, University of Hong Kong Libraries

Abstract

When three new positions for subject librarians were first established in July 2003 at the University of Hong Kong Libraries (HKUL), their purpose and the services to be provided needed to be explained and promoted, as this was an unfamiliar concept to both faculty members and library users. The rationale for the establishment of the three new subject librarian positions is examined in the context of the HKUL organizational structural changes, while highlighting the responsibilities of their roles. The focus of the chapter is to present the results of a survey undertaken to assess the faculty needs for subject librarians. The importance of customization in response to varied needs in formulating the action plans that guide future liaison activities is also discussed.

Introduction

The University of Hong Kong is a leading international university in Asia, whose language of instruction is predominantly English. The Libraries, which consists of a main library and five specialist libraries, caters to the multidisciplinary needs of 10 faculties—architecture, arts, business and economics, dentistry, education, engineering, law, medicine, science, and social sciences, as well as its 28 non-faculty academic units, and a number of research centers and institutes, serving a student population of about 19,000, including 11,700 undergraduate students and 7,300 postgraduate students, and a teaching faculty of over 1,200, including researchers.

Two major reasons led to the development of the faculty liaison program at HKUL. First, as a result of a review of the organizational structure carried out in 2003, it was resolved that the Libraries' structure be organized as much as possible around customers and their needs, rather than internal functions. Second, it was decided that the Libraries should shift the responsibility for collection development away from the faculty members and into the Libraries, as traditionally faculty members were primarily responsible for selection but many felt burdened and would rather have librarians take it up. The previous system of subject coordinators and selectors, all having other primary functional duties with secondary subject duties, did not work well due to conflicting priorities. A recommendation for a flatter functional team approach resulted in the restructuring. The Collection Development Team was one of the four operational services teams formed (the other three teams were Main Library Services Team, Branch library Services Team, and Technical Services Support Team).

In July 2003 the Collection Development Department was restructured with three new subject librarian positions through deployment from merging of operations in other parts of the library. Each subject librarian was assigned to oversee a disciplinary area, namely arts, social sciences, and science and technology. The goal was to offer more support in collection building, to better focus on meeting information needs through research consultation or advanced reference, and to provide current awareness and customized instruction in the use of library resources.

As HKUL moves from a hybrid library to a digital library, where resources are offered in large multidisciplinary packages often with complex licensing issues, faculty members need the expertise of librarians to rationalize print and electronic and to optimize use of funds. In the networked environment where an increased focus on collaboration and cooperation with new opportunities for resource sharing is arising, there is also a need for subject librarians to inform faculty about rationalizing between owned resources versus access to resources through inter-library loan, document delivery, and shared collections.

It is important to note that the rationale behind the HKUL model was to ensure that the function of collection development, which is to systematically build collections that meet the academic and research needs of the university community, remains user-centered and is directed at existing user needs. Thus, the reporting structure for the three new subject librarian posts is directly to the head of collection development rather than to reference. The HKUL model aims to deliver the personalized service one associates with special, branch, or departmental libraries without the cost of creating the physical branch, but operates within the strategic framework of collection development.

From its inception, it was considered a priority to develop a liaison program that ensures effective communication with all academic departments. Establishing an effective library liaison program to guide the Libraries in anticipating and fulfilling changing information needs was made one of the chief objectives of the Collection Development Department. The Collection Development Team brainstormed and came up with the most relevant activities and services appropriate for such a liaison program. The first opportunity to collaborate with faculty arose when feedback was sought through a survey, as faculty input and cooperation were considered crucial in successful implementation of the program. The results of the survey were used to refine the individual action plans aimed to address the particular needs of each department.

Roles of Subject Librarians

First, the definition of library liaison as "someone assigned to specific academic unit as primary contact, works closely with library representatives regarding issues related to library collection development, research, and teaching support in their subject area" was adopted.[1] This was necessary as the previous role of the subject coordinators/subject selectors was redefined to place more emphasis on targeting user needs by connecting users to appropriate resources other than purely materials selection.

The subject librarians at HKUL assume dual roles of building the collections in their assigned subject areas and also the role of faculty liaison. Subject librarians communicate information about collection development policies and strategies, such as budget allocations, book approval plans, collection goals and collection levels, acquisitions procedures, as well as information on library services and developments.

As faculty liaison, subject librarians are responsible for outreach to faculty and students, which may be through reference interview, specialized research consultation, and course-related user instruction. These activities are encouraged as part of their faculty liaison assignments, as they provide the opportunity to stay in touch with the faculty and students and to help subject librarians understand program and information needs. Building relationships with faculty will also enable librarians to take a more active role in the education process.[2]

Purpose of the Liaison Program

The new liaison program was intended to foster and strengthen links between library and faculty departments. The Collection Development Team identified the following goals to be achieved:

- Improve communication to establish rapport between faculty and librarians to facilitate collection building

- Collaborate with faculty to develop well-balanced collections

- Enable the library to meet information needs of users

  - Subject librarians to become more aware of course content and development through course-related instruction (customized and delivered on-site)

  - Subject librarians to keep current with research interests through faculty research consultations

- Connect users to the appropriate resources through promotion via Web pages or Web logs to increase awareness of library resources and services in support of teaching, learning, and research

- Increase visibility and credibility of the librarian's role

The six main areas of duties identified from brainstorming as the most relevant in support of teaching and learning were

- Collection building,

- Research consultation,

- Instruction on subject-specific library resources,

- Integrating library materials into teaching and learning resources,

- Promoting library services, and

- Fostering closer collaboration with faculty.

Faculty Needs Survey

The identified duties were used to formulate the questionnaire sent to faculty, which was intended to survey their needs and preferences for these services. To help faculty understand the nature of these duties, concrete examples were given (see Appendix 1, excerpt from the survey document). The aim of the survey was to seek faculty input in identifying the help most needed to support their teaching and research, and to help subject librarians develop a plan of action to guide their future collection development and liaison activities. A total of 457 personalized questionnaires was sent to members of the six faculties served by the subject librarians, and 143 replies were received (a 31% response rate).

Respondents were asked to rank the six areas (see Table 1) on the basis of their needs for subject librarians on a scale of 1 to 5 (1 being most important and 5 being least important).

Table 1

Department	Collection Building	Research Consultation	Instruction on Subject-Specific Library Materials	Integrating Library Materials into Teaching & Learning Resources for Specific	Promote Library Services	Foster Closer Collaboration With Faculty
	Mean (Ranking) ** *Ranking in descending order (1 is most important)*					
Faculty of Architecture	*2.33 (2)*	*2.33 (2)*	*3.22 (4)*	2.22 (1)	*3.22 (4)*	*3.44 (6)*
Faculty of Arts	1.48 (1)	2.64 (2)	3.04 (5)	2.76 (4)	2.72 (3)	3.28 (6)
Faculty of Bus & Econ	2.69 (2)	3.00 (5)	2.69 (2)	3.15 (6)	2.62 (1)	2.92 (4)
Faculty of Engineering	2.04 (1)	2.17 (2)	3.48 (6)	2.87 (3)	2.91 (4)	3.22 (5)
Faculty of Science	2.40 (1)	2.67 (3)	2.86 (5)	2.77 (4)	2.65 (2)	3.14 (6)
Faculty of Social Sciences	1.92 (1)	2.27 (3)	3.00 (5)	2.08 (2)	2.77 (4)	3.42 (6)
OVERALL MEAN :	*1.96*	*2.37*	*2.82*	*2.65*	*2.76*	*3.23*
OVERALL RANKING :	1	2	5	3	4	6

Generally, results based on the score and comments from the survey indicate an overall need for

- Collection building for most faculties, especially on identifying resources for emerging areas and new courses/programs, as well as identifying resources that HKUL lacks in specific subject areas;

- More research consultations for postgraduate students, also for final year undergraduates to prepare them for research;

- Assistance in integrating library materials into teaching and learning by helping faculty to identify resources pertinent to their needs, for example, creating links to subject guides and/or links from materials on reserve to courseware;

- More promotion of library service especially targeted to the undergraduate level;

- Systematic training for new undergraduates through "subject-oriented" library instruction relevant to them; and

- Closer collaboration with faculty members, since only through close collaboration with faculty (department) can activities be carried out to target their specific needs.

Table 1 shows the mean score at the faculty level, and ranking for each duty is prioritized based on the mean score. It was noted and expected that different faculties/departments have different needs or varying degrees of the same needs. For example, where collection building may be deemed at the faculty level as the most important need for a subject librarian, certain departments, such as history, with teachers who possess strong interest and dedication in developing collections, may deem another aspect to be more important.

Customizing the Action Plans

Subject librarians further analyzed the results with written comments of the survey at the departmental level to focus on department/individual needs and preferences. Prioritization was given to addressing the specific individual needs initially, and the larger needs gathered from the input and comments in the survey were to be addressed in a customized action plan. It was noted that some areas of need, for example, systematic training for new undergraduates, may require collaboration with other library departments.

The subject librarians then met with members of each department along with the faculty library representative to discuss and to seek feedback on the proposed action plan, which was formulated with the ranking of the duties in mind. Following meetings and consultations with departments, the subject librarians were ready to finalize and implement a plan that was practical and effective in addressing each department's information needs in the forthcoming term.

The activities in the action plans encompass a range of responsibilities that normally includes the creation and maintenance of Web sites and Web logs, faculty outreach, customized instruction given on-site, advanced reference consultation, and a variety of other tasks associated with public services among the major activities associated with collection development. Activities identified as expected, essential/preferred, and/or desired by faculty include

- Assisting in expending allocation, monitoring budgets, and managing the approval plan, if any;
- Identifying current information needs via research consultation or other means of contact;
- Developing Web pages to promote resources and services;
- Developing collections including materials selection and journal cancellation;
- Identifying the status of the collection, its strengths and weaknesses;
- Collection assessment projects in selected areas;
- Instruction on database searching, research methods, and Internet training;
- Assisting with e-reserve, document delivery, use of software for bibliography, online submission of requests, etc.; and
- Meeting with new faculty and attending events.

Addressing Information Needs

The subject librarians have taken on a more proactive role in the development of their collection in a systematic manner via approval plans and firm order selection. The result is a more balanced collection that aligns with the needs of users. Most faculty members expect librarians to use their knowledge about the university programs and research direction, the structure of the literature in the field, and the universe of publication to shape the collection and adjust priorities. Selection by faculty used to be a chore most often done as a last-minute resort to avoid forfeit of budget, but subject librarians have helped to avoid irrational last-minute expenditures.

The completion of a comprehensive collection analysis exercise conducted in consultation with faculty members yielded interesting findings that enable librarians to detect collection strengths and weaknesses and to identify areas that require more development and/or funding support. Depth indicators (numerical values 0–5), which describe a library's collecting activity, were assigned across the entire subject conspectus for the first time at HKUL to give an overall picture of the collection).[3] The indicators provide crucial information on how well the collections meet the information needs for teaching and research, and serve as a basis for future collecting priorities. Subject policy statements were also formulated for each of the academic subject areas describing the collections' coverage and areas of focus.[4] The faculty find this information on coverage useful for planning new programs when an assessment of library resources is required to implement the new program.

In advancing the digital collections, an advisory committee made up of faculty members and the head of collection development guides the development of digital collections to better target teaching and research needs, taking into account level of usage and acceptance. This collaboration with the faculty ensures robust growth in digital collections without neglecting the need for traditional formats. It also promotes a better understanding of how the use of material funds is optimized to enable effective budget shift from print to electronic.

To promote and enhance access to digital resources through instruction, the subject librarians have developed subject Web pages, subject Web logs[5] and other promotional programs to target announcement of resources for subject specific groups with the aim of increasing awareness and usage of resources. Faculty members find blog contents that deliver added-value information about current research and development in their field, such as conference/events announcements and enhancements of contents in existing resources, highly informative and desirable.

Through collaboration with faculty, the subject librarians are able to offer on-site course-related instruction with customized content that targets specific courses. Through their contact with students and faculty in designing subject-specific instruction, librarians become more aware of course content and the development of the curriculum. Research consultations that target postgraduates help librarians to keep current with the research interests of the faculty.

Although the action plans have only been implemented for just over one year since the fall semester of 2004–2005, the above-mentioned are just some of the activities that have yielded positive results. Many of the tasks undertaken would not have been feasible before the restructuring of the Collection Development Department and without full-time dedicated subject librarians working closely in consultation with faculty members.

Conclusion

The restructuring of subject librarians at HKUL was a timely one that reflects the shifting context of the new digital environment. As HKUL moves from a hybrid library toward digital collections, traditional collections and services are integrated with new digital resources and new information needs to be infused into teaching and learning with user education targeted at subject groups. Greater emphasis on liaison with users, developing digital library resources, connecting users to resources appropriate to teaching and research, involvement in integrating resources into education, and promoting collections and services are factors that attribute to the restructuring of the Collection Development Department with three subject librarians at HKUL.

The survey exercise provided an extra opportunity to promote the roles and responsibilities of the subject librarians in their new positions. It also helped to break the ice for the subject librarians and alleviated much of the apprehension in approaching the faculty members for the first time in their new role. The faculty perception of the subject librarians was better understood as a result of the exercise. The knowledge gained from the survey about faculty needs provided the framework for the subject librarians to formulate customized action plans for each academic department. The new public service role of the subject librarian in promoting the use of collections and offering course-related instruction and research consultations among collection development tasks has generally helped to raise the visibility of the librarians.

Notes

1. Raghini S. Suresh, Cynthia C. Ryans, and Wei-Ping Zhang. "The Library Faculty Connection: Starting a Liaison Programme in an Academic Setting." *Libraries Worldwide* 44, no. 1 (1995): 7–13.

2. Ada M. Ducas and Nicole Michaud-Oystryk. "Toward a New Enterprise: Capitalizing on the Faculty/Librarian Partnership." *College & Research Libraries* 64, no. 1 (2003): 55–76.

3. The University of Hong Kong Libraries, *Conspectus Table : Faculties and Departments,* n.d. [Online], available: http://lib.hku.hk/cd/policies/Classed%20Analysis.xls (accessed October 28, 2005).

4. The University of Hong Kong Libraries, *Subject Policy Statements,* n.d. [Online], available: http://lib.hku.hk/cd/ policies/ cdp.html#Sect8 (accessed October 28, 2005).

5. The University of Hong Kong Libraries, *Subject Blogs,* n.d. [Online], available: http://lib.hku.hk/cd/news.html (accessed October 28, 2005).

Appendix 1 Excerpt from the Survey Document

COLLECTION BUILDING

- Provide further help to faculty in the selection of library materials with particular emphasis on new courses/programs and emerging areas

- Work with faculty to identify subject areas with weaknesses or gaps in existing holdings and to strengthen the collections

RESEARCH CONSULTATION

- Give small group/individual consultation tailored to specific research needs/topics for faculty or students

- Provide Journal Citation Reports to help faculty identify high impact factor journal titles on a specific subject for publication or current awareness

- Provide citation index report for faculty to show number of times an author has been cited in journal articles

INSTRUCTION ON SUBJECT-SPECIFIC LIBRARY MATERIALS

Give instruction on subject-specific library resources to support curriculum

- in the Department
- in the Main Library

INTEGRATING LIBRARY MATERIALS INTO TEACHING & LEARNING RESOURCES FOR SPECIFIC COURSES/PROGRAMS

- Create subject guides/pathfinders/course guides/database guides/Webliographies for specific courses/programs
- Integrate course-reading materials via the use of electronic-reserve for specific courses/programs
- Provide assistance in identifying the appropriate library materials to be integrated in course management software for specific courses/programs

PROMOTE LIBRARY SERVICES

Introduce new and/or existing library services by live demonstrations and/online guides/faculty orientation. For example:

- ILL/Interbranch delivery/HKALL
- Hing Wai Store monographs/journals/document delivery
- E-reserve
- Book/journal/electronic resources/free web resources/recommendation online
- My library@hand (PDA applications and resources)
- MyLibrary
- Dissertations (for postgraduates)
- Help set up journal and database table of contents and article alerts
- New "additions" lists by subject/department., including books, journals, electronic resources and web resources

FOSTER CLOSER COLLABORATION WITH FACULTY

In additional to working with members of Faculty Library Committee

- Attend/speak at departmental meetings
- Meet with faculty members
- Meet with postgraduate students

The future of the book is still an important part of collection development. In 2005 we saw many speakers focusing on the importance of the printed or electronic book. Discussion on book issues included a look at Amazon approval slips, models for the scholarly monograph, budgeting for books, how scientist are using books, an online auctioning process for acquiring books, and electronic books.

Books

AMAZON APPROVAL SLIPS: MEETING THE CHALLENGE

Elsie Pritchard, Dean of Library Services, Morehead State University, Kentucky

Moving to an Online Book Vendor

In 2002, the Acquisitions Department at Camden-Carroll Library decided to experiment with purchasing books from Amazon.com. This decision followed several years of disappointing service from two traditional library book vendors.

Why Amazon? Our library decided that speed of delivery, fulfillment rate, and cost were the most important factors in selecting a vendor. Traditional library vendors are big on specialized services, but our library doesn't need many specialized services. We believed that online vendors such as Amazon could deliver books to us faster, cheaper, and more reliably. We selected Amazon because we had experience with it, but we could have just as easily chosen another online book vendor for our experiment.

Amazon seemed eager for library business and soon set up a new corporate account service with monthly billing so that we didn't have to use the dreaded credit card. Eventually Amazon even developed a libraries division. We were quite pleased with its performance on the big three (speed, fulfillment, cost), but Amazon's lack of experience in dealing with libraries continued to be evident. Even with the new emphasis on library business, corporate policies seemed to be developed without considering the effect on libraries. To their credit, the folks at Amazon were always cheerfully willing to admit mistakes and make changes. We moved more business to Amazon, but we retained our approval slip plan with a traditional library book vendor and so continued to place a portion of our orders with that vendor.

The Monthly Amazon Approval Slip

At the Charleston Conference in November 2004, I met Tony Small, Senior Product Manager at Amazon.com. I told Tony that we would order even more books from Amazon if it had an approval notice plan. After I explained to him what that meant, he seemed interested. Frankly, I didn't expect to hear back from him—but less than two months later he sent me a sample!

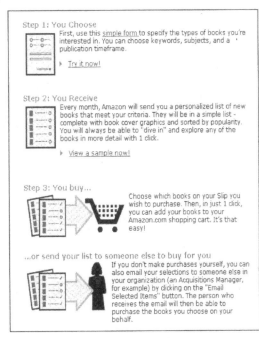

Create a Monthly Amazon Slip.

Tony's beta approval notice was an e-mailed link to a Web page listing "New Books Celebrating Black History." In typical Amazon fashion, the beta version was produced without any consultation with a librarian (to my knowledge) and was therefore unlike any other approval list I've seen. It looked terrific! Our selectors loved the book cover images, links to reviews, ratings, availability information, and e-mail and cart features, but they had plenty of suggestions for improvements. They asked for subject options, more academic titles and fewer popular titles, weekly lists, and more bibliographic information. Tony thanked us for the suggestions, and in March we received the second version.

The March version was a Web page called "Create a Monthly Amazon Approval Slip." At the time of this writing, it's still available at Amazon's "Librarians' Store" at http://www.amazon.com/exec/obidos/tg/browse/-/13753131/. We liked the ease of setting up our own approval notices, but the canned approach still didn't provide enough options. Selectors wanted more subject specificity, and they wanted to understand how the subjects were assigned. The form provided spaces for only five publisher names, and we were accustomed to an approval plan based on about 100 major academic publishers.

The Power Search Approval Slip

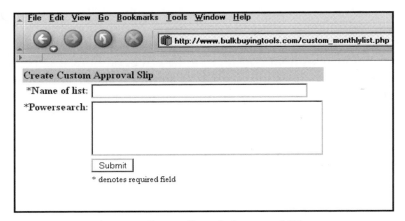

Amazon Power Search Approval Slip.

True to form, Tony took our ideas and returned with a new "power search" version in a few weeks, consisting of a free-text field with tags and Boolean operators and space for about 60 publishers. I serve as liaison with our university's music department, so I sent Tony a list of major publishers in the field, along with instructions to get all the books about music from those publishers, excluding textbooks. I wanted books in English only, and no reprints, although I believed that the publisher list would probably provide enough limitation by itself. Tony keyed in the data and sent me a link to the results. The list looked good to me, so for the first time I forwarded the link to my faculty contact in the music department. His response: "I visited the site and, of course because it is not only visual, but has reviews, etc., I like it much better than the other notices. While there, I saw an important book we should get, in case we have not ordered it. Good work!" He pasted the citation into the e-mail, missing the fact that he could e-mail the citation directly from the list.

Now we were in business!

Subject Profiling with Amazon

Once the power search version was in place, I wanted to verify that the results were reliable. It's important to know that our approval notices provide full coverage of certain publishers, so that we can save time by ignoring sales catalogs from those publishers. Libraries have more than a casual interest in approval slips. We rely on them to ensure that our collections are complete.

First, I needed to know how the subject profile was derived. Was there a controlled vocabulary? Could I view the subject hierarchy? Who assigns the subjects? Are keywords used? Which fields are included?

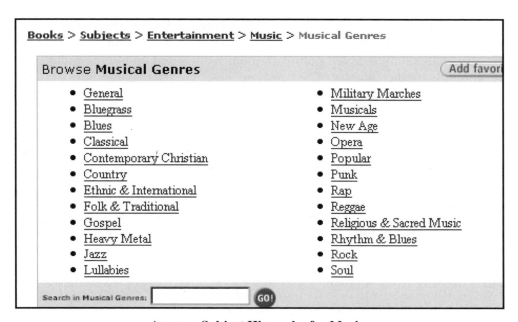

Amazon Subject Hierarchy for Music.

Tony's response: "There are two ways to search. One is using keywords, and the other is using subjects. For keywords, there is no pre-defined list. For subjects, these match closely to the books categories. To see these, start here: www.amazon.com/books and look at the left hand 'Browse' area. For example, you can click on the Entertainment subject and then drill down to the Music subject. So when designing a custom list, we can use both keywords and categories to tailor a list to meet your needs." According to Tony, Amazon's editorial staff assigns subjects to books in much the same way that traditional library vendors do. Based on this information, I decided to use the subjects instead of keywords, although I had some reservations about the fact that music falls under "Entertainment."

To test the subject coverage, I began to compile monthly lists of books from the Amazon approval slips to compare to the slips from our traditional library vendor, which we were still getting. In doing this, a huge problem was revealed.

The Dynamic List

I discovered that I wasn't able to go back to lists from previous months. The lists were dynamic, so only the current month of publications could be displayed. From Tony's viewpoint, it was ideal. From my viewpoint, I saw disaster for the typical selector or faculty member who waited until the end of the semester to catch up on ordering. Always accommodating, Tony created a permanent link for each month so that I could retrieve lists from previous months, but with the publication status updated. At this point, I didn't realize that the "dynamic list" problem was only partly solved.

Each list was created on the first day of the month with titles predicted to be published during that month, but if I pulled up the list later in the month, the titles were different. Some titles had appeared mid-month, while others had disappeared because publication was delayed. I began to obsess about titles that would be missed, depending on what day in the month the list was viewed. Titles with delayed publication dates appeared on the list month after month, creating more work for the selector. The solution? Now the lists appear only at the end of each month, after all the titles have actually been published. Acquisition may be somewhat delayed, but the list is more reliable.

Comparison to Traditional Approval Slips

We continue to receive and order from approval slips provided by our traditional book vendor, but comparing Amazon's subject coverage to that of the traditional slips is difficult. Subject assignments are not identical, and I elected to use a slightly different publisher list with Amazon. Since most titles appear somewhat earlier on Amazon's list, a month-by-month comparison wasn't possible. Still, after comparing about six months of data I was unable to find any titles missing from Amazon's lists that I would have expected to find.

Approval slips from traditional book vendors seem to use a more rigorous controlled vocabulary, along with a large selection of non-subject criteria. The bibliographic information is in a more traditional format. Because the slips are static, it's easier to assess the coverage. For libraries dependent on the range of services offered by traditional book vendors such as bibliographic records and physical processing, approval slips from the same vendor provide a necessary link.

Amazon's approval lists are more attractive than those from either of the traditional library vendors we've used in the past. The publication status is always current, and selectors like the book jackets and links to reviews. E-mailing the selections provides all the information necessary to order the books from Amazon. Using Amazon's approval notices allows us to use Amazon for a higher percentage of our orders, thus taking advantage of its speed of delivery, high fulfillment rate, and low prices.

If a librarian had designed approval slips for Amazon, I'm afraid the slips would have resembled those from traditional library book vendors. Tony Small had the advantage of not knowing what librarians expected. He was fast—amazingly fast, compared to the way librarians work. He didn't know anything about approval slips when we first met at Charleston in November 2004, but by mid-January 2005 he had developed a prototype and by the end of March he delivered a usable product. His solutions to problems weren't always the solutions I expected, but they worked.

What's Next?

Tony Small says that about 1,000 monthly approval slip forms have been completed by libraries. While the power search isn't publicized, it's available to libraries that ask for it. In the future, a more attractive, user-friendly interface may be developed so that it can be made available from Amazon's Web site. Amazon's library services may someday expand to include full-fledged approval plans. Our selectors have all been asked to work with Tony to set up approval slips through Amazon, with the goal of eventually discontinuing the use of traditional approval slips, and thus moving even more of our book purchasing to Amazon. But we aren't wedded to Amazon. If another vendor comes along with more to offer, we are open to change.

BOOK TO THE FUTURE: TWENTY-FIRST-CENTURY MODELS FOR THE SCHOLARLY MONOGRAPH

Colin Steele, Emeritus Fellow, Australian National University, Canberra, Australia

Abstract

There are many similarities between the fifteenth and twenty-first centuries in the impact of technological change on information flow and consequent cultural and societal impacts. New modes of distribution offer improved opportunities for access to and distribution of scholarship, particularly for the scholarly monograph.

Introduction

The digital information environment has ensured that the twenty-first century will be a global watershed, like the fifteenth century was in the Western world, for changes in the creation of and access to knowledge. By 1500 nearly 1,500 print shops had printed eight million volumes comprising 23,000 titles.[1] Vespasiano da Bisticci's Florentine manuscript scriptorium had gone out of business by 1478, with his 45 scribes made redundant. Who will be the twenty-first-century information chain equivalents?

The world of scholarly publishing is a complex one. At one end of the scholarly publishing spectrum are the annual multi-million-dollar profits of STM global publishers such as Reed Elsevier; while at the other is the plight of many university presses and learned societies. Cox has outlined the rise of Robert Maxwell and the Pergamon publishing empire, which was eventually incorporated into what is now Reed Elsevier.[2]

In 1951 Elsevier was a purely Dutch company, before becoming the largest STM publisher in the world by the end of the twentieth century. Over recent decades a number of other powerful publishing houses, notably Springer, Wolters Kluwer, Thomson Scientific, Blackwell Publishing, and Taylor & Francis, have expanded to take 52% of the global STM market, which totalled $9.2 billion in 2005. Reed Elsevier has reported an 11% rise in annual pretax profit performances for 2005. The 2005 adjusted profit before tax increased 9% to £1.002 billion ($1.75 billion), compared to the previous year.

Just as the Gutenberg revolution had profound work practice and publishing implications, so there is no divine right for any of the players in the information sector to survive on historical lines. The 2005 "Royal Society" debate in the United Kingdom on open access publishing and its implications saw some STM publishers arguing to the British government for a "level-playing field," but who determines the chronological playing field, and on what basis?

Per Saugman, who built Blackwell Scientific Publications (BSP) into one of the top scientific and medical publishing houses, died in January 2006. The first 15 years of BSP saw hardly any growth, and Saugman once said that there were only 50 good medical books to be published each year. Blackwell, like Elsevier, was a relatively small publishing player in the middle of the twentieth century, so again, when does one define the level playing field? Is it only when it suits major STM publishers?

In the context of the STM publication explosion, it is too simplistic and unrealistic to say, as some publishers have, that since R&D budgets have risen threefold, therefore library budgets should have risen accordingly. Most articles are still little read and little cited. The UK NESLI statistics in 2005 revealed that most useage of the UK "Big Deal" acquisitions by British universities came from a small number of journals.

One publisher who does not wish to be publicly named has said, "more research largely means we publish more crap!" Richard Charkin, the CEO of British Publisher Macmillan and currently the UK Publishers Association President, was particularly revelatory when he stated in the UK *Bookseller* in September 2005 that, "most of our words aren't read, so it's how you package it that really determines the profit."[3]

The profits of the major STM publishing multinationals are essentially based on sales to libraries, particularly of universities and research institutions in North America. Reed Elsevier publications absorbed half the University of California Library budget in 2002 for online publications, yet Elsevier titles accounted for only a quarter of the journal use.[4] Candee has noted that the University of California annual budget for licensed content by 2005 was $27 million.[5] How many of the articles purchased are actually used/read/downloaded, and how is "value for money" defined?

In addition to the quite significant double-digit price rises of the 1990s by the major commercial multinational publishers, the rise of the "Big Deal," that is, aggregated packages by publishers, has led to the STM access vote taking larger and larger proportions of a library's budget. This has usually been at the cost of the social sciences and humanities in general, and the monograph in particular.

Many North American University Councils and Faculty Boards have issued statements in recent years calling on scholars to change scholarly communication practice. However, few major practical changes seem to have resulted. The various "White Papers" issued in December 2005 by the University of California , however, promise to contain more "teeth" for institutional action.[6]

The University of California papers included the following words, which are relevant in terms of potential reconsideration of scholarly communication models in universities: "The current model for many publications is that faculty write articles and books, referee them, edit them and then give them to a publisher with the assignment of copyright. The publisher then sells them back to the faculty and their universities, particularly to university research libraries. While there clearly are costs of publication, a number of publishers (particularly, but not always, for-profit corporations) earn munificent profits for their shareholders and owners."

Most science researchers operate in Mode 2 research frameworks but resort to traditional Mode 1 formal publication for the dissemination of that research.[7] Many researchers have often distributed the contents of that research through electronic colleges or personal Web pages well before the formal publication process. Depending on one's viewpoint of the "Faustian bargain" between authors and publishers, the scholarly publishing environment has been in crisis for a number of years. While this has been particularly reflected in the debates on serials, many humanities scholars have experienced declining sales of their monographs and a lack of appropriate outlets for their research publications. There is no doubt that the last two decades have seen a very significant decline in the purchase of research monographs by university libraries.

The Future of the Scholarly Monograph

John Fell's ambitious program of publication for the Oxford University Press in the late seventeenth century led to the following comment from the Master of University College: "[T]he vending of books we never could compasse; the want of vent broke Bp. Fell's Body, public spirit, courage, purse, and presse."[8]

This budgetary crisis for Oxford University Press was subsequently overcome, and OUP is now one of the most profitable publishers in the world. However, its monograph production is extremely selective, and it no longer specializes in monograph publishing in several disciplines. Thompson has noted the distinctions between the dominance of OUP and the Cambridge University Press in the United Kingdom and the plethora of relatively smaller presses in the United States, to the benefit of the former.[9]

A number of university presses have tried to generate extra revenue by moving into general trade publications and by publishing fiction, travel, and cookbooks. It is debateable in 2006 whether this has been overall a successful policy, and the net result has been a continuing diminution of academic monographs being produced.

Mary Sue Coleman, president of the University of Michigan, affirms: University presses are "awash in red ink" and survive only with infusions of money from university funds. "The bottom line, for me and for you, is that our publishing houses and our authors can only benefit financially and reputationally from the widest possible awareness of books and their availability."[10]

The British Academy was sufficiently concerned in 2005 about the future of the scholarly monograph that it included a section about it in its report *E-resources for Research in the Humanities and Social Sciences.* The following words are extremely relevant in this context:

In the 1960s and 1970s, far fewer monographs were published than now, with routine global sales of 1500 or more. But these sales levels were not sustained, and a declining sales step-curve has been evident throughout the past quarter century, with a vicious circle of declining sales driving higher prices driving declining sales. Individual publishers have responded by issuing more and more individual titles, but with lower expectations of each. Global sales can now be as low as 250 or 300 in some fields. At some point in the 1990s, the UK academy ceased to be a self-sustaining monographic community: the subjects that have survived and/or thrived in this context have been those (like economics or linguistics or classics) with international appeal.

Thus even if major academic publishers can sustain some support of less popular titles across their lists, they cannot sustain large numbers of low-sales titles, however highly esteemed, in specialist fields. Moreover though authors now undertake the bulk, if not all, of the copy preparation in many cases, publishers clearly have large real costs both in handling hard copy distribution and, though to what extent they really contribute is not completely clear, in terms of marketing, as well as, usually, copy-editing costs.

The main barriers to primarily e-publishing for highly specialist monographs appear to be the general conservatism of much of the scholarly community, along with the fact that many specialist libraries are unable to handle digital materials effectively. Much of the conservatism, as with journals, comes from the entrenched belief that quality control of the scholarly object itself somehow evaporates with e-publication, even if the whole reviewing and editing process is electronically done; and, further, that this implies that the academic reputation that comes with monograph publication will be undermined.[11]

Cronin and La Barre indicated, from a survey of the major Ivy League universities in 2004, that a scholarly monograph is still an essential prerequisite for promotion and tenure in those universities, yet the outlets for monograph publishing via university presses have declined.[12] The Modern Languages Association in America highlighted in 2002 the problems of scholarly monograph publishing, particularly for the younger scholar. MLA returned to this topic in December 2005, deploring the "fetishization of the monograph" and called for a new metric to demonstrate scholarly worth, such as a body of articles, translations of works, electronic databases, etc.[13]

It makes little sense for researchers to spend many years writing a monograph, only to find either that there is no outlet for their publication or that their monograph is published in such a small edition that global or local distribution is extremely limited. Thompson has noted:

> The new millennium is proving to be a testing time for academic publishers . . . the problems are not temporary . . . but rather are symptomatic of a profound structural transformation . . . many academics 'depend on the presses to publish their work . . . yet they generally know precious little about the forces driving presses to act in ways that are sometimes at odds with the aims and priorities of academics . . . the monograph can survive only if the academic community actively support it . . . real benefits could be gained by using new technologies in the world of academic publishing . . . enabling publishers to exercise much greater control over the management of their resources and stock, through for example, digital printing and print on demand.[14]

Ironically, Thompson's own *Books in the Digital Age,* published in 2005, is not available in any electronic form. Thompson's manuscript was completed before the "take-off" of institutional repositories and e-press public good developments. Emerging models of 'public good' for dissemination of university research will impact publishing scholarly monographs. Columbia University, for instance, supports infrastructure for development of new models for organizing, presenting, disseminating, and sustaining digital scholarly communication.

When it was founded in 1895 Princeton University Press had as its mission "the promotion of education and scholarship and to serve the University." The twenty-first-century digital publishing environment allows for the same values as those stated for Princeton University, but distribution and access models are now radically different. Digital publishing technologies, linked to global networking and international interoperability protocols and metadata standards, allow for an appropriately branded institutional output to serve as an indication of a university's quality and also as an effective scholarly communication tool

Open Access, Institutional Repositories, and Publishing Practice

It seems likely that scholarly publishing will evolve along two distinct paths in the near future: one in which large multinational commercial publishers increase their dominance of the global STM market, and the other in which a variety of open access (OA) initiatives emerge and become commonplace.

Open access is here taken in its widest sense of making scholarly research available to readers through the Internet free of charge, notably through the mechanisms of placing research outputs in institutional/subject repositories, the "Green" strategy, and the "Gold" route of meeting publisher article costs to ensure OA.

Evidence from those publishers who provide material free of charge on the Web is that free access to books on the Web actually generates more conventional book sales. A South African open access publishing project made books available free of charge online, but then the sales turnover of the HRSC Press in question rose by 300%. The conclusion was that "availability of full text online for scholarly publications does push up sales."[15]

It is now time to consider new public good options, or rather old ones by universities returning to publishing their own scholars' output. Making such output free on the net with POD output is one of the major platforms of the new e-presses. The Australian National University e-press strategy is for all ANU publishing of scholarly works to be conducted through a single ANU E Press; open access to outcomes of ANU scholarship being a core value of the e-press; the e-press being built on a set of digital publication services provided centrally; and central services focusing on production platforms, Web-based discovery, and access.

The models exemplified by the ANU E-Press and the University of California eScholarship provide pointers for the future. The ANU 2005 figures are impressive for downloads from 15 academic titles. PDF book and chapter downloads totalled 55,000 in May 2005. This figure excludes additional mobile device downloads, etc. A sample survey in September 2005 revealed 1,905 downloads of the award-winning book *The Spanish Lake,* demonstrating a new digital market.

Most Ph.D. students in the social sciences and humanities will never see their dissertations published in traditional monographic form by a university press. Some publishers who see commercial potential in a thesis or dissertation require considerable reworking, but the vast majority of dissertations are of no commercial interest. Doctoral students would be better served by their supervisors (who are often locked in historical frameworks of publishing) making their dissertations available on the Internet through the various local and national digital theses programs.

In recent years, institutional repositories have developed and currently include material ranging from digital theses to books to digital objects. If these are included in new reward systems they could provide a framework for a fundamental shift in the processes of knowledge distribution. Institutional repositories have potentially significant benefits for institutions if they are integrated holistically into university frameworks. The place of the institutional repository within the university's mission and strategic plan is a crucial first step.

As Lynch has cogently stated: "At the most basic and fundamental level, an institutional repository is a recognition that the intellectual life and scholarship of our universities will increasingly be represented, documented, and shared in digital form, and that a primary responsibility of our universities is to exercise stewardship over these riches: both to make them available and to preserve them."[16]

It is arguable that institutional repositories and open access have much greater potential for scholarly distribution and access in the social sciences and the humanities than for the sciences, which by and large have a well-defined distribution system for their research, albeit often at high prices. Yet the number of humanities documents in institutional repositories is currently far lower than that in STM disciplines.[17] This result has been confirmed by a recent major German study, which in a survey of 1,000 researchers found that more doubts were expressed about open access publications by researchers in the social sciences and the humanities than by those in the sciences.[18]

Academics in the social sciences and humanities do not understand the potential of institutional repositories for the dissemination of their scholarship (which is often published in journals of limited distribution) and because an innate conservatism places them in outdated historical frameworks. The example of leading repositories such as the University of California needs to be more widely known. The University of California had 2,421,218 full text downloads by late January 2006 from its eScholarship Repository (http://repositories. cdlib.org), which offers faculty on the UC campuses a central facility for the deposit of research or scholarly output in a variety of forms.

Digital Textbooks

The book itself needs to be reconstituted for the digital era, both in the context of the tradition of the scholarly monograph and in the arena of the digital textbook. The latter may come more quickly, as students of the Google generation and publisher trends are likely to offer digital slices faster than academic conservatism allows. Thus, if it is priced too highly—no one will buy it; if can't be found—no one will use it; if can't be printed—no one will read it.

There is considerable movement in the area of digital textbooks and course readings as students, with less money than ever, try to adopt the iPod and music download frameworks into publishing. Will the scholarly textbook be ultimately transformed by such initiatives as the California Open Source Textbook Project (http://www.opensourcetext.org/), Libertas Academica (http://www.la-press.com/), and Wikibooks (http://en.wikibooks.org/wiki/Main_Page)?

The UK firm Taylor and Francis has seen a significant, if as yet still small as part of total revenue, increase in rental downloads for its textbook material. Chapters or whole books can be rented digitally for as little as one night. The new "digital natives" will play an increasing role in the determination of trends for e-learning information access.

Thomas and McDonald have stated that there is a need to achieve a balance between the traditional values of libraries and the expectations and habits of the wired generations.[19] Campbell has also explored the place of the library as a virtual destination and the implications for services in the twenty-first century.[20]

The digitization of material in the scholarly environment fits perfectly into the "long tail syndrome." Google Print, Microsoft, and Amazon's initiatives in this area allow for models that bring back out-of-print material into a global information environment. While the material may not be heavily used, the serendipity of searching and global user interest will provide sufficient momentum in this arena. We are moving from an era in which content is king to one in which convenience is king for most content.

Conclusion

Lynch has argued that "we are in the middle of a very large-scale shift. The nature of that shift is that we are at last building a real linkage between research libraries and the new processes of scholarly communication and scholarly practice, as opposed to just repackaging existing products and services of the traditional scholarly publishing system and the historic research library."[21]

Open access initiatives could have a profound impact on scholarly knowledge distribution. The process will be both liberating and disruptive; liberating in that it could release a large amount of scholarly material in a variety of forms globally without the financial barriers imposed by multinational publishers, and disruptive in that confusion may reign as access models bed down

Institutional programs of scholarly advocacy are needed in order to allow the global liberation of text. The new business models for e-presses are often predicated on "public good" foundations rather than a return to the investor in a shareholder context. Universities, however, will need to adopt an holistic approach to scholarly communication and information issues in the digital environment so that institutional budgetary and reward systems can change.

Access to knowledge in the twenty-first century could be liberated in terms of cost for the vast proportion of material created. As history since the fifteenth century has shown, the ability to predict knowledge access and transfer patterns is a complicated one. Without a doubt, the digital revolution has brought us to another set of information crossroads. While some information highways could lead to scholarly dead ends, hopefully there will be sufficient open access pathways, particularly for scholarly monographs, that can be implemented for the benefit of scholarship in particular and society in general.

Notes

1. E. L. Eisenstein, *The Printing Press as Agent of Change* (Cambridge: Cambridge University Press, 1979).

2. J. Cox, "The Pergamon Phenomenon 1951 to 1991: Robert Maxwell and Scientific Publishing." *Learned Publishing* 15 (2002): 273–78

3. Richard Charkin, *Bookseller,* September 23, 2005.

4. J. Willinsky, *The Access Principle: The Case for Open Access to Research and Scholarship* (Cambridge: MIT Publishing, 2005).

5. C. Candee, quoted in R. Poynder, *Changing the Paradigm,* 2005 [Online], available: http://poynder.blogspot.com/2006/01/changing-paradigm.html

6. University of California. Academic Council, Special Committee on Scholarly Communication, *Draft White Papers,* 2005 [Online], available: http://www.universityofcalifornia.edu/senate/committees/scsc/reports.html.

7. J. Houghton, C. Steele, M. and Henty, *Changing Research Practices in the Digital Information and Communication Environment.* Canberra: DEST, 2003 [Online], available: http://www.cfses.com/documents/Changing_Research_Practices.pdf.

8. Bodleian Library, *Printing and Publishing at Oxford: The Growth of a Learned Press 1478—1978* (Oxford: Bodleian Library, 1978), xiii.

9. J. B. Thompson, "Survival Strategies for Academic Publishing," *Chronicle of Higher Education,* June 17, 2005.

10. M. S. Coleman, *University of Michigan President Distresses Scholarly Publishers,* 2006 [Online], available: http://www.infotoday.com/newsbreaks/nb060213-2.shtml.

11. British Academy, *E-resources for Research in the Humanities and Social Sciences —A British Academy Policy Review,* 2005 [Online], available: http://www.britac.ac.uk/reports/eresources/index.html.

12. B. Cronin and K. La Barre, "Mickey Mouse and Milton: book publishing in the humanities." *Learned Publishing* 17 (2004): 85–98

13. Inside Higher Ed, 'Radical Change for Tenure," *Inside Higher Ed* (December 30 2005) [Online], available: http://www.insidehighered.com/news/2005/12/30/tenure.

14. J. B. Thompson, *Books in the Digital Age* (Cambridge: Polity Press, 2005).

15. Eve Gray and Associates, *Digital Publishing and Open Access for Social Science Research Dissemination,* 2004, p. 22 [Online], available: http://www.lessig.org/blog/archives/eve_gray.pdf.

16. C. Lynch, C. "Institutional Repositories: Essential Infrastructure for Scholarship in a Digital Age." *ARL Bimonthly Report* 226, no. 2 (2003) [Online], available: http://www.arl.org/newsltr/226/ir.html.

17. J. Allen, "Interdisciplinary Differences in Attitudes Towards Deposit in Institutional Repositories" (master's thesis, Department of Information and Communications, Manchester Metropolitan University, 2005).

18. Deutsche Forschungsgemeinschaft, *Publishing Strategies and Transformation?* Bonn: DFIM, 2005 [Online], available: http://www.dfg.de/dfg_im_profil/zahlen_und_fakten/statistisches_berichtswesen/open_access/download/oa_report_eng.pdf.

19. C. F. Thomas, and R. H. McDonald, *Millennial Net Value(s): Disconnects Between Libraries and the Information Mindset,* 2005 [Online], available: http://dscholarship.lib.fsu.edu/general/4.

20. J. D. Campbell, "Changing a Cultural Icon: The Academic Library as a Virtual Destination," *Educause* (January/February 2006): 17–30.

21. C. Lynch, "Research Libraries Engage the Digital World: A US-UK Comparative Examination of Recent History and Future Prospects," *Ariadne* (January 2006) [Online], available: http://www.ariadne.ac.uk/issue46/lynch/.

Colin Steele is Emeritus Fellow of the Australian National University. He was University Librarian 1980–2002 and Director Scholarly Information Strategies 2002–2003. He is the author/editor of seven books and over 300 articles and reviews, including *Major Libraries of the World* (1976). He has been an invited keynote speaker at conferences in a number of countries, including the United States, the United Kingdom, China, and South Africa.

BUDGET ALLOCATIONS FOR MONOGRAPHS: WHAT'S FAIR?

Rebecca Donlan, Head of Library Collections and Technical Services, Florida Gulf Coast University Library, Fort Myers

Library budget managers know that their resources are limited and that they need to distribute funds as fairly as possible. The most difficult part of this is defining what constitutes "fairness." At Florida Gulf Coast University (FGCU), we have devised a monographic allocation formula, which we have applied for the past three years. We believe our formula captures the most significant aspects of our institutional needs and, after just a few years, has begun to rectify some collection imbalances that resulted from inequitable distribution of funds.

At FGCU, we realized a few years ago that we needed a balanced approach to monographic expenditures. Some selectors were consistently overspending in a few categories because of faculty requests or personal interest. Other selectors were unnecessarily frugal and over-cautious, which funded the over-spenders and shortchanged important areas of the collection. In the face of this situation, we needed to develop a rational, data-driven formula for equitable monographic allocations.

An allocation formula should attempt to reflect its institution's values, not reform them. FGCU is a regional comprehensive university, with a stated emphasis on undergraduate and professional education. In our literature review, we identified several common variables of allocation formulas:

a) Existing budget

b) Student needs (i.e., undergraduate vs. graduate and the level of research support required by each)

c) Faculty needs (sometimes measured by productivity in terms of grant dollars received)

d) Credit hours per discipline

e) Levels of library usage

f) Resource costs

g) New program costs

h) Collection needs analysis (e.g., gap analysis)

The first variable—existing budget—is critical. This sets a limit on what is possible; we don't have, say, Harvard's budget, so we must maximize the effectiveness of the money we have. Admittedly, the larger question *not* addressed in this paper is how to determine appropriate levels of funding for broad categories of the collection (e.g., serials, monographs, electronic resources). Finding the proper balance of these variables is important and is something we hope to address in the next several years.

Here is a snapshot of the "macro allocation" of FGCU's 2003–2004 materials budget:

• Serials and standing orders = 43%

• Monographs = 32%

- Electronic resources = 16%

- Outsourcing costs = 9%

    ○ Cataloging and processing costs and supplies

    ○ E-resources management through Serials Solutions

In 2003–2004, $400,000 was designated for monographic purchases. Historically, this has been the amount we have spent on books, and we have attempted to keep serials expenditures reasonable through regular review and cancellation of underutilized journals. Also, our costs for electronic resources are much lower than they would be if we had to cover them separately. The state universities of Florida purchase many databases as a group, and we are fortunate to have separate state funding and consortia purchasing power. We think, too, that it is important to acknowledge that there are demands on our materials budget for services that are not, strictly speaking, materials expenditures. Outsourcing costs, for instance, are borne by the materials budget. Still, demand for new electronic resources and various services (electronic resource management, MARC records for e-journals, etc.) is strong, and yet another reason to have a well-reasoned and defensible monographic budget.

We have approval slip plans for 14 disciplines, each of which is assigned a fund code (e.g., ART, BUS, EDU, HEA, HIS, LIT, POL, SCI, etc.). For this pilot program, we chose to apply our allocation formula to these approval profiles, rather than attempting to cover every monographic purchase, such as firm orders that are not available from our primary vendors. Our ability to generate complete fund reports from our library management system is limited because of internal workflow. FGCU opened in 1997, with minimal staffing devoted to technical services and a heavy reliance on outsourcing. Some institutions generate orders from their catalogs and send them through their acquisitions module. We order from our primary vendor's Web site and batch-load its on-order records, which are eventually overlaid by full MARC records when the item arrives. But we do not have enough staff available to append an order record to each brief record, so we have depended on our vendor's financial reports.

Once we determined how much money was available and how the allocation formula would be implemented, we needed to work up the actual formula. For FGCU, a Master's I institution, we concluded that the variables of *credit hours by discipline, book price, and library usage* were most important. A large research library might, quite appropriately, place greater emphasis on faculty and graduate program research support.

Let us examine the individual variables. The first variable, credit hours per discipline, seemed to us to be the most obvious way to represent the subject content of student coursework. FGCU's Division of Enrollment Services provides us with an annual registration report; we total the credit hours for colleges and areas and assign them to the appropriate library fund/profile code. Each total is expressed as a percentage and multiplied by the entire budget available (i.e., $400,000). Some programs map one-to-one to their fund codes, like business and education. Other fund codes, like ART, reflect a number of different programs. Table 1 shows a sample of credit hours for the academic year 2004–2005.

Table 1. Sample of Credit Hours for 2004–2005 for ART

Fund	College	Area	Credit Hours 2004–2005
ART	Arts and Sciences	Art	591
ART	Arts and Sciences	Art History	330
ART	Arts and Sciences	Music: Ensembles	14
ART	Arts and Sciences	Theater	189
ART	Arts and Sciences	Theater Performance and Performance Training	189
TOTAL Credit Hours for ART = 1,313			

To convert these credit hours into usable data for our formula, we determined the percentage of the entire enrollment that the ART hours represent. The total number of credit hours for all courses taken at FGCU in 2004–2005 was 55,831. The total number of credit hours that map to the fund code of ART in that same time period was 1,313, so the percentage of credit hours that mapped to ART was 2.35% (1,313/55,831=0.0235). We repeated this process for all profiles; the total of all percentages must equal 1. (In our process, we call this "normalizing" the variable. Essentially, this just means treating the percentage as a decimal number, not as a percentage.)

The next variable we considered was book price by discipline. Costs of books in different disciplines vary considerably, and any formula that aims to be fair must acknowledge this. Many vendors will supply information about average book costs. Blackwell's, for example, publishes an approval coverage and cost study each year. This study presents information on the numbers of titles treated and their average list price, arranged both by Blackwell's subject areas and by Library of Congress Classification. We determined the average book price for each profile or fund code, totaled these prices by profile, and then added them to determine an aggregate average book price for the entire year. Table 2 shows the average book prices for the 2003–2004 academic year.

To convert these prices into usable data for our formula, we determined what percentage of the aggregate average book price the ART books represented. According to Table 2, the average book price for ART titles 2003–2004 was $55.41. Dividing the average ART book price by the aggregate average book price of $819.41, we find that ART books represent 6.76% of the aggregate average book price. SCI books, on the other hand, are 11.46% of the aggregate average. We repeated this for each profile and added up the normalized prices; the total of all percentages must equal 1.

Table 2. Average Book Prices for 2003–2004

Profile/Fund Code	Average 2003–2004 Book Price
ART	$ 55.41
BUS	$ 67.05
CJL	$ 63.59
EDU	$ 52.82
HEA	$ 46.96
HIS	$ 51.19
HOS	$ 63.28
LIT	$ 44.35
PHR	$ 56.36
POL	$ 52.71
PUB	$ 60.24
SCI	$ 93.95
SSI	$ 60.87
SWK	$ 50.63
Aggregate average book price	$819.41

Our third and final variable, library usage, is often represented in allocation formulas by circulation statistics. FGCU's approach is a little different. We came up with a ratio we call the "bookish multiplier" to capture the variable of library usage. The bookish multiplier is a ratio between circulation and credit hours (circulation/credit hours = bookish multiplier). This measurement seems to capture quite well the monographic dependence of disciplines, at least in the way that they are taught at our institution.

To determine the bookish multiplier for a profile, we consulted our annual cumulative report of circulation by LC range, which we then assigned to individual profiles. We divided the number of book circulations of a discipline (as defined by LC class number) by the number of credit hours in that discipline. For example, if the total circulation for ART in 2004–2005 = 1,839, and the total credit hours for ART in 2004–2005 = 1,313, then the bookish multiplier for ART in 2004–2005 was 1,839/1,313, or 1.4006.

To operationalize this variable for the formula, we determined what percentage of the total of bookish multipliers this discipline represents. Since the total of all bookish multipliers in 2004–2005 was 10.31, then the normalized bookish multiplier for ART was 1.4006/10.31 = 0.135890451. We repeated this process for all profiles, and the total of all percentages must equal 1.

Using the bookish multiplier reveals some interesting facts about the differences in book dependence among various disciplines. For instance, look at these statistics:

- History credit hours 2004–2005 = 1,492
- History circs 2004–2005 = 3,626
- History bookish multiplier = 3,626/1,492 = 2.4303
- Business credit hours 2004–2005 = 10,983
- Business circs 2004–2005 = 2,673
- Business bookish multiplier = 2,673/10,983 = .2434

These statistics indicate that history studies at FGCU are 10 times more dependent on monographs than are business studies. This does not mean that history everywhere is 10 times more "bookish" than business, although that might be true; it means that history students were using 10 times as many *books* as business students did at FGCU in the 2004–2005 academic year. We know from other statistics that our business students are heavy users of serials and electronic databases.

Many allocation schemes address the supposed higher demands of graduate programs by assigning higher weights to graduate full-time equivalent (FTE) students. While it may be true that graduate programs have higher *overall* library materials needs, that may not be true for the demand on individual components of the library's collection. An undergraduate program may have greater need for books than a large and heavily enrolled graduate program. For example, at FGCU in the 2003–2004 academic year, history, an undergraduate program, had 6.5 books charged per three credit hours. Education, on the other hand, with extensive graduate and undergraduate programs, had 1.5 books charged per three credit hours.

The bookish multiplier cannot be used as the sole source of information about the bookishness of disciplines. As mentioned before, some disciplines rely more on serials and databases. But low circulation may be an indicator of the need for more collection analysis and development. We are only in the third year of applying this allocation formula, so it is too early to determine whether circulation has increased in previously under-funded areas. Literature, for instance, was shortchanged for so many years that their low bookish multiplier may be a result of an inadequate collection. Table 3 shows the relatively low bookish multiplier currently assigned to literature. One would think, intuitively, that literature would be one of the top five bookish disciplines. We expect it to move up the scale after increased spending on monographs builds up the collection.

Table 3. Bookish Multiplier Assigned to Literature 2004–2005

Discipline	Bookish Multiplier 2004–2005
HISTORY	5.9
ART	3.4
PHILOSOPHY/RELIGION	1.8
EDUCATION	1.7
HEALTH SCIENCES	1.7
PUBLIC ADMINISTRATION	1.7
SOCIAL SCIENCES INTERDISCIPLINARY	1.6
POLITICAL SCIENCE	1.5
SOCIAL WORK	1.5
LITERATURE AND LANGUAGE	1.4
CRIMINAL JUSTICE AND LEGAL STUDIES	0.8
SCIENCES	0.8
BUSINESS	0.6
HOSPITALITY AND TOURISM	0.5

The last step in creating a budget allocation formula is to assign appropriate weights to the variables. Assigning every variable a weight of 1 would imply that each variable is of equal importance. This does not accurately reflect institutional mission and values. A high weighting of the cost variable, for instance, is appropriate for a research library that needs to collect deeply in a number of disciplines. The University of Maryland libraries, for example, assign a 50% weight to the "publishing universe" (variations in the volume of publishing, average price of publications, and the split between books and serials for various materials).[1] Such weighting distributes more money to disciplines with expensive books, ensuring that the library will be able to collect adequately in those areas.

With FGCU's emphasis on student education rather than research, we determined these weights:

Credit hours 2.50

Book price 0.25

Bookish multiplier 0.25

TOTAL 3.00

Admittedly, we have not yet discovered any purely quantitative way to determine the optimal weight for each variable. We relied on experience and understanding of our institutional mission. We tried weighting each variable as 1, and then weighting credit hours as 2 and the other two variables as .5, but the final allotments looked skewed. Some disciplines just got too much money relative to their number of majors. When we used this particular weighting formula, the final results looked appropriate.

So, how does one determine the amount of money that is available to a discipline? The percentage of the total budget that is allocated to a profile is obtained by adding the normalized and weighted factors and dividing that number by the total number of factors. The equation is (Credit hours + Price + Bookish multiplier)/3. The allocation for ART would be calculated as follows:

ART credit hours (0.0235 x 2.5) = 0.0588

ART book price (0.0676 x 0.25) = 0.0169

ART bookish multiplier (0.135890451 **x** 0.25) = 0.0340

0.0588 + 0.0169 + 0.0340 = 0.1097

0.1097 / 3 = 0.0365666

ART allocation = 3.66% of total monographic budget

3.66% x $400,000 = $14,640 for ART monographs for the fiscal year

Has our formula worked? We think it has. The problem that prompted us to create the allocation formula in the first place has improved through a more rational distribution of funds. Overspending in some problem areas has decreased, and disciplines that were lagging are catching up:

ART 03–04 53.7% over budget

ART 04–05 6.3% over budget

ART 05–06 72.0% remaining (end of Q1)

LIT 03–04 72.82% under budget

LIT 04–05 1.56% over budget

LIT 05–06 56.00% remaining (end of Q1)

The university faculty appreciate our allocation formula, knowing that their disciplines will not be shortchanged, and university administration appreciates our sound fiscal management. Interestingly, over the past three years the allocations have not changed dramatically. If this continues to be the case, we will probably only recalculate the allocations every two or three years, since the time involved in assigning credit hours and circulation statistics to disciplines is considerable.

In the near future we plan to expand the application of the allocation formula to all monographic expenditures, not just to those that are purchased through our primary vendors. Since we have recently migrated to a library management system with a more flexible acquisitions module (ExLibris's Aleph), it should be possible for us to automatically generate encumbrances for each on-order record we import from our vendors. Our vendors, too, have appreciated knowing how much money is available in an approval profile, so that they can work with our selectors to focus approval profiles more precisely.

We hope to eventually create a "macro" allocation formula that will allow us to determine the proper balance of funding of serials, monographs, and electronic resources. In the meantime, we are confident that the funds we have identified for monographic expenditures—whether or not they are adequate—are being allocated wisely and well.

Notes

1. University of Maryland Libraries, *Definitions of Categories and Variables Used in the Allocation Formula,* 1999 [Online], available: http://www.lib.umd.edu/CLMD/Formula/definitions.html.

Bibliography

Arora, A., and D. Klabjan. "A Model for Budget Allocation in Multi-unit Libraries." *Library Collections, Acquisitions, and Technical Services* 26 (2002): 423–38.

Clendenning, L. F., J. K. Martin, and G. McKenzie. "Secrets for Managing Materials Budget Allocations: A Brief Guide for Collection Managers." *Library Collections, Acquisitions, and Technical Services* 29 (2005): 99–108.

Copeland, L., and T. M. Mundle. "Library Allocations: Faculty and Librarians Discuss 'Fairness'." *Portal: Libraries and the Academy* 2, no. 2 (2002): 267–76.

Crotts, J. "Subject Usage and Funding of Library Monographs." *College and Research Libraries* (May 1999): 261–73.

Dinkins, D. "Circulation as Assessment: Collection Development Policies Evaluated in Terms of Circulation at a Small Academic Library." *College and Research Libraries* (January 2003): 46–53.

German, L., and K. A. Schmidt. "Finding the Right Balance: Campus Involvement in the Collections Allocation Process." *Library Collections, Acquisitions, and Technical Services* 25 (2001): 421–33.

Kalyan, S. (2003). Library materials budget allocation strategy for a mid-size academic library: a case study. *The Acquisition Librarian*, 29, 119–31.

Lafferty, S., P. Warning, and B. Vlies. "Foundation Resources: Formula-Based Allocation of an Acquisition Budget in a University Library." *Australian Academic & Research Libraries* 27, no. 4 (1996): 289–94.

Mulliner, K. "Why Who Gets What When: Ohio University's Acquisitions Allocation Formula after 20 Years." In *2000 Charleston Conference Proceedings: Is Bigger Better?,* edited by Rosann Bazirjian and Vicky Speck. Charleston, SC: Against the Grain, 2000.

Niemeyer, M., et al. "Balancing Act for Library Materials Budgets: Use of a Formula Allocation." *Technical Services Quarterly* 11, no. 1 (1993): 43–60.

University of Western Australia Library. *Information Resources Budget Formula,* 2003 [Online], available: http://www.library.uwa.edu.au/collection/acquisitions/formula.html.

Weston, C. V. "Breaking with the Past: Formula Allocation at Portland State University." *The Serials Librarian* 45, no. 4 (2004): 43–53.

Young, I. R. "A Quantitative Comparison of Acquisitions Budget Allocation Formulas Using a Single Institutional Setting." *Library Acquisitions: Practice & Theory* 16 (1992): 229–42.

DO ASTRONOMERS USE BOOKS?

Presented at the 2004 Conference but omitted from the 2004 proceedings.

Jane Holmquist, Astrophysics Librarian, Princeton University, New Jersey

Abstract

In the spring of 2004, lists of the astronomy books currently checked out of the libraries of 16 of my colleagues around the world were collected and compared to the list provided by Michael Kurtz of the top books cited in the Astrophysics Data System (ADS) database. I have subsequently analyzed the books cited by Princeton astrophysics undergraduates in their senior theses and graduate students in their doctoral dissertations (1980–2004), as well as book circulation and reshelving data for the Astrophysics Library for the past two years, in order to answer the question: Do astronomers use books?

I have served as the Astrophysics Librarian at Princeton University for the past 15 years; prior to that I served as the Plasma Physics Librarian for 10 years. So I thought that it would be interesting to look at patterns of book usage by astronomers for the past 25 years, a span of time that is generally considered to constitute a generation.

What prompted my investigation of book usage was the following statement made by a faculty member at a departmental meeting two years ago: "All one really needs in an astronomy library's collection nowadays—with so much available online—is about 500 books." Could this be true?

I look first at the evidence provided by citation studies—the books cited in the senior theses and Ph.D. dissertations from the Department of Astrophysical Sciences at Princeton University from 1980 to 2004, then the books cited in journal articles written by Princeton-affiliated authors between 1981 and 2001, and finally, the list of books most often cited in the Astrophysics Data System.

Table 1. Books Cited 1980–2004 in Undergraduates' Senior Theses and Graduate Students' Ph.D. Dissertations from Princeton University's Department of Astrophysical Sciences

	Senior Theses	Ph.D. Dissertations	Combined
No. of theses	51	77	128
No. of references	1632	8,621	10,253
No. of monographs cited	157	432	589
Percentage	9.6%	5.0%	5.7%
No. of unique titles	107	178	241
No. of conference proceedings cited	83	443	526
Percentage	5.0%	5.1%	5.1%
No. of unique titles	62	191	228

As shown in Table 1, of the 1,632 total references included in the bibliographies of the 51 senior theses written between 1980 and 2004, 157 monographs (9.6%) and 83 conference proceedings (5%) were cited. Most of the remaining references were to journal articles.

In contrast, graduate students cited the same percentage of conference proceedings (5.2%) but half as many monographs (5%). Most of the remaining citations were to journal articles, with a small number of technical reports, dissertations, and miscellaneous Web sites included in more recent theses. Graduate students averaged four times as many cited references as undergraduates: 112 to 32.

If we add the numbers for all the senior theses and Ph.D. dissertations, we find that 10.8% of the total citations were to books: monographs and conference proceedings combined. The number of unique titles was 469—astonishingly close to the 500 predicted by the faculty member!

Before I move on to consider the number of books actually "used" (charged out or reshelved) as opposed to "cited" in theses or journal articles, I thought you might be interested in seeing the titles of the top 10 books cited by undergrads and graduate students in their theses, the top 10 cited in journal articles, and the top 10 cited in the Astrophysics Data System, shown in Tables 2 through 4. I thank Nisa Bakkalbasi and David Goodman for the data from journal citations, and Michael Kurtz for the ADS data.[1]

Table 2. Top 10 Astronomy Books Cited in Princeton Senior and Ph.D. Theses, 1980–2004.

1.	Galactic dynamics/Binney & Tremaine
2.	Large-scale structure of the universe/Peebles
3.	Physical processes in the interstellar medium/Spitzer
4.	Computer simulation using particles/Hockney
5.	Numerical recipes in C: the art of scientific computing. 2nd ed./Press
6.	Galactic astronomy: structure, and kinematics. 2nd ed./Mihalas
7.	Gravitation and cosmology: principles and applications of the general theory of relativity
8.	Large scale structures in the universe/IAU Symposium (130th: 1987)
9.	Dynamics of star clusters/IAU Symposium (113th: 1984)
10.	Internal kinematics and dynamics of galaxies/IAU Symposium (100th: 1983)

**Table 3. Top 10 Astronomy Books Cited in Journal Articles
by Princeton-Affiliated Authors, 1981–2001**

1.	Galactic dynamics/Binney & Tremaine
2.	Principles of physical cosmology/Peebles
3.	Gravitational lenses/Schneider
4.	Structure and evolution of normal galaxies (1980: Cambridge, England)
5.	Critical dialogues in cosmology (1996: Princeton, NJ)
6.	Wide field spectroscopy and the distant universe (1994: Cambridge, England)
7.	QSO absorption lines: probing the universe (1987: Baltimore, MD)
8.	Galactic astronomy: structure, and kinematics. 2nd ed./Mihalas
9.	Inner space/outer space: the interface between cosmology and particle physics (1984)
10.	Astrophysics of gaseous nebulae and active galactic nuclei/Osterbrock

Table 4. Top 10 Books Cited in the Astrophysics Data System (ADS)

1.	Astrophysical quantities. 3rd ed./Allen
2.	Numerical recipes in FORTRAN: the art of scientific computing. 2nd ed./Press
3.	Galactic dynamics/Binney & Tremaine
4.	Large-scale structure of the universe/Peebles
5.	Physical processes in the interstellar medium/Spitzer
6.	Third reference catalogue of bright galaxies/de Vaucouleurs
7.	Gravitation/Misner
8.	Astrophysics of gaseous nebulae and active galactic nuclei/Osterbrock
9.	Gravitation and cosmology: principles and applications of the general theory of relativity /
10.	Bright star catalogue. 4th ed./Hoffleit

But surely astronomers use more than 500 books!

To bolster my claim, last spring I asked my astronomy librarian colleagues around the world to please send me lists of the books currently checked out of their libraries. I was gratified to receive their lists and to see that among the 16 of us, more than 2,500 unique titles were currently checked out and in use! So yes, astronomers around the world do use books! I was pleased to see that many people were borrowing popular books related not just to current research (Mars, the search for planets, life in the universe) but also many about the history of astronomy.

Finally, for the past two years we have been keeping track of all books borrowed and reshelved at the Astrophysics Library, and I am pleased to report that that number is approaching 1,500, three times the number of books cited, and three times the number of books the faculty member considered sufficient for an astronomy library's collection!

Time will tell. It is true that astronomers rely primarily on journal articles (see Kurtz et al. and Tenopir et al.),[2] but if one looks at the historical percentage of monographs cited by astronomers (see Abt),[3] we see that it hasn't changed that much since 1952, when it was 5.2%!

Notes

1. N. Bakkalbasi and D. Goodman, "Do Science Researchers Use Books?," in *Charleston Conference Proceedings 2004*, edited by R. Bazirjian (Westport, CT: Libraries Unlimited, 2005); M. J. Kurtz et al., "Worldwide Use and Impact of the NASA Astrophysics Data System Digital Library," *Journal of the American Society for Information Science and Technology* 56, no. 1 (2005): 36–45.

2. Kurtz et al., "Worldwide Use and Impact"; C. Tenopir et al., "Relying on Electronic Journals: Reading Patterns of Astronomers," *Journal of the American Society for Information Science and Technology (JASIST)* (forthcoming). Preprint available at http://web.utk.edu/~tenopir/eprints/tenopir_jasist_article_042503_preprint.pdf.

3. H. A. Abt, "Changing Sources of Published Information," *Publications of the Astronomical Society of the Pacific* 107 (April 1995): 401–3.

THE ELECTRONIC MONOGRAPH: CAN WE FIND A SUCCESSFUL BUSINESS MODEL?

Bob Nardini, YBP Library Services, Contoocook, New Hampshire

With Bonnie MacEwan, Auburn University Library, Alabama

Peter Potter, Penn State Press, University Park, Pennsylvania

In planning this talk, one thing Peter, Bonnie, and I decided right away was that I would speak last, after them. Whatever might happen with e-books, we reasoned, publishers would have a role and libraries would have a role. But, would book vendors?

That's why I'd like to point out that we book vendors are the original content aggregators. We brought together a lot of content—in the form of physical, printed books—and made it easy for libraries to buy the ones they needed and for publishers to sell those books to libraries. We earned our role by volunteering to take on much of the work required to carry out the many small transactions that occur when libraries buy books.

As for e-books, the first thing I'd like to know is, who decided they are books, anyway? Did they ask the rest of us? We know that print books and e-books share a text, at least we think that's normally true. Beyond that, though, there's not much in common between the two. For a publisher, the production of a print book and an e-book is the same to a point, but then they diverge. Libraries don't treat the two formats in the same way. Readers probably don't use them in the same way. Authors don't normally think about them too much at all. And I can say from experience that for a bookseller, selling e-books and selling print books are two very different experiences.

We know this because for most of this year, YBP has been gearing up to sell e-books, thanks to an arrangement between NetLibrary and our parent company, Baker & Taylor. What we are trying to do is replicate for e-books all of the services we provide for print books, from searching in our database, to profiling new titles, to accepting and placing orders, to reporting on expenditures. We've had to review nearly every one of our systems—all of which have been designed around print books—to ask the questions: Will this system work for e-books? Which systems can stand as they are? Which need to be modified? What new systems do we need? Once we have learned how to sell NetLibrary e-books, our plan would then be to incorporate e-books from other suppliers into the services we offer libraries.

We're now nearing the end of this project. It has demanded an enormous amount of work on the part of many of my YBP colleagues, some of whom who work in sales and marketing, others in systems, others in accounting and finance, and others as bibliographers. The meetings, the e-mails, the phone calls, the memos are just uncountable. We've had to write elaborate "functional specifications," as they are called, in four broad areas of our systems. One is for what we know as OOPS—our "online order processing system." This is homegrown software that filters all electronic orders that reach YBP, in whatever format, and parses them in such a way that our distribution and invoicing systems can allocate the right books to the right customers at the right price without staff getting involved in most transactions. Another system is our AS 400, the mainframe computer where all that matchmaking actually takes place. A third set of systems involves our technical services, where we provide cataloging records, shipping records, invoicing records, and other files to our customers. And a fourth system is GOBI, the interface most customers use to do business with YBP.

We have had to account for every situation we could think of, down to minutiae such as, what if a customer tries to order an e-book on a print book account? (Exception code "G" in our specifications, by the way.) Or, the reverse, what if a customer tries to order a print book on an e-book account? We've had to change the part of GOBI that enables rush ordering, to disallow rush orders for e-books. An e-book rush order would make no more sense than placing a spine label on an e-book, but some user will surely attempt to do it. We've had to create rules for the copying of bibliographic data from the print books we've already examined over to the equivalent e-book. Can we safely assume, for example, that the title of an e-book and its print companion are the same? We think so, but that's really only an educated guess, one of many we have had to make.

We've created new data categories for e-books, categories that aren't necessary or don't exist for print books, and have integrated these new categories into our systems. "Downloadable," for example (yes/no are the choices). "EBook supplier" (as opposed to publisher) is another example. "Consortial rights" is a third. (Is a library buying this e-book as itself, or as a member of a group under different business terms?) "International rights" is yet another. (Are we permitted to sell this particular e-book to a library located in this particular country?)

The other thing I'd like to know then is, who decided that costs for handling e-books were low? I don't know who that person was. But we have decided that the considerable costs of reconfiguring our systems are worth taking on. And that's because we do believe there is a role for the traditional book vendor in the supply chain for e-books.

We are placing certain bets. One is that print books and e-books will coexist for a long time. Another is that libraries will be willing to pay for e-books, that they will not become more or less advertising vehicles for print—available for free—or will not move into some kind of open access model. Another is that sales for e-books will not cannibalize sales for print books, as sales for simultaneous paperbacks have done for sales of cloth books. A fourth bet is that book vendors can add value for libraries by enabling them to coordinate decisions about buying a title as a print book, or as an e-book, or both ways. We are setting up our internal systems and GOBI in such a way that all of a library's activity on a given title—no matter the format—is brought together and displayed in a convenient way, so that unintentional duplication of content can be avoided.

And finally, we think that book vendors will have an e-book role if libraries buy them title-by-title, at least much of the time, instead of buying in bulk. Recently, for example, I visited a library and told them about our NetLibrary plans. "Oh yes," the librarian said, "we bought 10,000 e-books a few years ago. We will probably buy another 10,000 next year." Believe me, I wish we could sell print books that way.

Another question is, will there be many suppliers of e-books, or just a few? The more suppliers, the greater a book vendor's technical challenges, since systems for loading of titles, ordering, invoicing, and everything else will need to be looked at, one supplier at a time. If Penn State Press, for example, decides to go it alone with the Romance literature series, instead of giving over these e-books to NetLibrary and/or other suppliers, we would need to be sure that YBP had a good way to place an order on behalf of a customer for one of these e-books, that Penn State could accept and acknowledge our order, and then provide the right library with the right e-book under the right terms. If we master these technical challenges, though, our marketing role will be stronger, since tracking and doing business with many different e-book suppliers will be difficult for libraries. They will need help, as they need help in buying print books published by the multitude of publishers.

If, on the other hand, there turn out to be a relative handful of e-book suppliers, the technical barriers will be lower, since we would need to establish fewer business relationships. But our marketing position would be correspondingly weaker. Libraries could the more easily keep track of a smaller number of suppliers. And maybe those suppliers would prefer to sell to libraries direct, as only a generation or so ago many book publishers preferred to do it (as some still do). Of course that will increase the chance that our ongoing "serials crisis" will have a twin, the "e-book crisis."

Another role that has been suggested might emerge, one that is purely a marketing role, whereby book vendors, through their various alerting mechanisms, would announce availability of new e-books but would not necessarily be the agent to sell them. That would avoid some of the development costs necessary actually to sell e-books. Who would pay for this service? Would publishers pay a book vendor to announce their e-books? Would libraries pay for a vendor's subscription alert service for e-books the vendor could not necessarily sell to them?

Once again, are e-books really books? If it turns out the answer is anywhere close to yes, then we book vendors will almost certainly play a role similar to the one we have established for print books. If the answer turns out to be no—that e-books are not very much like books—then we book vendors, along with publishers and libraries, have ahead of us many lessons to learn.

ELECTRONIC REFERENCE SOURCES: THE LIBRARY CONNECTION

Kathryn M. Crowe, Interim Associate Director, University of North Carolina at Greensboro

Electronic reference sources provide librarians with the exciting opportunity of offering their users authoritative content 24/7, regardless of location, to resources that previously were available only in the library. Publishers have developed a variety of purchasing and pricing models from which to choose. These online resources also provide new possibilities for virtual reference and information literacy.

Opportunities

It's beyond redundant to say that a vast amount of information is available freely on the Web and that we all rely on it. Answers to what we used to call ready-reference questions can easily be found through Google searches. When more thorough information is needed, however, teachers and librarians struggle to educate students to use reliable published sources. Reference and instruction librarians have long used subject encyclopedias to provide introductions to topics and background information. As wonderful as we think they are, however, Millennials and Generation Y have grown up with the Web and are highly unlikely to use print reference sources. At the same time, this proprietary information offers users high-quality content and more substantial alternatives to what's found on the Web. Reference sources were among the last to convert to the online format, and it's been gratifying to be able to offer them more widely to users. As reference has expanded beyond the traditional desk, we can now offer valuable content beyond the library walls.

Issues to Consider

With new opportunities there are always issues to consider. Although e-journals took off immediately, e-books have never been quite as popular. Printing an article to keep is very convenient, but using an entire monograph online or printing it is quite awkward. Reference sources, however, adapt well to the online format since users usually just need a few pages of material.

Content issues have arisen as well. Some publishers have not been able to acquire rights to graphics and illustrations. Because these can be crucial to certain subject areas (e.g., art), librarians may choose to retain print for some titles. And while the younger generation embraces anything online, older librarians are still accustomed to print resources! Experienced reference librarians are used to browsing their well-known shelves for good information and to using traditional indexes. Some of that valuable browsing capability is lost in the online versions.

Purchasing and Pricing Models

Publishers have devised several business plans for purchasing online reference sources. Some, including the Oxford Reference Center and Routledge Reference Resources Online, offer bundled collections of titles for a subscription fee. Usually these packages tend to be sources that were one- or two-volume works in print. Librarians need to determine if the amount of new content each year warrants the subscription price. Other publishers, such as Thomson Gale, XREFER and the Oxford Digital Library, offer the option of choosing specific titles. These resources are primarily ones that were multivolume titles in print. Pricing models for these are based on the print model; each title is purchased on a one-time basis and an annual access fee is charged for maintenance.

Collection Management Decisions

Librarians have many decisions to make when selecting online reference sources. There are, of course, obvious factors such as curriculum or user needs and affordability. Online reference resources often cost more, and so libraries on a tight budget may not be able to afford them. The bundled packages may include sources not really needed. Another factor to consider is whether to duplicate print and online or choose one format. For the most part, print is usually canceled in favor of online since most users prefer it, but librarians need to be cautious that important content is not lost. As mentioned above, the availability of graphics and illustrations is also a consideration Campuses will need to consider distance education and commuting student needs, and public library systems how much their users access resources remotely. Online resources also offer the possibility of consortial purchases, which may save libraries money to devote to other unique materials.

User Access

Online reference sources provide new opportunities for librarians to push content to users in addition to the traditional reference encounters. Databases such as the Gale Virtual Reference Library or Oxford Reference Center may be added to federated search engines so that reference sources may be searched along with other online resources. These search engines may also be customized to specific subject areas. For an example, see the Business Multisearch at the University of North Carolina at Greensboro (http://library.uncg.edu/dbs/subject/busadm.asp). Individual titles may be cataloged in the OPAC so users can find them in a subject search. Reference databases and individual titles may be included in online guides for subject areas or specific courses. At the University of North Carolina at Greensboro, librarians have developed lists of online reference sources for each major or program at the University (see http://library.uncg.edu/depts/ref/courseguides.asp) as well as including them in guides for specific classes. Such guides can also be pushed to students through course management software such as Blackboard.

Information Literacy

Subject encyclopedias have long been promoted by instruction librarians as a starting tool for students to begin their research. Instructors may now display an article on the screen and explain its usefulness. An article can be scanned to find keywords. An entry from a bibliography can be chosen and located in the Library OPAC to illustrate how to continue research. This technique is much more appealing than passing print sets around the classroom, and students are much more likely to use the sources if they're available 24/7.

Bibliography

Albanese, Andrew Richard. "The Reference Evolution." *Library Journal* 129, no. 19 (November 15, 2004): 10+.

Tyckoson, Dave. "Facts Go Online: Are Print Reference Collections Still Relevant?" *Against the Grain* (September 2004): 34+.

Wilkinson, Frances C., and Linda K. Lewis. "Reference eBooks: Does an eBook on the Screen Beat One on the Shelf?" *Against the Grain* (September 2005): 1+.

YOU ARE THE TOP BIDDER! BEGINNING THE ONLINE AUCTION PROCESS

Amy J. Carlson, Head, Serials Department, University of Hawaii at Manoa

Regardless of their size, most libraries have specific acquisitions policies. Such policies create efficient processing and ensure a reasonable cost and a timely receipt, but limit more creative purchasing. Policies offer convenience. But the cost of these limitations outweighs the convenience if the library cannot acquire specialized or important materials due to the policy itself. Through my presentation, I discussed the investigation and use of online auctions to purchase materials, including changes in auctions, policies and procedures at the library, and training needs for the staff.

The University of Hawaii at Manoa Acquisitions and Serials Departments previously had a policy that excluded the use of online auctions. The policy was created soon after the advent of such auctions as eBay and was upheld in 2000 and again in 2003. What happens when a bibliographer stands next to my desk, excited about the possibility of purchase, with the auction clock ticking away? No matter what established policies technical processing departments fall back on when faced with an unusual request, usually acquisitions librarians look into the request. In April 2005 our Russian bibliographer stood at the edge of my desk, eBay printouts in hand, pointing to the auction deadline. I had no choice but to open another investigation in 2005.

World of Online Auctions

I began the process by examining online auctions themselves. In the late 1990s and early 2000s I made personal purchases through eBay, but had since sworn off a highly addictive albeit useful "garage sale." The world that greeted me in 2005 was a highly polished, streamlined, and easy-to-use version of the world of my previous experiences. Over 12 million items are up for sale by purchase or auction on the 10-year-old eBay. It boasts 150 million regular users worldwide. In the course of its 10 years, eBay has conducted three national advertising campaigns, including one that began in November 2005. Yahoo! and Amazon.com provide auctions, but as a component to a larger offering of services to their users. Their auction services are newer and smaller, and they have conducted advertising on their auction services, but have concentrated on their services as a whole package.

In the course of the last few years, online retailing has been established as an option for the mainstream consumer. Where early experimenters were buying online in the late 1990s to early 2000s, many consumers had adopted the convenience and ease of purchasing over the Internet by 2005. Grewal, Iyer, and Levy cite type of product, access to information, price, convenience, and novelty as some of the reasons for the growth of Internet retail sales.[1] Hardesty and Suter suggest that the consumers perceive lower prices online as compared to physical stores but they neglect to factor in the shipping costs. In addition to their perception of lower costs, most consumers expect e-tailers to provide lower prices due to their reduced overhead. The maintenance of an online store is quite a bit less than the cost of renting a space, employing people to run and work in the space, cost of phones, computer systems, and other overhead costs. Online auctions may influence expectation of pricing as well.[2] Online retailing has become another outlet for the shopping experience and continues to influence consumer expectations of service and price.

The e-tailers have made a number of changes in the last few years to adjust to consumer purchasing. With the success of its own Web site storefront, Amazon.com has expanded to run storefronts for national retailers such as Target and Toys R Us. eBay fosters a unique version of a storefront, allowing smaller sellers to create a kind of "garage sale" or boutique for all of their items. The buyer can bypass the auction altogether and "Buy it now" with an established price from the seller, and many items on eBay no longer have the auction feature but are available through a set price only. Amazon.com, which also has an auction service on the Web site, also provides the "get it now" type feature, which allows one to bypass the auction. Yahoo Auctions has many of the features of eBay and Amazon.com, but on a smaller scale. In looking at the three auctions sites, I found more similarities than differences. eBay, in moving away from the auction process and providing storefronts for its sellers, is moving closer in business model and services provided to the consumer to an e-tailer like Amazon.com. Amazon.com, by offering auctions in addition to its new and used media and books, is moving into the eBay target audience. Overall, I found the changes allowed the shopper to easily find products and make purchases, while offering a community of possibilities.

Local Background

The University of Hawaii at Manoa is the flagship campus in a 12-campus system of community colleges and universities called the University of Hawaii System. The university offers 286 degree programs and is one of a handful of universities that is a Land, Sea and Space grant institution. It is located on the Island of Oahu, very close to the famous Waikiki Beach and the city of Honolulu. Over 20,500 students attend the university: 14,250 undergraduates and 6,300 graduate students.

The University of Hawaii at Manoa Library is a medium-sized, research library. A member of ARL, the library holds 3,356,031 volumes, adds approximately 74,000 each year, and employs 150 librarians and staff. Our materials budget is approximately $5.3 million. We subscribe to 19,889 active serials and over 37,000 electronic resources. We spent $4,552,578 on serial subscriptions in fiscal year 2005.

The library acquires materials through two different departments. The acquisitions department orders and receives the monographic and media purchases. The serials department orders, receives, claims, and provides copy cataloging for all serials and most standing order publications. The two departments work together closely, particularly to solve the mysteries and problems of the types of resources that make up a grey area in between the two absolutes. Many of our purchasing policies must agree between the two departments, although the general processing can vary quite a bit. Previously, the head of our acquisitions department and her staff had investigated the use of online auctions. But the reason why I became involved in this particular case was because the pieces up for auction were serials.

Each institution, particularly a state-run university, has procurement peculiarities. The University of Hawaii at Manoa Library is no different. By state and university laws and regulations, all payment documents must be in original, paper form. We require signatures on paper for all purchase requests or worksheets. Although both the acquisitions and serials departments have purchasing or credit cards, the process requires extensive paperwork. Potential vendors must fill out additional paperwork in order for us to purchase from them. We must fill out a form justifying any invoice over $2,500. In general, the regulations and paperwork process highlight a fiscally conservative institution. One would assume online auctions could be troublesome.

On October 30, 2004, the Manoa stream diverted through the campus. A giant wall of water, mud, and debris crashed into the mountain-facing side of the library, destroying the entire ground floor of the building, which housed the Collection Services, Government Documents, and Maps Departments as well as the library and information science program. Drywall melted, commercial shelving twisted under the water pressure, maps and books floated down to the other end of campus. The estimated damage for the collections lost in the flood is about $28 million. Beginning in 2005, we began to replace lost or ruined pieces in addition to the usual purchasing. In other words, we had twice as much to purchase and process.

"For Decisions and Revisions Which a Minute Will Reverse"

Before the Russian bibliographer came to my desk with her auction printouts, the University of Hawaii at Manoa library did not purchase materials officially from online auctions. The most recent look at online auctions came in 2003. When I spoke with a supervisor from and the head of the acquisitions department, both told me that fiscal concerns were the main reason.[3] Some of the secondary concerns related to staff time, responsibility, and training. I wanted to find out how many other institutions faced a similar situation, how they resolved their concerns in order to use online auctions, and if it had become a viable form of acquiring materials.

I began by conducting a search of library literature. I found successful cases of online purchasing, but limited information regarding policy and purchasing through online auctions. To the SERIALST and ACQNET listervs membership, I sent out a questionnaire containing four questions: Do you use online auctions? Does your institution have a policy in place for using online auctions? What prevents you from using an online auction? and What is your library type (university, college, public, specialized)? Out of 16 responses, 8 people asked to see the responses that I received, only one institution had an established policy, and most were from smaller libraries. I solicited information from three librarians who had made purchases from online auctions and received their policies through e-mail exchanges. A few of the respondents said that their institutions would not allow them to use auctions or that they did not have the time. When auctions were used by other libraries, it was for specialized materials (such as a special collection of cookbooks or local photographs for the Special Collections). I found that concerns about fair pricing were a secondary concern for most institutions and that those places who were using online auctions were using them sparingly or for very particular items.

How many materials had been lost to us over the last few years because of our policy? I contacted the selector librarians at the University of Hawaii at Manoa. I interviewed five selectors, in addition to the Russian bibliographer. Three out of the five were from the Special Collections, one from the Music Collection, one from the Science and Technology Collection.[4] All had made personal purchases on an online auction over the last few years for their collections, either for reimbursement from or for donation to the library. Occasionally they would check on the auctions for items, but these kinds of sites were not part of their regular searches for materials. I asked if any of the book dealers had begun to use an auction site, such as eBay, as their online presence or storefront, but most responded that for established vendors they preferred the direct source. Only one responded that she had found a new vendor through the online auctions. Concerns about time and the bidding process were the primary constraints to finding more materials online. Concerns about the preservation and shape of the materials were another limitation voiced by most of those interviewed. Although limited by a policy against the use of online auctions, the policy itself did not limit the purchase of these materials by the library's selectors.

In talking with one of the acquisitions department's supervisors, I found out that fiscal concerns were not the greatest drawback to using online auctions. After seeing some of the new features, the supervisor suggested that she was not entirely opposed to using eBay, but processing factors prohibited her. eBay is a gigantic community of sellers and buyers; for each different seller, we would require a different vendor record in our library management system. Training and staff time used to check and maintain auctions was another problem, when the staff was shortened by open positions and overworked with additional flood-related orders. She found that use of the purchasing card at online sites or through the Amazon.com corporate account was far easier and efficient. The cost of staff time, when staff time is already in limited supply, was too great a drawback in her mind to justify use of the auctions, except in certain circumstances.

I asked the fiscal officer a series of questions.[5] He in turn contacted the University of Hawaii's main procurement office (Office of Procurement, Real Property and Risk Management or OPRPRM). He suggested that we could purchase from online auctions, especially now following our devastating flood. OPRPRM had considered the flood and the limited time and opportunity to repurchase materials as a factor in the decision to authorize bidding. This ability came with a few caveats. We could not use PayPal, the service that allows buyers to use credit cards to purchase from some of the eBay vendors, due to an indemnity clause in the agreement authorizing use. For some materials, such as DVDs, we would have to be wary of receiving copies rather than the original form of the materials. Tracking sellers through the ratings systems would be an important part of the use. But international vendors were not a problem. In general, from a fiscal standpoint the library could obtain materials through online auctions if it were treated as the exception rather than the rule in purchasing.

Setting Up a Policy

Although my process seemed lengthy, certain steps became vital. When thinking about the use of online auctions or bidding for materials, you should first check with your fiscal officer or procurement specialists. Determine whether the library can bid for items; who would have the authority to make the bids; who would create the top bidding price, such as the acquisitions staff or the selecting librarian; and whether you could use a service such as PayPal. Once you are authorized to use the service, you must also decide if you will bid or use the "Buy it now" type service. This usually costs more, but it guarantees the purchase, without having to follow the auction process. Establish who will monitor the auctions: Will the selectors monitor the auctions and give the results to the acquisitions staff after winning the auction, or will the acquisitions staff follow from the first point of bid? Some sellers allow for other forms of payment, such as check or money transfer. You may need to resolve preferred forms of payment or a priority list of payment types. Who will make the contact with the seller? You may need to question the seller regarding the condition of the materials or preferred form of payment. In addition, you should determine who will contact the seller at the completion of an auction.

Once you have the ability and the set-up to use an auction, you should set a guideline for when you would use such a service. In many cases you may decide not to use an auction. Availability may be the first factor. If you cannot find the photographs for a specialized collection from an established vendor, but an entire set is on auction at Amazon.com, it seems straightforward to consider the auction. But other factors to consider are the limited knowledge of the condition of materials, sellers' ratings (or lack of), increased staff, or efficiency cost. From an established vendor, you may have certain expectations regarding quality of materials and service, which may triumph over momentary availability. Online auctions may create a space to meet new vendors or make you thankful for your current vendor list. Having a basic framework for your online auction policy will help you to fill it in with detailed information from your own experiences.

Conclusion

The investigation into use of online auctions opened up a new avenue of purchase for the University of Hawaii at Manoa library. However, we have used this ability with mixed success. The initial use, the purchase of Russian-language serials, came before the completed investigation. Although we were able to make the purchase, and the Russian bibliographer herself has since obtained more materials from the original seller, we had to circumvent the auction process. Making purchases away from the online auction is in violation of the policies for most of the services, and your buying privileges will be revoked if you are caught doing this more than once. The relaxation of the procurement rules will help us to find more creative ways to buy flood-related materials, although the general policies on price and vendors remains a paperwork burden on library staff. This process has allowed us to change the policy on online auctions, but we look at the use of auctions on a case-by-case basis. The most valuable lesson learned in the process is to continuously explore creative opportunities for acquiring materials and to balance these opportunities with staff and processing costs. After all, we collect these materials and resources not for ourselves, but for the community surrounding our libraries.

Notes

1. Dhruv Grewal, Gopalkrishnan Iyer, and Michael Levy, "Internet Retailing: Enablers, Limiters and Market Consequences," *Journal of Business Research* 57 (2004): 706.

2. David Hardesty and Tracy A. Suter, "E-tail and Retail Reference Price Effects," *Journal of Product and Brand Management* 14, no. 2 (2005): 130.

3. Interviews with Thelma Diercks, Head, Acquisitions Department, University of Hawaii at Manoa, April 13, 2005, and October 24, 2005.

4. Interviews with Patricia Polanksy, Russian Bibliographer, University of Hawaii at Manoa, April 13, 2005, and October 20, 2005; interview with Dore Minatodani, Selector, Special Collections, University of Hawaii at Manoa, September 24, 2005; interview with Karen Peacock, Pacific Curator, Special Collections, University of Hawaii at Manoa, October 4, 2005; interview with Gregg Geary, Selector, Music Collection, University of Hawaii at Manoa, September 22, 2005; interview with Eileen Herring, Selector, Science and Technology Collection, University of Hawaii at Manoa, October 24, 2005.

5. Interview with John Awakuni, Library Fiscal Officer, University of Hawaii at Manoa, October 3, 2005.

Bibliography

"eBay—If You Can't Beat it, Join it." *Strategic Direction* 21, no. 6 (2005): 11–13.

"eBay: What am I Bid for World Domination." *The Times*, August 19, 2005, 4.

Grewal, Dhruv, Gopalkrishnan Iyer, and Michael Levy. "Internet Retailing: Enablers, Limiters and Market Consequences." *Journal of Business Research* 57 (2004): 703–13.

Hardesty, David M., and Tracy A. Suter. "E-tail and Retail Reference Price Effects." *Journal of Product and Brand Management* 14, no. 2 (2005): 129–36.

Vincelli, Nick J. "Online Auction Services Orders: An Order Librarian's Reflections on OLAS." *Against the Grain* 14, no. 4 (2002): 30–34.

Consortia deals continue to be a major topic at the Charleston Conference. Librarians heard about the "Big Deal" and the pros and cons of consortial buying. A deal that may work to one library's advantage might not help another, because libraries are all different in size, vision, and nature. The contributors in this section look at these issues and focus on the advantages and disadvantages of consortial purchasing based on experiences at their libraries.

Consortia Deals

THE BIG DEAL: WHAT'S IN IT FOR ME?

Tim Bucknall, Assistant Director for Electronic Resources and Information Technologies, University of North Carolina at Greensboro

The Big Deal is an agreement between two partners: publishers and libraries. Clearly, for any deal to grow and prosper, it has to benefit both parties. After all, if the problems outweigh the benefits for either side, then that party will withdraw its participation.

The perception that the Big Deal is indeed mutually beneficial seems to be widespread, because the number of both library and publisher participants has grown in recent years. National data on these trends are difficult to obtain, but in North Carolina compared to a couple of years ago, there are now more than three times as many schools participating in these deals, and there are more than three times as many publishers who have Big Deals with North Carolina schools.

This growth seems to indicate that libraries and publishers feel the advantages of the Big Deal outweigh the associated problems. This chapter covers those advantages from a library's perspective.

No deal (or, for that matter, no e-content and no e-service) will benefit all libraries equally. Therefore, the Big Deal probably benefits some libraries more than others. But it isn't readily apparent exactly where that inequity lies.

The conventional wisdom is that large libraries are getting a significantly worse deal than smaller libraries. Such arguments often hinge on a cost-per-title figure. Certainly a large library paying $1 million for a Big Deal package of 2,000 titles is paying 10 times as much per title than a smaller library paying $100,000 for the exact same content. But that formula completely ignores two of the most important elements of collection development: actual usage and the size of the collections budget.

According to a news release on its Web site, Cornell dropped its Science Direct deal in 2003, noting that its Elsevier bill was consuming 20% of its total serials expenditures. A quick check of the University of North Carolina at Greensboro's (much smaller) serials budget determined that we were spending 20.5% of our serials subscription budget on Science Direct. If this pattern holds true elsewhere then, while ARL libraries spend more absolute dollars on titles in Big Deals than do smaller schools, once the expenditures are indexed to the relative sizes of collection budgets, the inequities between large and small libraries are reduced or eliminated.

Of course measuring only collections budgets, costs, and numbers of titles ignores the primary reason we provide journals in the first place, which is to ensure that our faculty, staff, and students can readily use them. It may be that a large research institution pays 10 times as much for a given package, but because of its expanded research emphasis and larger student and faculty population, it may well get more than 10 times as much use per title as a smaller school, which would yield a lower cost-per-use figure in larger institutions. I'm not aware of any research that compares these figures, and unfortunately it would be hard to obtain accurate data because much of the Big Deal pricing is secret. But if smaller schools are paying about the same percentage of their serials budget for the Big Deal and are seeing roughly comparable cost-per-use figures, than it is very difficult to argue that they are somehow getting a much better deal than larger institutions.

Because inequities in the Big Deal probably do exist, and because no one has yet conducted any definitive studies of usage and collection budgets to pinpoint those inequities, it is difficult to determine the perceived benefits of the Big Deal for libraries with any specificity. That's especially true because not all Big Deals are equal. These deals vary tremendously in terms of upcharges, cancellation terms, dual format costs, access restrictions, shared title lists, etc.

So, given that not all Big Deals are equal and that not all types of libraries benefit equally from any given deal, the overall benefits of the Big Deal to libraries can only be examined in general terms. I have divided them into three categories: costs, patron satisfaction, and sharing.

Costs

Real costs are often difficult to compare because exact pricing formulas are frequently treated as proprietary information by publishers and consortiums. But there are several general cost advantages to participating in the Big Deal.

The one that is discussed most frequently is the one that is the least illuminating: cost avoidance. That figure compares the actual expenditure for the total package to the sum of all the published list prices for the separate titles in the package. For example, if a school pays $2,500 for a large group of titles that would have cost $1.2 million if each title were purchased independently, then that generates a cost avoidance of $1,197,500. That's a large number and is often equated with a tremendous benefit. While it is indeed a good, big number to use to impress people, it isn't a very realistic "savings." No library would ever want to pay the separate price for every single journal from a large publisher, and avoiding something you wouldn't want to do isn't truly much of a budgetary accomplishment.

A much more concrete cost benefit is actual out-of-pocket savings, but this may be the exception rather than the rule in libraries. In assessing the fiscal effect of UNCG's participation in three Big Deals via the Carolina Consortium in 2005, I developed a spreadsheet that included all additional upcharges and other costs, and all savings generated by the deals. Through large reductions in pay-per-view usage, the cancellation of alternative means of accessing the same journal content, and through the difference between the price caps and a projected 9% serials inflation rate, I determined that UNCG would come out $140,000 ahead over the life of those three contracts. That figure does not include cost avoidance for something we wouldn't have done anyway; it is a real reduction in actual costs for equivalent content.

Another related issue is cost containment and predictability. With a multi-year deal and inflation caps, a library can determine in advance exactly how much it will be spending on a given publisher's titles. In the absence of a multi-year deal, libraries are at the mercy of inflation rates set by publishers each year. Libraries find that inflation caps are particularly useful for foreign publishers because it reduces the volatility of exchange rate fluctuations. Price predictability allows better planning, which can help libraries stave off unexpected serials cancellations.

A final cost benefit relates to economies of scale. By centralizing negotiations, title list generation, and some licensing issues through a consortium deal, libraries can reduce duplicative work and save money. In most cases it takes a lot less time for one person to do something on behalf of lots of schools through a consortium than it would for all of those schools to each perform that same function on their own.

Patron Satisfaction

In assessing the benefits of the Big Deal, many librarians talk about all the new serial titles that are now available in their institutions. But that isn't quite accurate, because no academic library has been in the business of denying journal articles to its faculty and students; unsubscribed titles have always been available through ILL or other means.

But ILL doesn't offer the instantaneous access that today's students and researchers have come to expect. The Big Deal eliminates the ILL wait time for large numbers of important titles.

Unlike ILL, pay-per-view is a real-time delivery alternative to the Big Deal for non-subscribed titles, but at UNCG we found it to be a more expensive option. We also found that pay-per-view offered significant barriers to users. The majority of patrons who pursued a pay-per-view title at UNCG did not complete the transaction. Even though the library fully subsidized the service, some patrons had a lingering concern that they might be charged. And some patrons didn't follow through because they thought that $25 was an exorbitant cost for an article, not realizing that it was a much better deal for the library than a subscription to a seldom-used journal.

The Big Deal can put more articles in our patrons' hands more quickly. And that can only increase patron satisfaction.

Sharing

Most libraries want their public collections (including their subscriptions) to be used as broadly as possible so, in general, libraries are all very supportive of the concept of inter-institutional resource sharing. Many Big Deals allow libraries to fulfill that goal on a regional basis.

These deals may also foster other modes of mutually beneficial sharing and cooperation among libraries. For example, within our UNC-System Science Direct deal, UNCG dropped 30 Elsevier titles duplicated elsewhere in the group, and instead picked up unique titles that then became available to most of the schools in the UNC system as shared titles, at no cost to anyone. And when The Citadel needed to pick up titles to join the Carolina Consortium Wiley deal, it deliberately selected titles to which no one subscribed, because that created a broader serials collection for the entire group of 36 schools. These, and many other similar instances of cooperation fostered by the Big Deal, have laid a positive groundwork that has allowed libraries to move forward on many other types of shared regional endeavors.

Sharing also serves to reduce the inequity between information "haves" and "have-nots." Through participation in a shared-title Big Deal, even small liberal arts schools, and HBCU's and other historically underfunded institutions, can have access to large journal collections that were previously only within the financial reach of large academic research libraries.

While sharing is a great benefit in theory, it only becomes truly beneficial if the shared titles are actually used. Fortunately, my early data show this to be the case. After eight months of participation in the Carolina Consortium Wiley Big Deal, I found that seven of the top twenty most heavily used titles were not subscribed locally and were available only because they were shared through our consortium deal. Overall, just over 50% of our Wiley journal use was of unsubscribed titles.

The benefits of sharing titles is supported by anecdotal evidence as well. Susan Whitt, the Collection Development Librarian at UNC Pembroke, sent me the following e-mail: "A couple of weeks ago I had a call from one of our professors asking for a new title. We were able to access it through our Wiley deal. The journal itself was $5450, more than what we paid to be a member of the Wily deal and one of the other deals combined. This past weekend I worked reference and I referred a student to a title that we again had through our Wiley deal. The cost of that title is $3898. I worked reference last night and one of our chemistry professors was in and I showed him the new titles be had in biotechnology. He is working on a biotechnology grant project and was psyched about these new resources. I am really excited about being able to respond so positively to the needs of our faculty and staff. As they get excited about it, the word will make it around campus."

Conclusion

Ultimately each school will have to carefully weigh the many pros and cons before making a decision to participate in any specific Big Deal. But participation can yield potentially significant advantages in terms of cost savings, enhanced patron satisfaction, and resource sharing. Perhaps that largely explains the growth in interest in the Big Deal on the part of both libraries and publishers.

EVALUATING THE BIG DEAL: THE CAROLINA CONSORTIUM'S EXPERIENCE

Tim Bucknall, Assistant Director for Electronic Resources and Information Technologies, University of North Carolina at Greensboro

The Carolina Consortium is a "buyer's club" for electronic resources in North and South Carolina. The group was formed in 2004, with 38 institutions participating in some or all of three large academic journal "Big Deals" from Wiley, Springer, and Blackwell. At the end of its first year of operation the consortium had made as many as 2,300 high-quality titles available to more than 150,000 students and faculty, while saving approximately $70 million for the group.

Those are large, impressive numbers, but they aren't very meaningful. The cost savings comes from comparing the price of complete packages to the price a school would pay when buying the equivalent titles individually, although no school would ever do that. And while the potential audience for the group's journals is large, that's not very relevant if actual usage is low. So, the numbers most frequently cited by consortia to justify their existence—savings, number of titles, and audience size—are not all that helpful in determining the group's success or failure. Instead, relative success can probably be more accurately assessed by examining other types of data, especially those related to issues of usage and cost effectiveness.

Usage and Cost Effectiveness

These two measures are very closely aligned. Higher usage levels yield a lower cost-per-use ratio, and cost-per-use is the most common measure of cost effectiveness. There are a couple of different ways we can examine statistics on these interrelated issues.

Are Targeted Subscriptions a Viable Alternative to the Big Deal?

If a school can accurately select the exact titles needed by its faculty and students and subscribe to only those titles, then perhaps there is no need to join a "Big Deal." By comparing the direct Wiley subscriptions at the University of North Carolina at Greensboro (UNCG) to the Wiley usage levels after joining the Carolina Consortium Wiley deal, we can see if careful title selection is an adequate substitute for the more "shotgun" Big Deal approach.

UNCG had 39 direct Wiley subscriptions prior to consortium membership. After joining the deal, the number of accessible titles rose to 290. With this greatly expanded title set, if almost all of our Wiley usage is of those same 39 titles we already had, then joining the consortium deal was of no benefit.

The data are somewhat mixed, despite a long-term and intensive title selection and cancellation policy involving both subject experts and teaching faculty at UNCG. After joining the consortium deal and having access to 290 titles, 7 of the top 10 most heavily used journals were ones to which UNCG subscribed. And of the top 20 most used, 13 were subscribed titles, while 7 were titles that were accessible through our consortial sharing arrangement. After ranking all 290 titles by use, 12 of our 39 subscriptions fall in the bottom half in terms of use, while 2 had no uses at all during the first eight-month period of our participation in the Carolina Consortium Wiley deal.

So, the time-consuming and intense effort at UNCG to subscribe to our most relevant titles has yielded mixed results. A majority of our most heavily used titles are ones we had selected for subscription, but other heavily used titles are ones to which we had never subscribed. And nearly a third of our subscriptions fall below the median when all currently accessible titles are listed in order by usage. It certainly appears that UNCG's careful selection of subscribed titles was not adequate to support the research needs of our faculty and students, and that our researchers are indeed benefiting from access to a greatly expanded title set.

But perhaps other schools could be more effective in subscribing to only the most heavily used titles. In that case, could it still be desirable to join a Big Deal? The answer depends on how concentrated or diffuse usage is. If a school is successful in subscribing to all 20 of the 20 most heavily used titles, its clientele may still be unhappy if, in fact, the top 50 journals receive a significant amount of use.

UNCG's Blackwell usage data show that 64% of our 809 accessible titles received some use in the first eight months of participation in their Big Deal. Based on the statistics thus far, more than a quarter of the total number of titles will be used 10 or more times this year.

The combination of a wide number of titles being used and difficulty in selecting the most heavily used titles makes it extremely difficult for most schools to meet their constituents' research needs solely through targeted subscriptions. Joining a Big Deal through a consortium seems to be a stronger option for providing broader access to needed materials.

Are There More Cost Effective Alternatives to Direct Subscriptions and the Big Deal?

Most libraries that join Big Deals state that they have added hundreds or thousands of new journals, but that's not really the case. After all, these same journals have always been available to faculty and students via inter-library loan (ILL) or, in some cases, alternative delivery mechanisms. If these delivery options are more cost effective and produce similar levels of patron satisfaction to the Big Deal, then the Big Deal is a bad deal.

At UNCG, we filled about 4,000 journal article borrowing requests with one FTE staff person in 2005. Also, in that year our usage of non-subscribed titles through the three Big Deals amounted to nearly 16,000 transactions. If we had had to fill all those requests through ILL, we would have had to add at least one more person to ILL, and the combined salary and benefits would have exceeded the amount we paid to join the Big Deals. Therefore, the Big Deal has proven more cost effective than ILL.

But obviously all those 16,000 transactions wouldn't have turned into ILL requests. Most patrons would simply have given up once they found that the article was not immediately available. ILL, then, is not only more expensive, but also provides a lower level of service than the Big Deal.

Unlike traditional ILL, pay-per-view (PPV) offers real-time access to articles. But again, the customer satisfaction is dramatically lower with PPV than with the Big Deal. UNCG has used PPV for years and has seen that less than a quarter of the patrons who started a PPV transaction carried it though to the end—even though the Library fully subsidizes the cost of each article. This may be because there is some lingering fear that the patron will receive a bill, or perhaps a feeling that articles simply aren't worth more than $20 each. With the Big Deal, each click takes the user directly to the article (without the extra screens of most PPV services), so nearly 100% of interested patrons end up with the full article on screen.

The Big Deal can also be significantly cheaper than PPV. For example, in 2004 UNCG paid $5204.50 for PPV articles from Kluwer. In 2005, UNCG gained free access to all non-subscribed Kluwer titles through a Big Deal with no extra charge, thus eliminating the need for incurring any more PPV costs for those titles,

Neither ILL nor PPV would be a good alternative to the Big Deal at UNCG. Both services reduce patron satisfaction significantly, and both are less cost effective than the Big Deal.

Growth

Another way to assess the success of a consortium is by using the traditional business measures of growth and customer retention. By both these standards, the Carolina Consortium is doing quite well as it moves into its second year, with a 100% institutional retention rate, a growth rate of 56% in the number of schools, and a more than fourfold increase in the number of consortium deals.

Conclusion

For a consortium to be successful it must meet the needs of both the group and the individual participating schools. As a group the Carolina Consortium has grown and prospered. The experience at UNCG has shown that individual schools can benefit significantly from the consortium's deals. The new titles made available through the group are widely used at UNCG, and, although alternative access modes exist, the Carolina Consortium's Big Deals are more cost effective and offer higher levels of patron satisfaction.

MAKING THE MOST OF A "BIG DEAL": BUILDING A CONSORTIAL SHARED LIST TO RECLAIM TITLE-BY-TITLE EJOURNAL SELECTION FOR LIBRARIES

Jason S. Price, Ph.D., Life Science Librarian, The Claremont Colleges, California

Introduction

The Statewide California Electronic Library Consortium began its ScienceDirect contract in late 2001 with a total of 12 institutions signing on after a semester of access to the complete collection. By mid-2004 there were 10 institutions left, and the size of our financial commitment to the deal had grown greatly thanks to the acquisition of Academic Press by Elsevier in 2002. My sciences journal budgets were overspent, and we were seeking ways to control costs within the package. At the same time, we had user requests for some titles we lacked access to, and use statistics showed that we were paying for access to hundreds of titles that were not being used. I lamented the loss of title-by-title control to Elsevier's batch-marketed subject collections, and the Unique Title List they were offering appeared to be a step in the wrong direction. Then came a rare bit of good news: We could build our own lists, as long as they were shared among institutions. Here I provide specific reasons why we felt the subject collections and UTL were inadequate, describe the process of building the shared title lists we assembled as an alternative, and provide an initial evaluation of their effectiveness.

The ScienceDirect "Big Deal"

The bad news. Institutional customers agree to be "locked-in" to a subscription commitment for the life of the deal. They commit to maintain their Elsevier print subscription total plus a fixed annual price increase, often called a price cap (e.g. $0.5x\%$), presumably because it is lower than the market rate increase. In "return" they gain perpetual e-access to these *subscribed titles* for a percentage of their list price, say $x\%$. Although this e-access fee is less than Elsevier charges for e-access outside of the deal, it is still a significant additional commitment. Although some contracts include an annual cancellation allowance (0.1 to $0.2x\%$), it is not large enough to allow libraries to balance their budgets within the ScienceDirect Package (given a fixed annual inflation rate that is at least 2.5 times the cancellation allowance). Thus the Big Deal requires that libraries forfeit the ability to balance their budgets by canceling a sufficient number of Elsevier titles when Elsevier's prices go up faster than the library budget.

Putative good news. The benefit that theoretically balances this significant and ever-increasing commitment is low-priced leased access to *unsubscribed titles*. Although other publishers' Big Deals may not charge separately for this additional access and/or may open their entire collection, Elsevier charges fees that usually limit libraries to a subset of the complete collection.

These collections take one of two forms. The older model is to lease selected prepackaged subject collections with prices apparently varying from 0.1 to $0.5x\%$ of list. Presently, there are 24 subject collections containing 1,788 Elsevier titles (See Figure 1). The newer model is to lease access to a Unique Title List (UTL), which is based on the consortium's subscriptions. UTLs consist of a deduplicated list of all titles subscribed to by at least one member of the consortium and are priced similarly to subject collections. Both models have significant drawbacks.

- Agricultural and Biological Sciences
- Arts and Humanities
- Biochemistry, Genetics and Molecular Biology
- Business, Management and Accounting
- Chemical Engineering
- Chemistry
- Computer Science
- Decision Sciences

- Earth and Planetary Sciences
- Economics, Econometrics and Finance
- Energy
- Engineering

- Environmental Science
- Immunology and Microbiology
- Materials Science
- Mathematics
- Medicine and Dentistry
- Neuroscience
- Nursing and Health Professions
- Pharmacology, Toxicology and Pharmaceutics
- Physics and Astronomy
- Psychology
- Social Science
- Veterinary Science and Veterinary Medicine

Figure 1. ScienceDirect Subject Collections as of November 2005.

Shortcomings of subject collections. Subject collections are the worst of these two evils, for a number of reasons:

1. **Publisher-fixed subject collections prevent quality-based selection**. By definition, large subject-based collections tend to have a few high-use journals and many low-use journals. Thus libraries that lease subject collections are unintentional accomplices in supporting low-quality journals. An unfortunate corollary is that dropping even a relatively low use collection requires the loss of at least a few valuable titles.

2. **Publisher-fixed subject collections force collection gaps**. While they may be suitable for very specialized schools (e.g., medical, veterinary, or dental), even a school of natural sciences would need to purchase at least half of the collections to approach comprehensive coverage. This problem often forces decisions as to which departments to support and which to deny.

3. **Publisher-fixed subject collections result in double and triple payment.** Subscribed titles that are duplicated in subject collections are paid for both through the e-access fee and the subject collection fee. Double payment is quite common, because institutions tend to lease collections in subject areas in which they also have a large number of subscriptions. Triple "payment" occurs when these titles are included in more than one subject collection. One analysis shows that pairs of subject collections

can have up to 50% duplication, and the percent of unique titles in any one collection ranges from as low as 5% (!) to a high of just 75%.[1] These two common forms of overlap make it meaningless to calculate percent of list price for individual subject collections—accurate values can only be calculated for the complete set of leased titles after the aggregated subject collection list has been deduplicated internally (i.e., within all leased titles) *and* externally (i.e., against the subscribed title list). Thus discounts are not nearly as large as they appear, because libraries commonly pay two or more times for e-access to the same titles.

4. **Publisher-fixed subject collections are not really fixed!** Titles are added and moved on an annual basis as Elsevier acquires new titles and seeks to optimize marketing of the collections. I am not aware of any case in which Elsevier intentionally revoked subsequent access to a title that was part of a collection in the first year of the lease. It is clear, however, that subject collections with the same name purchased in different years will have different title lists and that later versions lack some of the titles contained in earlier versions. Titles are also added to these collections over time. The resulting disarray grows with time as Elsevier attempts to manage 24 subject collections times five years and counting. This results in inevitable inconsistencies between library e-journal catalogs and actual availability that do not serve users well.

5. **Publisher-fixed subject collections are not priced consistently over time.** For SCELC, at least, recent changes in our invoices make subject collections less attractive. They have recently begun to be priced relative to their total list price rather than equally per collection, though the percentages were adjusted so that there was no effect on the current bottom line. This change suggests that future cancellations or additions will be priced in this way, despite the overlap mentioned above.

Shortcomings of unique title lists. UTLs are an improvement over subject collections. They solve the duplicate payment problem because they are deduplicated by nature and are discounted based on each institution's subscribed title list. However, their other selling points are dubious at best:

1. **Based on legacy subscription profiles.** Elsevier suggested that gaining access to all of the titles subscribed by other institutions in the consortium would ensure that we were only leasing important titles and would therefore be an improvement over the subject collections. But important to whom? Given that most institutions had far more titles on their leased title (subject collection) list than on their subscribed list, we had little confidence that a list based on subscribed titles would include all of the most valuable. Legacy subscribed titles (so named because they were established far in the past and cannot be changed) become less and less relevant with increasing electronic access and use of leased titles. Our subscription lists are likely to be hazy reflections of the sets of titles that have become most valuable to our users. Put another way, it seemed foolish to give up the high (and low) use titles out of our subject collections in favor of titles that had been chosen by other institutions in the distant past. We knew which titles were most important to our users (at least within our collections): the ones that had received the greatest online use in recent years.

2. **One size fits none.** UTLs do allow broader coverage, since they do not force choices between disciplines. The flip side, however, is that they are a one-size-fits-all solution: They do not accommodate specialized schools that might want to focus on particular disciplines. They are also biased toward larger budgets; either you can afford to lease the whole list or you can't. When there are major differences in the size or focus of institutions in the consortium, UTLs favor larger schools in that 1) they can afford to lease a large list, and 2) they get a greater discount on the list because they have more overlap between their subscription list and the UTL. Thus Elsevier's UTLs cost smaller schools more than larger schools, lacking size and subject flexibility.

3. **Higher priced titles?** Priced as a percent of list minus any overlap with an institution's subscribed titles, UTL pricing is indeed more transparent. We also expected, however, that each institution was subscribed to a number of high-priced titles deemed necessary for its programs, or left as a legacy of a more affordable past. Combining these, then, seemed to make it likely that a UTL would contain a preponderance of high-priced titles, especially since these are the very titles that cannot be canceled under the meager $0.1-0.2x\%$ cancellation allowances. We wanted a chance to eliminate some of these legacy behemoths from our leased title list.

Clearly then, after a brief discussion of the UTL option, our Consortium's 10 ScienceDirect subscribers agreed that it was *not* a viable alternative.

Truly good news. When presented with our lack of interest, Elsevier's Barbara Kaplan provided the first really good news since the start of our contract: *Elsevier doesn't care which titles are on our "UTL."* Elsevier was even willing to manage more than one list to allow for differences in size or subject emphasis (even for subsets of our 10-institution consortium). After repeated confirmation that we had understood correctly, we were left with a single question: Which titles should be on this *shared* title list or lists? The simple answer: each institution's most used titles. But of course, the devil is in the details . . . .

Building the Shared Title Lists

A shared title list (STL) differs from a unique title list in that the consortium gets to select the titles that are included and can change the list as often as once a year. The other significant difference is that a consortium can build more than one list. Otherwise, the terms are identical to UTLs: access to titles on the list is leased by annual payment of a small percentage (e.g., $0.25x\%$) of the list price of all the titles on the list that the institution does not subscribe to. Thus every institution that opts for a shared title list has access to the same titles but pays a different amount for that access.

The goal of this project was to merge each institution's historical subject collection use data to form a shared list or lists that represent the ideal compromise between the subject collections and the UTL, providing access to the most valuable titles at the lowest possible price.

These were our guiding principles:

1. **Base the contents of the list on the history of use by the consortium's users.** Hereafter, "use" of an individual article from a title, whether a view of HTML or PDF full text, will be referred to as a view. The proportion of these articles that are actually

used is a subject for another paper—the relationship between views and ILL requests would be of particular interest.

2. **Guarantee needs of *all* institutions are addressed** by including every title that was requested more than a fixed number of times at any institution.

3. **Keep the list as small as possible** to cut costs while increasing collection quality.

4. **Weed out high price-per-view titles**, preferentially removing these when possible.

5. **Recognize that building this list allows for future flexibility**, allowing the list's shortcomings to be improved title by title in future years.

Collecting the data. I collected the COUNTER-compliant statistics for 2003 from all 10 ScienceDirect members with the goal of combining these numbers to select the most used titles from each institution. Most were sent by the individual library, with Elsevier filling in some holes (the sharing of use data within consortia is permitted). Ideally we would have used data from at least two years, but SD was not COUNTER-compliant until 2003. I strongly recommend that at least two years of data be used by others who are seeking to build a shared title list.

Removing subscribed titles. Institutions are locked in (or "guaranteed") ongoing electronic access to their subscribed title list. One way to limit the size of an STL is to remove these titles from each institution's data, allowing us to focus on leased title (subject collection) use. Subscribed title lists with ISSNs were readily available, and Microsoft Access "Find unmatched query wizard" was used to remove each institution's subscribed title data from its overall electronic use data.

Looking at the subject collection use data. Use distribution patterns formed three rough groups (Figure 2a-c), with each set conforming well to Zipf's Law: The majority of each institution's views were from a minority of its titles. Group (a) consisted of three schools that had much lower overall use, reflecting their smaller size. This showed that they would need a smaller, more affordable list. Elsevier had ignored their holdings when constructing the UTL proposed to the consortium and had made no accommodation for their smaller size.

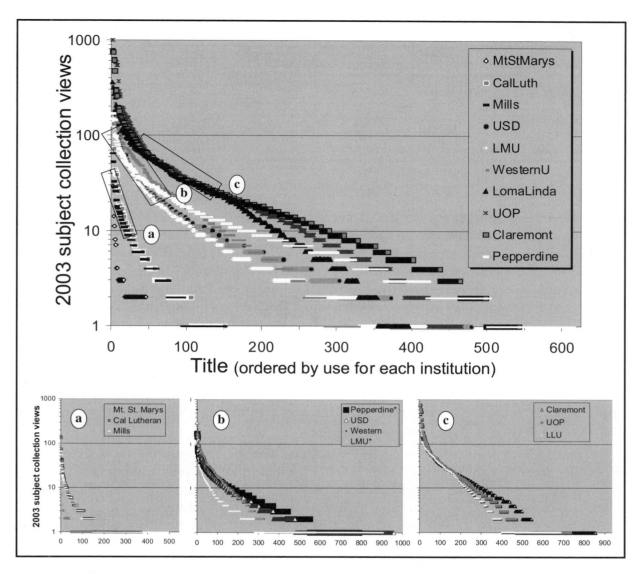

Figure 2. Patterns of ScienceDirect Subject Collection Use by SCELC Institutions.

The distributions of use among titles were visualized by plotting the COUNTER "total number of full text article requests" on a log scale versus journal title for each institution. The journal title (x) axis was sorted from high to low use separately for each institution. Zero use titles were ignored in the composite graph for clarity. Panels (a) thru (c) include the zero use titles (raw view data were transformed by adding one use for every title since log (0) is undefined).

Group (b) had more titles in the 10 to 100 view range, yet still noticeably fewer than group (c). This can be seen in the still negative exponential curve in (b) versus the more sigmoidal curve for (c). These two groups lose their distinction, however, when the number of titles used 0 to 10 times is considered. It is interesting to note that Pepperdine users seemed to use a wider variety of titles than their peers, as evidenced by a shift from clear membership in group (b) in their higher use titles, crossing over to group (c) type use for titles used less than 10 times. This anomaly may be explained by the impact of a series of Elsevier-led training sessions (held only at Pepperdine in 2003) that encouraged use of ScienceDirect as an A&I database. Finally, it should be noted that on average, more than half of each institution's subject collection titles went completely unused in 2003 (Fig. 1a-c; mean = 50.8±4.9% SE).

Table 1. Description of Smaller Schools in the SCEL Consortium ScienceDirect Contract

Institution	Subject Collection Titles*	Subject Collections
Mount St. Mary's College	575	4
Mills College	445	4
California Lutheran U.	370	3

*Indicates the number of unsubscribed titles in the leased collections previously held by each institution.

Determining inclusion criteria. Graphically described, the task was to fairly determine where to truncate each distribution and which titles made the cuts. The smaller schools had leased subject collection access to between 370 and 575 titles (Table 1). Separate spreadsheets for each institution allowed determination of 1) percent of total views in each title, and 2) cumulative percentage of views in highest use titles (after sorting from highest to lowest number of views, e.g., see Table 2). Analysis of each of the three schools' data showed that a 53-title shared list could be certified to include either (1) every title used at least once a month at any of the three institutions, or (2) all of the most frequently viewed titles representing the top 66% of use at each institution, whichever included more titles. One institution requested the addition of two titles to this list, and the resulting list priced out at less than the cost of two subject collections. It was agreeable to downsize to this degree, because this group was particularly concerned about shrinking their ScienceDirect commitment (which for schools of this size consists mostly of their leased title holdings).

The larger schools' inclusion criteria were more complicated, even for the first cut. Subject collection title number ranged from 600 to 950, and equitable treatment required a compromise (see Table 3). The first three schools contributed every title viewed more than once a month, as before. This covered 68% of their total subject collection views (on average). Applying this criterion to the last four schools would have overrepresented their collections (i.e., covering an average of more than 91% of their views). To compensate, I doubled their minimum use criterion to include all titles viewed more than twice a month. Although this would appear to be a disadvantage to these schools (in terms of absolute use per title), it was still the case that a greater percentage of their total subject collection use was represented (Table 3, average 82% vs. 68%). Under this scenario, 766 titles were selected, yielding a deduplicated list of 400 titles (we'll call this list A). The base price of list A was equivalent to about 5.5 subject collections. So the quality of this list should be improved over subject collections, but it did not provide significant savings.

Table 2. A Sorted Use List with Cutoff Point (Triple Line)*

TITLE	ISSN	2003 e-use	% of total views in title	Cumulative use
Animal Behaviour	'00033472	41	25.95%	
Epilepsy & Behavior	'15255050	28	17.72%	
Brain and Language	'0093934x	13	8.23%	51.9%
Contemporary Educational Psychology	'0361476x	10	6.33%	
Cell Biology International	'10656995	7	4.43%	
Biochemical and Biophysical Res…	'0006291x	6	3.80%	66.5%
Journal of Experimental Child Psych…	'00220965	3	1.90%	
Religion	'0048721x	3	1.90%	
Biological Journal of the Linnean Soc…	'00244066	2	1.27%	
Brain and Cognition	'02782626	2	1.27%	
…..	…..	…..	…..	
Total		**158**	**100.00%**	**100.0%**

*For this institution, cumulative use of 66% was satisfied by the top six titles, which included all titles viewed an average of at least once every two months.

Table 3. Criteria for Shared Title List Inclusion of Higher Use Titles from the Seven Largest Schools in the SCELC ScienceDirect Agreement*

Institution	Subject Collection Titles**	Inclusion Criteria	
		>12 views	>24 views
Loyola Marymount University[†]	900	64% (45)	[40%]
Pepperdine University [†]	800	66% (117)	[44%]
University of San Diego	950	74% (101)	[57%]
Western University of Health Sciences	600	[87%]	74% (78)
Claremont Colleges	850	[90%]	77% (146)
Loma Linda University	700	[94%]	85% (133)
University of the Pacific	750	[93%]	85% (146)
Average >>	787	76% (109)	

*Subject Collection Titles is the number of unsubscribed titles in the leased collections previously held by each institution, which defines total use for the inclusion criteria values. Inclusion criteria columns refer to the set of titles viewed more than once or twice a month at each institution, with values indicating the percent of total use covered by that set, and (parentheses) indicating its number of titles. Shaded boxes indicate the criteria that were selected for each school. [Bracketed percentages] indicate the percent of total views that would have been included had the alternate criteria been used.

**Rounded to the nearest 50.

[†]Two schools chose to keep some of their subject collections because they had already bought corresponding backfile collections. Data from these subject collections (for these two institutions) were removed prior to analysis and list building.

List A was based on individual institution needs and use patterns. It seemed appropriate to base the second cut on SCELC-wide numbers in order to balance individual needs with the value of titles to the consortium as a whole.

Thus I determined the SCELC-wide price per view for List A based on 2004 price (0.25x% list/2003 combined views). Although all 400 titles met our criteria for "high" use (at least once a month by at least one institution); more than 20% had a price-per-view greater than $10 (see Table 4 for those over $20). Their median list price was $3,570. Placing these 87 titles on the "chopping block" allowed our consortium to play a small part in fighting journal inflation by cutting support for as many high-priced titles as possible. This cut (had it been permanent) would have brought the STL to 313 titles with a base price equivalent to three subject collections (called List B).

Table 4. The 31 Highest Price-per-View Titles for the SCEL Consortium*

Title	2003 SCELC views	2004 list price	Total SCELC price per view
Archives of Biochemistry and Biophysics	#######	$4,578	$61.63
Journal of Materials Processing Technology	#######	$4,701	$58.76
International Journal of Food Microbiology	#######	$3,282	$41.03
Journal of Organometallic Chemistry	#######	$10,545	$36.91
International Journal of Biochemistry…	#######	$2,873	$35.91
Carbohydrate Polymers	#######	$2,750	$34.38
Chemical Physics Letters	#######	$11,750	$33.17
Marine Geology	#######	$3,375	$32.81
Chemical Geology	#######	$3,627	$31.74
Remote Sensing of Environment	#######	$2,496	$31.20
The Journal of Steroid Biochemistry and …	#######	$4,659	$29.12
Clinica Chimica Acta	#######	$5,097	$27.87
Agricultural and Forest Meteorology	#######	$2,497	$27.31
Insect Biochemistry and Molecular Biology	#######	$2,045	$25.56
Developmental & Comparative Immunology	#######	$1,872	$25.20
Peptides	#######	$3,598	$25.19
Mutation Research…	#######	$4,314	$25.17
Polymer Degradation and Stability	#######	$3,732	$25.12
Comparative Biochemistry and Physiology…	#######	$3,555	$24.89
Vision Research	#######	$3,250	$24.73
Journal of Immunological Methods	#######	$5,088	$24.06
Palaeogeography, Palaeoclimatology…	#######	$3,571	$24.04
International Journal of Production Economics	#######	$2,002	$21.90
Journal of Aerosol Science	#######	$2,247	$21.85
Thermochimica Acta	#######	$8,591	$21.79
Journal of Chromatography A	#######	$12,344	$21.60
Journal of Banking & Finance	#######	$2,331	$21.47
Journal of Financial Economics	#######	$1,881	$20.57
Biochemical Pharmacology	#######	$6,603	$20.27
Plant Science	#######	$3,795	$20.13

*Number of views is intentionally hidden to avoid revealing specific terms of the contract.

The response to the List B proposal was mixed—some argued we should cut more high-priced titles; others contended that we needed to add the majority back. In the end we agreed on an intermediate value that each institution could add back, and it was up to each institution whether to request restoration of some of the 87 titles cut from List A or add other titles. The final list (C) contained 425 titles (more than List A!), but at a base price equivalent to five subject collections, demonstrating success in bringing down the average price of titles (versus List A, which had 400 titles for the price of 5.5 subject collections).

Evaluation of the Shared Title Lists

STL adoption and benefits and costs relative to subject collections. Seven of nine institutions chose to replace their subject collections with a shared title list. All three of the schools with lower use overall elected to lease the 55-title list. This STL allowed them to cut their lease payments by at least half in return for relinquishing access to 9 out of 10 of their subject collection titles. This may seem extreme until it is realized that 60 to 70% of their titles were not used even once in 2003.

Five of the seven larger schools selected the large STL. Although it represented a 30 to 80% decrease in the size of an institution's leased title collection, its potential impact on each large institution's bottom line was much more variable than for small schools (see Table 5). For two of the seven, it represented a sizable *increase* in price over their subject collections. Perhaps not surprisingly, one of these two schools chose not to lease the STL, citing the recent addition of two more subject collections, increasing use in 2004, and the feeling that subject collections were sufficient to cover their relatively narrow range of needs. The other school that decided against leasing the STL tied for the lowest price decrease, had bought backfiles of at least one subject collection, and perhaps most important, could not be convinced that less is more (i.e., that fewer higher quality titles is better than many more with very low use). Zipf's Law did (of course) hold for large institution subject collection use as well: 30 to 70% of each large institution's leased titles were not used in 2003.

Table 5. Shared Title List Benefits and Costs*

Institution	Overlap with subscribed titles	Credit for overlap	Savings vs. subject collections	% fewer titles vs. subject collections
Small List	(Total of 55 titles)	—	—	—
A	1	0.2%	61%	91%
B	0	0%	61%	88%
C	1	0.2%	48%	85%
Large List (C)	(Total of 425 titles)	—	—	—
D	175**	48%	59%	70%
E	275**	47%	45%	79%
F	75**	18%	35%	49%
G	25**	5%	13%	58%
H	25**	5%	13%	55%
I	50**	20%	-26%	47%
J	25**	17%	-31%	29%

*Shaded rows indicate schools that selected the STL. Overlap with subscribed titles indicates the number of titles that appeared both on the STL and the school's subscription list. Credit for overlap is the percent of STL base price saved, and savings versus subject collections compares each institution's STL price after overlap credit to the price it would have paid for its subject collections.

** Rounded to the nearest 25.

Difference from UTL. Another subjective evaluation of the STL is to ask whether it is notably different from the SCELC UTL offered by Elsevier. Our expectation that the set of shared subscriptions in the UTL would *not* contain the titles that were most used at other institutions was borne out: The two lists had fewer titles in common than were unique (see Figure 3).

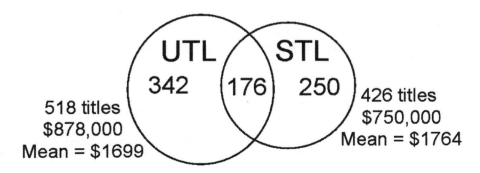

Figure 3. Venn Diagram Comparing the Subscription-Based Unique Title List Offered to SCELC by Elsevier to the Use-Based Shared Title List Designed as an Alternative.

Dollar values indicate the total and mean 2005 list price.

Choosing quality over quantity. The STL has nearly 100 fewer titles than the UTL we were offered, with a similar average list price. On average, adopting the STL meant loss of access to more than half of an institution's leased titles (58%). Although those who see this as a significant loss can be easily countered by the observation that an average of 50% of subject collection titles had zero use, this still lessens the extent to which users and accreditation agencies can be impressed by the large total number of subscriptions an institution has access to. Indeed, in every case the percent of titles that became inaccessible (after replacing the subject collections with the STL) exceeded the percent cost savings. The challenge I believe libraries must rise to is that of interpreting this as an appropriate choice, because it enhances our collection quality and may put pressure on Elsevier to maintain the quality of its journals (rather than simply constantly increasing the quantity).

Future assessment. Objective tests of the effectiveness of the shared title lists can be performed after a year of use of the new collections. Do the new lists decrease the number of titles getting no use? Is there a lower individual or SCELC-wide cost per use for leased (STL) titles? In addition to these questions, it remains to be seen how well these lists will adapt to changing needs and new SCELC ScienceDirect members, but they are almost certainly more flexible than the UTL, and subject collections are still an option. In addition, it might be interesting to examine impact factor per dollar of the STL versus a set of subject collections.

A clear benefit. One thing is certain: These lists have restored the ability of the SCELC libraries to add individual Elsevier titles in the future. No longer will we need to make excuses (though they may have been valid) about not being able to add access to high-priced ScienceDirect titles because they can only be purchased in packages or at full list price. Shaving off the lowest use titles and replacing them with more desirable ones is second only to an unlimited budget, and may even bring a touch of efficiency back into this market!

Conclusion

It's not the number of titles that counts, but their quality and value to local users. Sharing use data to build the optimal shared access list represents one way consortium members can work together to improve the quality of a product for their users. Library vendors (even some of the most notorious) are willing to work with consortia to increase the value of their products—even if it means at least a temporary loss to their bottom line. Collection development, serials, acquisitions, and electronic resources librarians must take issue with the least attractive pricing models and negotiate with publishers to develop viable alternatives in order to be effective in a world where things are seldom what they seem.

Notes

1. G. Ives, "Content Overlap of the Elsevier ScienceDirect Subject Collections: Book Series, Current Journals, and Journal Backfiles" (Paper presented at the 9th World Congress of Health Information and Libraries, 2005) [Online], available: http://www.icml9.org/program/track2/activity.php?lang=en&id=7 (accessed January 27, 2006).

The Charleston Conference is a venue for all types of presentations. This section includes an interesting look at challenges with metadata, how to be a good manager or supervisor, issues libraries face when dealing with pornography, and how to engage your community in using the library.

Miscellaneous

CHALLENGES AND OPPORTUNITIES IN THE REALM OF METADATA

Jin Ma, Electronic Resources Cataloging Librarian, The Pennsylvania State University, University Park

Introduction

In addition to traditional MARC standards, libraries are adopting a variety of new and emerging metadata standards for both non-electronic and electronic resources. This chapter introduces metadata implementation and use at the Penn State University Libraries: metadata for digital projects, for electronic publishing, and for Web content management.

The author also discusses the challenges and opportunities in such areas as metadata and cataloging, standards and interoperability, and skills and training, and concludes that it is a librarywide strategy that can transform challenges into opportunities in the realm of metadata.

Metadata for Digital Projects

The Pennsylvania (Penn) State University Libraries have undertaken a broad range of digital projects. Metadata plays an important role in these projects.

VIUS (Visual Image User Study)[1] was a 30-month period project funded by the Andrew W. Mellon Foundation. The purpose of the project was to assess the requirements for a digital image delivery system. VIUS studied user needs through focus groups, surveys, observational analysis, and other data collection methods; constructed two prototypes of image delivery systems—a traditional centralized database service and a peer-to-peer system in a distributed environment[2]; and assessed these prototype services for usability and sustainability.

An "application profiling"-like metadata approach was adopted for the VIUS project; that is, adopting metadata elements from different schemes using a "mix and match" approach.[3] Three emerging metadata standards were proposed and implemented: VRA (Visual Resources Association) Core Categories,[4] Dublin Core,[5] and IEEE Learning Object Meta-data (LOM).[6] The focus on images suggested the use of VAR Core, which consists of a single element set to describe works of visual culture as well as the images that document them. Dublin Core is a standard for cross-domain information resource description. The purpose of the LOM standard is to facilitate search, evaluation, acquisition, and use of learning objects. Attig, Copeland, and Pelikan[7] have described the metadata implementation in detail in "Context and Meaning: the Challenges of Metadata for a Digital Image Library within the University." The basic assumption of the metadata design for the VIUS prototype database was that each of these three metadata standards needed to be supported because images included in the database might include metadata elements in any one or more of these standards. Given these objectives, a "merged superset" of all the elements in the three standards was created. The authors tried to preserve the context of the metadata created with each standard and provided mappings to support searching across the entire database. Unfortunately, it was not possible to test this metadata scheme in the prototype. CONTENTdm,[8] a digital collection management system, was selected for the prototype. The software's data structure cannot accommodate the superset scheme. The final metadata for over 10,000 images was created using a single Dublin Core standard.

Though the "merged superset" was not implemented for the VIUS project, the Libraries gained invaluable experience in understanding metadata standards, creating and managing metadata, and coordinating different units and personnel for collaborative projects.

The Mira Dock Forestry Lantern Slides project is the result of collaboration among subject librarians, catalogers, technical staff, and faculty and students, who collaborated in digitizing 468 forestry glass lantern slides from the collection of Mira Lloyd Dock (1853–1945). Dock was a native Pennsylvanian who was very active in the City Beautiful movement in the early 1900s and extremely influential in the founding of the Pennsylvania State Forestry Academy at Mont Alto in 1903.[9] The subject expertise of faculty and students in the forestry program helped implement the International Plant Names Index (IPNI)[10] to assign family, genus, species, and common names to plants and trees in the collection. Other completed and ongoing digital projects include Pennsylvania German Broadsides and Fraktur, Hershey Medical School instructional materials, digital monograph collections, and Pennsylvania geological surveys.[11]

Metadata implementation is rarely a discrete process but usually a critical component of a digital project and should be integrated into various stages of the project. The Digital Technology Advisory Group (DTAG) coordinates digital project implementation at Penn State. The metadata librarian is a member of the group and works with other DTAG members and other project stakeholders regarding any metadata decision during the metadata implementation process: analyzing metadata requirements, choosing metadata schemes, creating metadata content, ensuring metadata search and retrieval, evaluating metadata, and sustaining metadata maintenance. While early metadata decisions were made on a project-by-project basis, the DTAG is working toward general metadata templates and guidelines to ensure that best practices are followed to the extent possible and that metadata is consistent across projects and collections.

Metadata for Electronic Publishing

The role of libraries in the landscape of scholarly communication is evolving. A partnership between the Penn State Press and the University Libraries has formed to create an Office of Digital Scholarly Publishing (ODSP) at Penn State.[12] Its mission is to use new media technologies to advance scholarly communication at Penn State and beyond. One of the current tasks of ODSP is a partnership with the Cornell University Library in the DPubS (Digital Publishing System)[13] project. DPubS software was originally created by Cornell University Library for Project Euclid, which supports both academic libraries and independent publishers of mathematics and statistics. Working together, the libraries at Cornell and Penn State are now enhancing and extending DPubS to create an open source, general purpose publishing platform for online scholarly literature in diverse disciplines. DPubS will feature peer review, administrative functionality, and interoperability with other open source repository systems such as Fedora[14] and Dspace.[15]

The Penn State University Libraries have digitized the back issues of *Pennsylvania History —A Journal of Mid-Atlantic Studies,* which published the best of current scholarship on the history of the Commonwealth and the region. Since 1934 *Pennsylvania History* has been the official journal of the Pennsylvania Historical Association (PHA).[16] All issues published prior to 2000 have been loaded into DPubS and are now publicly available online via the Libraries' server.[17] In the near future, refereeing, editing, and production of the journal will migrate to a digital environment using DPubS software.

Penn State has adopted and modified the DPubS Document Type Definition (DTD) developed by the Cornell University Library. The XML DTD is a set of tags and rules defined in XML syntax that describe the structure and elements of a document. It is used for encoding journal issues including both issue and article level metadata for submission to DPubS. The issue metadata elements include series, journal volume number, issue title, issue number, issue publication date, start page, end page, and editorial board. "Record" is a high-level wrapper element for bringing together all the metadata for a submitted document (typically a single article). A tag dictionary specifies the details of each metadata element, including description, characteristics, attributes, examples, etc., and guidelines on how to encode metadata.

Penn State will use DPubS software for the electronic publishing of conference proceedings in conjunction with the Penn State University's Outreach programs and faculty conferences. As part of the DPubs project, the Penn State Libraries are trying to come up with a DTD that can be used for building XML descriptions of conference proceedings.

The purpose of the DTD for either journals or conference proceedings is to capture the metadata necessary to provide the functionality in a publishing environment instead of bibliographic control. What data, and what structural relationships, does a publisher want to display? How is content to be arranged for browsing? Are there kinds of information useful to researchers that are routinely omitted from bibliographic records that might be included in an XML description of conference proceedings? These are the questions that need to be answered before a DTD is designed.

Metadata for Web Content Management

Day Communiqué Content Management System (CMS)[18]

The Penn State University Libraries are in the process of implementing Day Communiqué —a commercial content management system for managing the Libraries' Web sites. The CMS Metadata Expert Team is charged with recommending how metadata standards can be applied in the context of a content management system, and to develop a glossary that will be applied to the CMS. The tasks of the charge include, but are not necessarily limited to, determining

- if the metadata needs of the intranet and public Web site are the same or different, and if different, then to specify the needs of each;

- which elements of metadata are required or optional;

- which elements of metadata should be published to the Web and which are strictly for administrative purposes; and

- if and when controlled vocabularies are appropriate and how they should be created and maintained, and by whom.

The group brainstormed a list of action items to be completed by early 2006:

- Examine Web logs to learn how visitors use the Libraries' Web site.

- Examine the pages of organizations that use the same CMS.

- Examine the features of the CMS that will allow more efficient use of data.

- Develop a test suite to include elements from the intranet and public sites; suite should include text, images, audio, and video if possible.

- Draft a list of commonalities: what elements are found on every page (or most pages)?

- Determine metadata elements with usage guidelines.

- Create a model that encourages the reuse of data whenever possible.

- Draft a list of Content Types such as "Subject Guide" and "Documentation" to classify content.

Taxonomy for Penn State's Web Project

Historically used by biologists to classify plants and animals, taxonomy is a hierarchical structure for the classification or organization of data in content management. Taxonomy is a means of organizing content and metadata further describing it.

The Taxonomic Tags Group was formed as a university-level group, with representatives from Information Technology, Business Administration, and the Penn State Libraries. The mission of the group is to develop a taxonomy model, expressed as metadata tags and systematically applied across the university's Web pages. It could

- make Web search more efficient and effective,

- make it easier to find specific pages from among the University's nearly 1,000,000 public Web pages,

- simplify Web content management tasks, and

- come up with a durable data model that remains useful amid increasing adoption of content management systems or as search engines continue to evolve.[19]

The Tags Group has developed recommendations to address these issues, including the development of a controlled vocabulary, along with synonyms for Penn State departments, colleges, administrative units, etc.; a mechanism to resolve common names or "nicknames" to authorized terms; and a set of practices for its maintenance over time. The vocabulary would be incorporated into both into Web pages and the University's LDAP (Lightweight Directory Access Protocol) system.

The Group has recommended that a broadcast search mechanism be developed for the main Penn State Web search screen. Under this system, user search terms will be submitted both to a Web search appliance and to the university's LDAP system. The results will be combined, identified, and presented to the user.

Challenges and Opportunities

Since the middle of the 1990s, when the term "metadata" began to be used more frequently in the library and information community, especially with the creation and promotion of the Dublin Core Metadata Element Set in 1995, there have been many discussions about metadata and its use in the library field. Challenges at the same time embrace opportunities as libraries are moving toward a new information environment.

Metadata and Cataloging

Metadata is often called "data about data." Libraries have been creating data about data, in the form of cataloging. Though some only apply it to the description of electronic resources, the ALA Task Force defines metadata as "structured, encoded data that describe characteristics of information-bearing entities to aid in the identification, discovery, assessment, and management of the described entities."[20] This definition indicates at least two points. First, the information must be structured and recorded in accordance with some metadata scheme. Second, the metadata must describe an information resource, including electronic and non-electronic resources. This definition suggests a broad definition of metadata, covering both MARC standards and new emerging metadata schemes. Instead of being territorial, traditional catalogers and metadata librarians should work on applying the established principles to new initiatives, bringing together new access systems and traditional catalogs, and providing linkages between various access systems.

Standards and Interoperability

In the context of information community, standards are generally developed to be used in data exchange and retrieval for the purposes of interoperability, portability, and reusability. Many new metadata standards have been developed by various communities. We should make use of the standards being developed and make contributions to any initiatives that facilitate metadata interoperability in a networked environment. We should participate in the development of new standards with other communities, bringing to the table a wealth of experience and expertise from our own profession.

Skills and Training

Some libraries have created metadata-related positions with various titles such as "metadata specialist," "metadata librarian," "metadata coordinator," and "electronic resources librarian." The role of such positions is to coordinate and manage metadata implementation. What skills are necessary to ensure the success of metadata implementation? How do "metadata specialists" acquire the skills and knowledge that are involved in their jobs?

It is generally agreed that cataloging professionals can apply established principles and rules to new environments. Catalogers are familiar with MARC and are used to working within standards and with controlled vocabularies. Using metadata may involve use of new digital tools, systems, and applications, and having a good understanding of how digital library systems work is crucial, as are communication skills and problem-solving skills. In addition, understanding XML technologies is a plus since it has been widely used in digital information management.

Acquiring new skills is important and should be ensured by reading, studying best practices guide from other institutions, talking to people with experience, attending workshops or conferences, etc. What's more important is to apply new skills to practices and to think creatively with each new challenge.

Summary

The implementation of metadata is generally a librarywide venture, involving not only cataloging and metadata librarians, but also subject librarians, technical staff, and other personnel. It is important to debunk the metadata myths across the whole library to create an open and productive environment. This is a librarywide strategy that can transform challenges into opportunities in the realm of metadata.

Notes

1. Visual Image User Study (VIUS) Web site, 2003 [Online], available: http://www.libraries.psu.edu/vius/ (accessed January 5, 2006).

2. Lionshare Web site, n.d. [Online], available: http://lionshare.its.psu.edu/main/ (accessed January 5, 2006).

3. R. Heery and M. Patel, (2000). "Application Profiles: Mixing and Matching Metadata Schemas," *Ariadne* 25 (2000) [Online], available: http://www.ariadne.ac.uk/issue25/app-profiles/ (accessed January 5, 2006).

4. VRA Core Categories, Version 3, n.d. [Online], available: http://www.vraweb.org/vracore3.htm (assessed January 5, 2006).

5. Dublin Core Metadata Element Set, n.d. [Online], available: http://dublincore.org/documents/dces/ (accessed January 10, 2006).

6. IEEE Learning Object Metadata, n.d. [Online], available: http://ltsc.ieee.org/wg12/ (accessed January 10, 2006).

7. J. Attig, A. Copeland, and M. Pelikan, "Context and Meaning: The Challenges of Metadata for a Digital Image Library within the University," *College and Research Libraries* 65, no. 3 (May 2004): 251–61.

8. CONTENdm Digital Collection Management Software, n.d. [Online], available: http://contentdm.com/ (accessed January 10, 2006).

9. A. White, J. Ma, and L. Wentzel, "Digitizing Glass Lantern Slides: The Mira Lloyd Dock Project at the Pennsylvania State University," *Microform Imaging & Review,* 34, no. 2 (2005): 81–90.

10. *The International Plant Names Index,* n.d. [Online], available: http://www.ipni.org/index.html (accessed January 14, 2006).

11. Penn State Digital Library, n.d. [Online], available: http://apps.libraries.psu.edu/digital/index.cfm (accessed January 14, 2006).

12. "Publications Go Digital; New Partnership to Offer High-Tech Opions for Distributing Scholarship," *Penn State Live* (March 15, 2005) [Online], available: http://live.psu.edu/story/10874 (accessed January 14, 2006).

13. DPubS Digital Publishing System home, n.d. [Online], available: http://dpubs.org/ (accessed January 17, 2006).

14. Fedora Web site, n.d. [Online], available: http://www.fedora.info/ (accessed January 14, 2006).

15. DSpace Federation Web site, n.d. [Online], available: http://www.dspace.org/ (accessed January 17, 2006).

16. Pennsylvania Historical Association Web site, n.d. [Online], available: http://www.pa-history.org/ (accessed January 17, 2006).

17. *Pennsylvania History: A Journal of Mid-Atlantic Studies*, n.d. [Online], available: http://cip.cornell.edu/DPubS/ UI/1.0/JourNav?authority=psu.ph&type=home (accessed January 17, 2006).

18. Day Communiqué Content Management System, n.d. [Online], available: http://www.day.com/content/site/en/ index/products/content-centric_applications/overview.html (accessed January 18, 2006).

19. Michael Pelikan et al. "Searching for the Needle in the Haystack: Taxonomies, Tags and Targets," in *Proceedings of the 32nd Annual ACM SIGUCCS Conference on User Services 2004, Baltimore, MD, USA, October 10-13, 2004,* 256–61. New York: ACM Press, 2005. Also available: http://portal.acm.org/citation.cfm?doid=1027860 (accessed January 18, 2006).

20. *Task Force on Metadata Final Report*, June 2000 [Online], available: http://www.libraries.psu.edu/tas/jca/ccda. old/tf-meta6.html (accessed January 18, 2006).

THE HUMAN SIDE OF MANAGEMENT

Tinker Massey, Serials Librarian, Embry-Riddle Aeronautical University, Daytona Beach, Florida

This preconference session was designed to be a workshop on helping supervisors understand the human aspects and advantages of management. In attendance was a mixed group of middle managers, supervisors, and upper management people from various regions of the country and various sizes of institutions, but they were all academically oriented environments. Some people discussed problems they were having with their subordinates and others talked about problems with their peers and upper management. Since the discussion was designed to be collegial in nature, all levels of management shared their views about themselves, their colleagues, and workflows that did and didn't work. We discussed possible programs that might work to remedy situations and analyses that would help them diagnose and solve problems in their own environments.

There were handouts and bibliographies that could give them new ideas and afford further reading on various aspects of problem solving, mentoring, coaching, communication, and non-confrontational intervention. Each person was allowed to state why he or she was attending this session and what information he or she hoped to acquire. If that information had not been presented, we stopped and did so at that point, which usually spurred a new discussion.

The basics of communication patterns and ways to achieve them were presented, as well as non-confrontational negotiations in the workplace. Each person was allowed time to vent and present his or her case, and other attendees commented about positive ways to achieve changes and cope with the stresses. We had a short discussion on change as a grieving process and how to support people through the stages. The main emphasis was on positive ways to make change and control it in the work environment. Some breaks included times for individuals to sit one on one for special tutoring on various aspects of self-development and coping. I appreciate the interactive participation of the attendees. Everyone wanted to share business cards to follow up on each other throughout the year.

VICE SQUAD

Mark Herring, Dean of Library Services, Winthorp University, Rock Hill, South Carolina

Vice is a monster of so frightful mien," wrote Alexander Pope nearly more than 300 years ago, "As to be hated need but to be seen. Yet seen too oft, familiar with her face, We first endure, then pity, then embrace." There may not be a better history of pornography than this one, and it is to this succinct history that I shall again refer.

Standing before a host of librarians, myself a librarian now for more than a quarter of a century, I feel a bit like the man accused of killing his parents who, as he stood before the court, asked for leniency since he was, after all, an orphan. I haven't really killed anyone, but over the course of my career, whenever I have stood up and argued that, au contraire, the First Amendment is neither absolute nor implacable and that, more recently, filtering is not only not a bad idea but also one we should wholeheartedly embrace, I have been treated almost as contemptuously as that man before the court.

I am not unaware of the irony, if we can call it that (as opposed to calling it an outrage), of a librarian defending what some have incorrectly called censorship. My position has always been one of defending not only what the First Amendment does, in fact protect itself, and allows, but also what librarians have always done in the area of collection and acquisitions. More about that later.

Let us get to the heart of the matter and talk dirty for a few minutes. I mean, about pornography. Pornography is one of the nation's largest industries. Whether soft- or hardcore, pornography earns more money annually than CBS, NBC, ABC, ESPN, FoxNews, and CNN *combined*. Indeed, as Catherine McKinnon—hardly a conservative stalwart—points out: "the industry was said to gross $ 4 billion a year in the 1980s, between $ 10 billion and $ 14 billion in 2001 and by 2005, adult video rentals alone were estimated to earn $ 20 billion a year in the US, $ 57 billion globally—its distributors no longer live under rocks. Legitimate corporations now traffic pornography, often through subsidiaries, their financial stake as immense and established as it is open."[1] In Los Angeles alone, more than 10,000 hardcore porn films were made last year versus Hollywood's annual output, 400 films.

Vice Is a Monster

Porn is everywhere you look: it's in rock music videos and not just on the X-rated labels. Whether it's Brittany Spears confusing herself, as she said to *Good Morning America's* Diane Sawyer, that "masturbation is sacred," or California (natch) gubernatorial candidate and porn-starlet, Mary Carey, you can't seem even to run from it. All of the hotels you're staying in during this conference have everything from skin flicks to hardcore readily available for a small price. Peer-to-peer file-sharing for child porn, for example, has increased fourfold since the national Center for Missing and Exploited Children began tracking child porn in 2001. There are now more than half a billion porn sites on the Web, and those sites are growing at an astonishing rate. I once argued that when people cease to defend virtue publicly they will no longer practice it privately. Nostradamus should have been so right.

Of Such Frightful Mien

Porn star Ron Jeremy now shows up in mainstream films like *The Rules of Attraction,* while Jenna Jameson, the on-again, off-again—no pun intended—porn star, has her own best-selling book and is the first skin-flick star to earn more than a million a year. Hugh Hefner now does commercials for Carl's Jr., and your own young children, whether adolescent or junior or senior highs, wear clothes that say "porn star" or hang hand-cuffs from their rearview mirrors. So called kiddie porn sites on the Web have grown from about 1,400 in 1998 to more than 30,000 in 2003. Porn on the Web has grown more than twenty-five-fold in less than five years.

As to Be Hated Need But to Be Seen

Hollywood has, of course taken up the gauntlet. *The Girl Next Door* is a story about the porn star next door, while Jeff Bridges stars in a movie about a small town that makes a porn movie in *Moguls. Deep Throat*, the first such widely publicized movie, required dark glasses and a trench coat to view it in a seedy part of town in a theater that was itself a biohazard. Today, no such disguises are required. Finding porn on the Web is also easy. Not only can you type in the obvious, but the not-so-obvious will also get you there. Lolita is far more likely to get you to the subject matter of Nabokov's book than it is to retrieve Nabokov himself. From 1996 to 2004, the FBI reported a twenty-three-fold increase in the number of child porn cases.

Yet Seen Too Oft, Familiar with Her Face

Of course librarians want into the act, so we have the sexy librarian and a host of other such sites with soft porn. Lately, one librarian group did the unthinkable, for a number of reasons. They are now selling calendars featuring naked librarians, books, and other familiar library accoutrements covering most of the unmentionable and in some cases unsightly parts. And of course who can forget Paris Hilton's two-fold rise to stardom. She's always been filthy rich; now, with the advent of the Internet, we discover she's also just plain filthy. Now we know she's as likely to blow a few thousands in some Rodeo Drive boutique as she is to . . . .

We First Endure, Then Pity, Then Embrace

Now to this introduction some might say, what's the problem, and what has that to do with librarians? Since it's everywhere, why should we librarians care? We're just one more cog in the wheel, and eliminating this spoke will do positively nothing to curb what has become America's newfound obsession (I nearly said possession). Besides, it is argued, porn is harmless, right? We should be proud of our bodies—or, well, some of us should—and if we believe and defend civil liberties, as we say we do, we must also be in favor of porn. Elizabethan playwrights Beaumont and Fletcher were right after all: "Vice gets more in this vicious world than piety."

I simply do not have enough time to go into all the harm that porn has done. There will be no time to talk about the objectification of women, nor will there be any time to talk about how men have been reduced to only one anatomical part (some women will doubtless say it has *always* been that part, but let's move on). Whatever we can say, it is safe to say that porn has not been good for anyone, men or women, neither those who participate in it nor those who are duped into thinking that porn has something useful to say about sexual relations. Getting sex education from a porn site is like getting your geography from www.flatearthers.com.

Nor will we have time to talk about the fact that four of five men surf porn at least once a month, and this is *self-reported*. Nor that, even in this audience, even in this gathering of austere and serious-minded folks, some of you have a problem with porn; either you have it yourself, or your spouse does, or you have a good friend who is struggling with it. We will not have time to talk about the harm of pornography even though ALA's position is that it doesn't do any harm at all because it is private and between somewhat consenting adults.

We have all heard of the "butterfly effect." This is the notion that if a butterfly flaps its wings in Argentina there may well be a hurricane in New Orleans. It's the idea that everything is connected, we are all part of a unified whole, that there are six degrees of separation. And yet ALA's position on this issue of porn is that it is harmless. Dear me, if a butterfly flapping its diaphanous wings in Argentina can cause Katrina in New Orleans, then surely Jenna Jameson flapping, well, her "wings" in Los Angeles, can cause at least minimal trouble right here in River City.

There is also no time to talk about the beautiful human body, but certainly the gyrations and contortions of porn sites are not a very good place to discover that. To coin a line from that old Seinfeld episode about his nudist girlfriend, many such contortions on porn sites are "not a good look" for either the men or the women. And whether one's tastes yield to weare18.com or the more horrific sites that feature the unimaginable, one would be hard pressed to argue that such sites proffer any useful information about sex that is not itself degrading, or at the very least untoward, not to mention altogether likely painful for one or both partners.

But the issue of the First Amendment is one about which I do want to say something briefly. The basic assumption about filtering is that it somehow violates or repudiates the First Amendment. This is patently untrue. Filtering, it is argued, is in direct contradistinction to the First Amendment; ergo it is wrong, as indeed any censoring is. This argument is true, however, only if one misreads the First Amendment as an absolutist doctrine: no speech anywhere, at any time, may be restricted ever at all. Should anyone be able to present such evidence, the argument might hold some weight constitutionally.

But it specifically does not. Granted, the Court has been very liberal, that is, expansive, in its opinions about what speech is, citing everything from dance to the wearing of arm bands as constitutionally protected "speech." It's been clear that whatever the form, not all manners or modes of expressing oneself are First Amendment safe. Court after court has held that *some forms* of speech are not protected.

For example, in *Roth v. United States*, obscenity is one such exception. Roth developed a lucrative mail order business out of New York City dealing in erotica and obscene works. In *Roth*, the government argued that *not all speech is equally protected by the First Amendment*, and that, further, *some expressions, such as obscenity, should not receive much protection, if any at all*. Moreover, Brennan, hardly a name immediately associated with conservatism, held that not only was obscenity "utterly without redeeming social importance," but it also into the same category as libel. Since libel had already been held to be speech not protected under the First Amendment, or at least not speech as defined by the First Amendment (*Beauharnais v. Illinois*), the precedent had been set.

Roth has held sway since its inception and has not been overturned. More recent courts have made adjustments, most notably to what is commonly referred to as the "Roth Test." But the fact of the matter is that no new cases have overturned the central argument in *Roth*: that some speech is not protected. In *Memoirs v. Massachusetts*, the book known as *Fanny Hill* furthered the agreement in *Roth*, though the book in question passed the obscenity test. As liberal a judge as Potter argued that the Constitution protects all but "hardcore" (Potter's words) pornography. That Potter specifically mentioned the word "pornography" instead of "obscenity" should give pause to those who hide behind the semantics of one to excuse the other.

The last most important case, *Miller v. California,* merely augments this argument. Here, community standards are defined and become a further test. While some will argue that *Miller* changes the constitutional view, it in fact places more of the burden on communities and therefore local (and often elected) judges. It does not overturn either *Roth* or *Memoirs*. If anything, *Miller* gives some credence to the conservative argument that Supreme Court justices interpret less than they define the Constitution. For clearly, the only change between *Memoirs* and *Miller* is the face, literally, of the latter court compared to the former.

But one need not resort to court cases of historical importance. It is by now proverbial that one cannot shout "Fire!" in a crowded theater when there isn't one. Surely this restricts one's right to "free" expression. The court, however, ruled that such expressions, whether speech or not, *are not constitutionally protected.*

I labor this argument for the simple reason that it is so little known. The First Amendment is neither absolute nor ambiguous. Since our founding as a country, obscenity and pornography have not been protected forms of speech, regardless of the court, and regardless of the medium used to portray that speech. If the First Amendment allows that some forms of speech are not worthy of protection, then why is ALA so intent on preserving pornography?

Another argument made about filtering runs like this: Even if it does not violate the First Amendment outright, it is repugnant on its face because it restricts the free flow of information. There is the *chance*, some argue, that *some* form of information may be lost via filtering, and so it cannot be allowed.

This would be a persuasive argument if the practice of librarians themselves did not run counter to it. If hypocrisy is wrongheaded, it must be wrongheaded regardless of who does it. First, to argue that we must not filter anything for fear of filtering something is equal to arguing that we must not convict anyone of a crime for fear of convicting the innocent. And while I am aware there are those who make such arguments, they are not, thankfully, in positions of jurisprudential power. Police often pull you over for speeding even when others have zoomed by you. Should we outlaw violations of the speed limit because we cannot be sure of catching everyone equally? Moreover, for all the hoopla about the potential loss of important literature, the fact remains that we have lost nothing. *Ulysses*, to take a particularly innocent example, remains on shelves as unread by the vast majority as ever.

The argument that we *may* lose some information and therefore the risk is too great is already impugned by our practice. We lose good, solid information daily. Furthermore, it's *our* fault. Librarians censor most often in the most odious of ways: money. Hardly a librarian alive has not rejected some very valuable resource simply because it consumed too much of his or her materials budget. Further, we censor not only accidentally but also intentionally. We do not, rightly I think, buy books on gay-bashing or about the glorification of the KKK. The list could go on, but my time grows shorter. Is "filtering" bad only when *others* attempt to do it but not when we choose to do so based on our own ideologies and selection and acquisitions statements?

Another argument brought to the fore is that filtering does not work, or can be worked around. I find this to be the weakest of all arguments because we use incomplete technology all the time and do not find that a compelling reason to discontinue it. We all know that many database vendors perform their own version of cut and paste, clip and snip, and yet we do not see anywhere in the press a call to outlaw databases. Indeed, if present benedictions continue we'll see a hagiography for Bill Gates by most library associations, so enamored are they of the possibilities of technology, so dismissive are they are any of its obvious failures. I would be happy if all technology worked as well as filtering. As for the workarounds, it is possible, but we also know that it's possible for patrons to steal our books, and yet that has not stopped us from buying expensive book detection systems. We know that OPACs often give either false or dispositive results for various kinds of searches, sending users either to no information or to wrong results. I have yet to see even one call to remove these fallible OPACS from our libraries.

Let us not forget, too, that filtered information can be unfiltered. It may not be easy, and it may require greater technical expertise on the part of the librarian. But it *can* be done. Indeed, it is being done, and quite successfully. It does not follow that if we filter weare18.com, we will also filter www.komen.org, a site dedicated to education and research on breast cancer causes, treatment, and the search for a cure. Nor does it follow that filtering out www.hooterville.com will prevent users from finding www.thebreastcancernsite.com. Why, then, the objection to filtering?

What are we to make of ALA's abnormal fear that we are curtailing information? How many of you out there take *Screw* magazine? Why then are we "subscribing" to such on the Web? Our collection and acquisitions management of materials has never allowed for an unfettered access to any and all material. And may I please remind everyone that only 10 years ago we did not have any of this information, good or bad, and we were none the worse without it. Why, now, all of a sudden, must we have every possible snippet or witness the end of civilization as we know it?

I am happy to say that the growing majority of public opinion is siding *with* filtering, not against it, making ALA's bewildering protection of pornography and pornographers even more disconcerting. Some of our own professional organizations have made statements that conflict with ALA's ne plus ultra views. Finally, what about those who say they do not know what pornography is? This is mere cant. No one is "getting off" while reading the Bible or the *New York Times,* or watching FoxNews or CNN. They aren't even "getting off" while reading something as racy as *Moby Dick.*

Make no mistake about it: This is not a call to censoring. I have dwelt on porn because it is the most despicable of what's on the Web, but it is surely not all. With eight billion pages on the Web, and more added each day, much on the Web is useless, pointless information that for any number of reasons would never have made its way into a library. It would not have made its way there because it is wrong, it is disinformation, it is mal-information, or it is simply too silly to occupy our shelves. My desire is not so much to close these sites as it is to curtail library support of them, inadvertent or no. My aim is to remind us why we are in libraries and why we are a value-added addition to the libraries we serve. If we are to defend pornography, then someone must come forward and explain its value. A colleague once told me it was for art students to draw the human figure. This is like saying we must preserve the writings on the walls of men's restrooms for they are the legacy we leave behind. Dear Lord, let's hope not.

If we select everything for fear of censoring anything, then there is no reason for us or for our libraries. If we agree that everything's on the Web, then let's close our doors now and let the Gates foundation take all our places.

If on the other hand, we as librarians understand that we have an intellectual role to play in the calculus of information access, then let us exercise that intellect by passing all our information—print or nonprint, Web-based or no—through the same lenses we always have. I contend that filtering is as much a part of that process and always has been. If you feel better about calling it selection, then please, be my guest.

ALA must reconsider its position on filtering and begin accepting the defensible case for it. The sad fact of the matter is this: If ALA does not make the case that hardcore pornography can be filtered defensibly, then others will make the logical deduction that nothing can. Once that realization is made, we will have lost our voice in the public forum. For if Huxley was right, that the true intellectual is one who finds something other than sex to be interested in, then librarians will be excluded as intellectuals with anything useful to say. Not only will we lose our public voice, but, more important, we will lose our public standing, not to mention our public. We do not want to be accused of liberating fantasy, as Wendell Berry said, while killing imagination. If you thought our image was bad before, just wait. "Hot cross-buns" will have an entirely different meaning in our pornified future.

Notes

1. Quoted in Ariel Levy, *Female Chauvinist Pigs: Women and the Rise of Raunch Culture* (New York: Free Press, 2005).

Bibliography

Paul, Pamela. *Pornified: How Pornography Is Transforming Our Lives, Our Relationships, and Our Families*. New York: Times Books, 2005.

Shapiro, Ben. *Porn Generation: How Social Liberalism Is Corrupting Our Future*. Washington, DC: Regnery, 2005

United States. Congress. House. Committee on Government Reform. *Stumbling onto Smut: The Alarming Ease of Access to Pornography on Peer-to-Peer Networks*. Hearing before the Committee on Government Reform, House of Representatives, 108th Congress, 1st session, March 13, 2003. Washington, DC: U.S. Government Printing Office, 2003.

United States. Congress. House. Committee on the Judiciary. Subcommittee on Crime, Terrorism, and Homeland Security. *Child Abduction Prevention Act and the Child Obscenity and Pornography Prevention Act of 2003*. Hearing before the Subcommittee on Crime, Terrorism, and Homeland Security of the Committee on the Judiciary, House of Representatives, 108th Congress, 1st session, on H.R. 1104 and H.R. 1161, March 11, 2003. Washington, DC: U.S. Government Printing Office, 2003.

ENGAGING YOUR COMMUNITY: LIBRARIES AS PLACE

Robert Martin, Professor and Lillian Bradshaw Endower Chair, School of Library and Information Studies, Texas Woman's University, Denton, Texas

Louise Blalock, Chief Librarian, Hartford Public Library, Connecticut

GladysAnn Wells, Director, Arizona State Library, Archives and Public Records, Phoenix, Arizona

Introduction and summary by Milton T. Wolf, Director, Rita E. King Library, Chadron State College, Nebraska

> *The children using the libraries represented by the American Association of School Librarians today are the students who will be using the libraries represented by the Association of College and Research Libraries tomorrow, and all of them are the Public Library Association's patrons of the future. These are not separate universes. United, they are the roadmap for a productive lifetime of reading, learning, and fulfillment.*—Leonard Kniffel, *American Libraries* (September 2005).

The Faceless User Looking for Faces

For the majority of people looking for information today, the search process usually begins on the Web. For scientists in particular, the next step is usually an examination of pre-prints in their discipline (or e-mail inquiries to colleagues). The third step of investigation generally occurs at conferences, either through formal presentations or networking. And the fourth step finally involves looking at book(s). So books, what many associate with the library's traditional raison d'etre, are no longer the research/information draw that once brought patrons to the library—even the public library.

And while library circulation, especially in public libraries, is way up, many, if not most, come to the library to access e-mail, the Web, or other electronic resources; but since electronic resources, even if paid for by the library, can generally be accessed remotely by those with computers at home, office, or wherever, there are no longer the traditional reasons for visiting the library, especially in the academic environment. Yet the "faceless user" has actually made libraries more desirable for its faces, for the opportunity to meet and form communities!

Even "virtualReference," which has swept across the country and is an excellent example of how libraries are learning to bridge the gap to the "faceless user," is but another reminder that libraries are transforming socially. In many places this service is 24/7, yet few realize that the majority of those seeking virtual reference services are teenagers! According to the Pew Internet and American Life Project,[1] teenage use of the Internet has burgeoned immensely, so much so that the majority of teenagers between 12 and 17 are online with great regularity. They are not only playing games; they are seeking a variety of information topics, including health information. They seem to understand intuitively that "what you don't know can really hurt you in life!"

This is just one more example of how different generations are reacting to and using technological advances in the information field. And believe it or not, the largest demographic group of new e-mail users are those 55 years and older!

At the same time, the library as place, as a cultural context in which society renews and refreshes itself, where community reshapes and energizes itself, has emerged as a cornerstone of the library's essence. However, a library that only understands part of the demographic mosaic of its clientele, or worse, thinks its clientele all want the same thing, is not going to fare well in building community or evolving the library as "place." Even on academic campuses, only a third of the 16 million students are the traditional 18- to 22-year-old full-time cohort, so if the library is to become a catalyst in bringing the diverse elements of community together, it must learn to cross generational divides as much as digital and technological ones.

While the concept of library is going through a monumental sea change that is, in many ways, bringing it back to its philosophical roots—the agora, the place where people "meet and greet," exchange pleasantries and news, have something to eat and drink, and even gather information—and while technology has made it possible to access information from home, hotel, or wherever the computer can be connected, people are social creatures and are attracted to the library because it is one of the few institutions that has a long history of welcoming the diverse groups that create community—all without charging fees!

After all, the user of the school library often goes on to become a user of the college/university library and the public library, especially as our nation becomes ever more one of lifetime learners. Realizing that libraries, whether they serve town and gown or more specialized commercial interests, are more alike than different when it comes to serving the interests of its community, Milton T. Wolf, director of the King College Library at Chadron State College, invited three of the best thinkers and practitioners of the art of building communities to share their insights at the 25th Annual Charleston Conference.

These three notable public servants were asked to present and discuss the importance of "community" in institutions and how to develop, encourage, and sustain it. The three speakers, Dr. Robert Martin, formerly the director of the Institute of Museum and Library Services (IMLS) and now serving as the Lillian Moore Bradshaw Endowed Chair at Texas Woman's University; Louise Blalock, chief librarian at the Hartford Public Library and past recipient of *Library Journal*'s prestigious "Librarian of the Year" award; and GladysAnn Wells, director of the Arizona State Library, Archives and Public Records and past president of COSLA, all agreed that librarians must stimulate their constituents and act as a catalyst in making the library a "place" for community expression.

Remarks of Robert S. Martin

My thinking about this subject has lately been informed by the arguments that Mark Moore makes in his very important book, *Creating Public Value: Strategic Management in Government.* Moore is a professor at the John F. Kennedy School at Harvard. He has spent a lot of time working with public sector managers. He has developed a detailed analysis of what public managers should do and a framework for judging their success.

Moore asserts that just as the aim of the manager in the private sector is to produce private value, in the form of revenue, profit, and capital growth, so too the aim of managerial work in the public sector is to produce public value.

In a sense, really, this is a no-brainer: If public enterprises do not create value for the public, then why would they be formed or continue to exist? The problem, of course, is how we define and measure public value.

Moore describes a number of frames of reference or standards that have been used for reckoning public value, and concludes that none of the standard approaches or concepts really provides the best way to define public value. Moore argues that value is rooted in the desires and perceptions of individuals. In the private sector, private individual consumption is the final arbiter of value: Profit and capital growth results from the accumulation of a myriad of individual decisions to satisfy desires by purchasing a product or a service. In the public sector, politics serves as the final arbiter of public value. The desires and perceptions of individuals are expressed through representative government. And therefore managers need to pay attention to politics to define the value that they are expected to produce.

There are three key concepts in Moore's discussion about public value that I would like to call to your attention. The first of these is that value is determined not by the providers of services, but by the consumers. In other words, we do not get to decide what is valuable, our users or customers do. And this means that if we want to offer services that the public will value and support, it is imperative that we listen carefully and systematically to our elected officials and resource allocators to understand fully their agendas, their concerns, and their goals. And then we need to take care to explain how libraries can help them achieve their goals and advance their agendas.

This is essentially a marketing approach. I am both amused and dismayed by the way librarians usually talk about "marketing." In the discourse of our profession, "marketing" is often used as a synonym for "advertising" or "selling." We use it to describe efforts to create awareness about services we provide and to promote appreciation for the work we do. That's not marketing, that's sales. In the business world, trying to convince an individual or group to purchase the product or service that you make or provide is called selling. Marketing, in contrast, is asking an individual or group what product or service that they want to buy, and then developing a product or service that meets the identified demand.

So what we need to do is real marketing. We need to use marketing tools like focus groups and surveys to provide structured ways to listen to the communities we seek to serve. And we do not need to ask them about what we do that they like and do not like. We need to pursue truly deep inquiries into what they want and need to make their lives better. And then we need to fashion programs and services that meet those needs and desires. For example, it is far less important to ask users what hours they want the library to be open than it is to ask them what their goals and needs are, and then think creatively about what we can do to help them achieve their goals or fulfill their needs. Ask them what are the issues in their daily lives that they care most about, and then respond appropriately.

The second key concept in Moore's discussion of public value is the notion of distinctive competence, the thing that is core to the organization and that it does better than any other organization—what one of my professors used to call "our propitious niche." To succeed in strategic management, it is imperative to focus on the core of the enterprise, to stick to our knitting. First, however, we must carefully define what our core business is.

Contrary to what we often hear in the rhetoric of the profession, the distinctive competence of libraries is not in providing access to information. Although libraries and librarians are indeed good at acquiring, organizing, and retrieving and transmitting information, there is nothing distinctive about that competence. There are many other professions (from accountant to information architect) that can claim such expertise, and many other organizations that can provide good information services.

Instead, I think, the distinctive competence of all libraries is to provide the resources and services that stimulate and support the creation and dissemination of knowledge—in other words, education. Perhaps it would be better to say that libraries—all libraries—are in the business of creating and sustaining learners—learners of all ages.

It should not be necessary to argue that the primary function of school libraries and academic libraries is to support education—that is their raison d'etre. But in recent years I think that we have forgotten that the primary role of the public library is education, in the broadest and best sense of the term. In developing resources and services in response to identified and defined needs in the communities we serve, we must take care to remain focused on this distinctive competence. Education is what the public expects from the library, and education is what communities value.

Another key element in Moore's analysis of creating value is that we have to evaluate and demonstrate impact. That is one reason why the Institute of Museum and Library Services has been providing training to all grantees in outcome-based evaluation and is requiring grantees to develop outcome-based measures for the success of their projects. We librarians simply have to do a better job of demonstrating the value that we provide to the communities that we serve. This does not mean that we have to quantify everything—good stories are important too. The best kind of evaluation of outcomes is when the library is so enmeshed in its community that the community cannot imagine operating without it.

Of course, none of this focus on creating and demonstrating value is really new. In 1920 John Cotton Dana wrote "All public institutions . . . should give returns for their cost; and those returns should be in good degree positive, definite, visible, measurable. The goodness of a [library] is not in direct ratio to the cost of its building and the upkeep thereof, or to the rarity, auction value, or money cost of its collections. A [library] is good only insofar as it is of use. . . . Common sense demands that a publicly supported institution do something for its supporters and that some part at least of what it does be capable of clear description and downright valuation."[2] I believe that the foundation for successful advocacy for libraries lies in ensuring that libraries create public value.

In her article in the November 2002 issue of *American Libraries,* Joey Rodger of the Urban Libraries Council draws a clear distinction between being an advocate and being a player. "Advocates go out into the community and say 'library, library, library'," Rodger says. "Players go out, listen, and then say 'economic development, child safety, literacy. Here's how we can help.' There's no question about who is welcome at more tables, or who is more valuable," she says.[3]

A colleague of mine likes to say that everything that libraries do is about solving problems. Individuals come to libraries not to find information, for example, but to solve some problem. That problem may be serious, like how to cope with a life-threatening disease, or how to prepare for licensure in one's occupation. Or it may be as trivial as how to waste an afternoon in pleasant relaxation. Libraries solve problems, for individuals and for communities.

The point is simple: We who love libraries and who see ourselves as library advocates do not advocate for libraries because we like libraries. We advocate for libraries because we believe in the good work that libraries do, the difference that they make in our lives and in our communities. So if we want to be successful in helping libraries achieve those goals of community service, we need to stop being perceived as advocates for libraries, and start working to be perceived as advocates for community solutions. We need to align ourselves with the agendas of our elected officials and resource allocators. Whether it is the local councilman whose primary priority is economic development, the congressperson who is most interested in workforce development in his district, or the University provost who wants to provide demonstrable measure of teaching and learning achievement on her campus, libraries can offer indispensable assistance in achieving those goals. We should strive to find the appropriate place for the library at the tables where decisions about these issues are being made.

Another way to look at this is to return to the original definition of "advocate": one who pleads the call of another. From this frame of reference, librarians (and library supporters) cannot really be library advocates, since in pleading the cause of libraries they are pleading their own cause. Perhaps what is more important, they are perceived by others as pursuing their self-interest. Instead, we need to be advocates for the priorities of our resource allocators and elected officials, and for the communities that we seek to serve.

Here are the things I think we need to do to create public value and thus become players and partners rather than advocates:

1. Focus on our distinctive competence, which is in providing the resources and services that support learners of all ages;

2. Use marketing effectively, listening to our elected officials and our communities to identify their needs, and responding in creative and innovative ways to deliver what they want and need;

3. Evaluate our services for value, and communicate effectively about the value that we provide our communities;

In short, do not be an advocate, be a player, solve problems, create value. If you do, you will find that you have gone beyond advocacy to being a partner in the political process.

Remarks of Louise Blalock

Louise Blalock implored the audience to "get out from behind your desks" and "walk the local beat" to find out what their community wants and needs. Louise quickly "bulleted" the audience with these questions:

- Is your library relevant in the face of

    ○ rapidly changing modes of learning?

    ○ rapidly changing faculty research needs and teaching strategies?

    ○ a rapidly changing student body?

    ○ rapidly changing technology?

- Are your audiences changing faster than you are?

- Are you a boomer—and they're millennials?

- Does the campus community value the library's services?

- Are the Web and increasing amounts of free scholarly material making your library obsolete?

- Are fiscal restraints making it increasingly difficult to meet rising expectations from students, faculty, and the community?

I think the reason these questions may be eating at you is because you are in the same place I found myself when I arrived in Hartford. Then, we were not engaging our users. We were serving fewer and fewer customers—with yesterday's services! But we were safe behind our desks! Where are you? Are you behind your desk? I think you need to engage every segment of your—to link their needs to your resources and expertise—developing and changing resources as you listen and learn.

When I say, YOU—I mean *all* library staff members. Involve all library staff—at all levels —from the librarians to the circulation staff. ENGAGE! Everyone needs to get face-to-face—that's where the possibility of change takes hold:

- observe

- listen actively

- learn what users need

- learn what users value

Include EVERY SEGMENT:

- students—F/T, P/T, young and old

- faculty—research and course work

- administration

- Deans

- alumni

- parents

- citizenry

As you get face-to-face and begin to respond—links occur! You want—you need —the campus community to link to the library (and don't overlook the football, basketball, swimming teams, etc.).

When the faculty and the students get your message—they spread your message. For example, we worked with neighborhood outreach workers to get people into our bilingual financial management classes. When people know and experience, firsthand, what the library provides they will be selling the library to others.

Nothing is more powerful!

Nothing has more potential for change!

In 1995, we had zero people in adult learning programs. This year, 9,753 people attended our classes, workshops, and training programs. Sure, technology drove some of the change—but the real change was people-driven!

We were out there—learning about our community—getting responsive! First of all, we did it with what we call Neighborhood Teams. More than 60% of our staff attends community meetings, such as revitalization and civic associations, to identify issues and concerns and learn about what information is needed.

Doing this kind of work is now a part of every job description at the Hartford Public Library. We also bring in community leaders to talk to our staff about current issues including homelessness, youth at risk, and housing.

To put it another way, we need to be out "walking the neighborhood like a beat cop," to get acquainted on the street, to bring ourselves face-to-face with our constituents.

We also serve other agencies and departments of governments with enthusiasm.

We make the mayor's initiatives our initiatives:

Home ownership

Early literacy

Public safety

We connect needs to existing services—and sometimes help create new services. Let me tell you what can happen when we are out there where it is actually happening. Our Youth Services Manager, for instance, a 20-year veteran librarian, attended a community meeting in one of the poorest sections of Hartford. With a long history and a historic name, Dutch Point had become simply a 50-family public housing project that was so deteriorated that it was slated for demolition. And there were no plans for rebuilding. The neighborhood was angry and frustrated because the Hartford Housing Authority said funding was only available for large-scale projects—but not their needs! The community wanted to challenge the lethargy of the Authority.

Our librarian really heard the anger and frustration and came back to the library and did the research; she discovered that the Feds did have money for small projects. This information gave the Dutch Point residents the impetus and information they needed to engage and challenge the local Housing Authority. In the end, the Hartford Housing Authority became the successful applicant for $20 million for a small-scale family housing project in the Central Library's neighborhood. And the Dutch Point people will have housing! They broke ground for the project yesterday! And our librarian was there!

Since our folks have been engaging our communities, people see the library as

• Relevant;

• Flexible;

• Respected;

• Valued; and

• And from our point of view, most important, a place to USE!!

When you are face-to-face with your community, you will learn so much about who they are and what they need and want, and you will serve them better and better.

Your services will be tailored to real interests and needs. And you will be able to more fully participate in distance learning and access to electronic resources. Also, you will be recognized by decision makers outside of your community of users, for example, by government officials, philanthropists, and other academic institutions.

In my experience at a public library, involvement at the community level does capture the attention, and often the assistance, of the decision makers and the policy makers. I believe there are similar implications and opportunities for you in the academic community. Take a first step in getting out into your communities . . . before the semester ends, attend classes for one week, find out what goes on and learn what students really need that you could provide, attend a department meeting, administrative meetings; learn to see them as your customers, even your guests—help them with grant research. Connect them to your expertise!

Let me share another story about the results of real community engagement. The children's librarian at our Mark Twain branch in the Asylum Hill section of Hartford is a tall, young man from Sierra Leone. Last year there was a resettlement of many Somalian and Liberian immigrants into his Asylum Hill community. He knows what it is like to be a stranger in a new land and not to able to speak the language. So he went to the schools to see what could be done for the immigrant kids who had been placed in the fifth grade because they are tall and of "an age" to be in the fifth grade—even though they spoke very little English and could read even less of it.

Our librarian began working with the media specialist and the teachers—and now the children come to the library after school and he reads and works with them using their common language, Pathois, to learn English.

He also goes to their homes and finds the preschoolers who are not enrolled in school because parents find it too complicated to register them. Now the parents attend ESOL classes and work with a Somalian language tutor at the library. And the library's manager for multicultural education is getting them connected—through the classes—to the preschool providers.

It's just that we need to be where they are in order to do the work:

• Obtaining relevant information for people to use,

• Connecting them to services they need, and

• Understanding their cultural background and experience.

All I can tell you is that once you get out in the community and start responding to the needs you learn about, nothing will be the same again! And that's good!!

Sure it is challenging and a bit scary. You initially feel you are giving up a lot of control, but what you get in return is opportunity after opportunity to do things that really make a positive difference, and you realize that you do have the needed information! Or that you know how to get it.

I believe that the situation you are facing is very similar to the one we in the public library system have faced and are facing. Let me leave you with one final story that is a result of the kind of outreach I am urging you to undertake.

We had learned from talking to teens that their view of the city of Hartford was a dark one. We also knew of their interest in using computers and learning new skills—teens want to learn by doing. Now the drop out rate in Hartford is horrendous!

The failure to achieve! To read! To graduate! To go on! It's an enormous concern!

But we believed that focused and sustained attention in a highly interactive program—utilizing the hook of technology and our strong connections to the neighborhoods—could make a difference. We called this project COLT, for Capital Opportunity through Technology, and also because COLT Arms Manufacturing Company became the subject matter for the project. The COLT program used state-of-the-art communications technology to have students share knowledge with peers, decision makers. and the greater community about the history of Colt Manufacturing and the history of Coltsville as a future national park. Teens loved the program!

Academic performance improved, student attendance improved, there was more participation in class discussions in school, mastery test scores are higher, and more students stayed in school. All these results have been documented. It's a story with great results, but it is FIRST and foremost about being out and about—engaged in the community! Teens helped us understand what needed to be done and how we could go about doing it.

I'd like to hear from you about what you know, because we in public libraries have a lot to learn from your experience.

You are working with the "millennials" and X, Y, and soon Z—and your experience, discoveries, and models can help us as the millennials replace the boomers as our primary customers. These new patrons were brought up on e-mail, cell phones, MP3s, and Web surfing. They collaborate more than previous generations. You can help us understand what their needs will be, how we can make them comfortable and welcome.

And, increasingly, we see ourselves as important players in the education process. As academics you only have a short time with students—to sell the product! But throughout their lifetime your students could be using academic resources—increasingly making career changes and going back to community or other colleges for new learning.

In the library we see all those single mothers in parenting classes who want to go to college for the first time. We have an opportunity to collaborate here!

- How to keep people aware of what's available in colleges

- How to support career change and life enrichment

The students you pass on will—on the strength of their positive academic library experiences—support our bond referendums and tax levies; they will bring their children to use the public library. These are the children we will pass on to you. And you will pass them back to us! Libraries are for lifelong learning and we are in this together!

And we may give them back to you in retirement! Back as elders—able, in the leisure of retirement, to learn with more vigor than ever before!

Let's stay connected! The success of each of our libraries benefits ALL libraries.

Remarks of GladysAnn Wells

GladysAnn Wells reminded us that communities "change," that they are not static demographic groups, that in less than 10 years a community may change its coloration and needs. She agreed with Louise Blaylock that the most important aspect of community building is the ability to "listen." As Arizona's state librarian she is ever mindful that there are major changes occurring as public institutions are transforming from a largely print world to a more digital one, and has never lost sight of the fact that libraries are community centers, no matter what format the information containers!

During her tenure as the director of the Arizona State Library, Archives and Public Records she has brought in more grant money than the library budget provided by the state. She has done this by making the State Library the hub of the libraries, museums, archives, and information centers for all of Arizona—including strong relationships with the academic community. She understands that servicing a diverse group of users demands a diverse approach to administering services. What works for one group won't necessarily work for another. In Arizona, libraries are well positioned to reach people of all ages and education levels.

By far one of the largest demographic cohorts in Arizona is that of older adults. It is no secret that Arizona libraries are national leaders in meeting the needs of active older adults. GladysAnn's comments follow.

Our libraries are finding innovative ways to reach the untapped resource of Baby Boomer experience while providing Boomers with connections to meaningful work and civic engagement. Model programs for lifelong learning like those listed below are starting or underway in libraries across the state. Because of our innovative library leaders, we have been cited as "Statewide Laboratory for Change."

Chandler Public Library is part of a coalition bringing all community resources together under the umbrella of one exciting boomer Web site, www.myboomerang.com—a Next Chapter project. The site provides links to resources on everything from health and wellness to re-careering and volunteering.	Phoenix Public Library has made assessing community needs and redesigning services for older adults a strategic priority. . . . It is one of the first Lifelong Access Libraries to be named a Center for Excellence and Innovation.
Glendale Public Library began "Directions & Connections: Life Options for Mature Adults" with a grant in 2004 . . . In 2005, Boomers and Seniors continue to benefit from an array of programs including those focused on their top concerns: health and financial information.	Scottsdale LifeVentures sponsored by Scottsdale Community College begins with a physical meeting space on campus—a welcoming space that will be replicated in satellites throughout the community via partners like the Scottsdale Public Library.
Mesa Life Options includes Mesa Community College, the City of Mesa and Mesa Senior Services . . . Peer Mentors in this Next Chapter project meet with people looking to retire and guide them through self discovery assessments. The, mentors will also guide people to community resources that fit their plans.	Tempe Connections is a citywide initiative to create a comprehensive one-stop resource within the library followed by satellite locations throughout the community—a Next Chapter project.

Parker Public Library earned a Community Development Block Grant for its Lifelong Learning Center. Now Parker is working with Arizona Western College to train and empower adults to research independently.	The Bonus Years: Connecting @ the Carnegie includes a core bibliography of books, articles and websites for people in transition…Managed by The Carnegie Center, a unit of the Arizona State Library, as part of a larger program for Boomers.
Arizona is one of the first states to support the national EqualAccess Libraries initiative in collaboration with Libraries for the Future, a national organization that champions the role of libraries in American life and works to strengthen libraries and library systems. Over 30 libraries across the state have participated in this program to develop libraries as centers for civic engagement. EqualAccess programs foster collaboration, outreach and use of technology to bring innovative services to Arizona communities.	Arizona has four Next Chapter projects underway: Chandler, Mesa, Scottsdale, and Tempe. The Next Chapter projects (described above) promote access to meaningful choices for work, service, learning and social connections. The premise is that these activities, and libraries, play a crucial role in the vitality of older adults and can enrich community life. They are led by Civic Ventures, a national non-profit working to expand the contributions of older Americans to society.
Libraries for the Future has worked closely with the Arizona State Library for nearly five years to bring together local leaders, library leaders and legislators as partners in crafting and implementing a vision for library programs including those with a focus on lifelong access.	Arizona is a member of the National Advisory Committee for Lifelong Access Libraries. The 25-member group includes leading gerontologists, social workers, government officials and other specialists on aging. It guides an effort to transform libraries into centers for productive aging.

It is easy to see from the list above of the various associations that Arizona Libraries has brought together to provide services to the older adults of Arizona that Arizona librarians have "gotten out from behind their desks!" And closely allied with the baby boomer issues, but also of the concern to all age groups, is health care. Here again the Arizona State Library has worked with numerous groups to so that Arizona libraries are a seminal place to get relevant information on all aspects of health care.

Arizona libraries provide the following:

Access: accessible to all ages and backgrounds, on-site or remotely; bringing communities together in rural and urban Arizona.

Trust: highly trusted & neutral, allowing partnering groups to work together on health issues/concerns.

Programs, services, and training: health literacy, evaluation, consumer health information.

Resources: diverse informational sources, no fee electronic information. Libraries provide the solution for the increased need for Health Information. Health information consumers are faced with complex and varied sources. Patients increasingly have less personalized time with medical professionals. With rapid medical advancements and informed patient requirements, it has become more and more essential to have guidance. Increased information on health related topics is available on the

Internet, but much of the information is outdated or false. Libraries provide assistance with evaluating resources and providing valid, trusted sources in a neutral environment.

Health initiatives in Arizona include the following:

• AZ Health Sciences Library; University of Arizona (http://www.ahsl.arizona.edu/)

• Library is open to everyone and all library materials and computers are available for use within the library. All Arizona library card holders can request materials at no charge through their public library. Free "Ask a Health Librarian" online resource is available. Arizona residents may purchase a library card for $60 per year.

• The U.S. National Commission on Libraries and Information Science (NCLIS) winner for the 2004 NCLIS

• Blue Ribbon Consumer Health Information Recognition Awards for Libraries. CHILE: Consumer Health Information Links for Everyone (http://www.chilehealth.org/)

• Consumer health information collaboration between Tucson-Pima Public Library and the Arizona Health Sciences Library, University of Arizona. Includes information on Diseases, Insurance, Medication, and Providers.

• Funded in part with Federal funds from the National library of Medicine, National Institutes of Health.

• EqualAccess (http://www.lff.org)

• Professional development initiative for public libraries provided by Arizona State Library, Archives and Public Records, in partnership with Libraries for the Future.

• Fifteen libraries each year are selected to participate and receive training on needs assessments, planning, programming and outreach for underserved populations.

• Get Real, Get Fit! (http://www.lff.org)

• National library-based program promoting physical fitness and healthy eating made possible by a grant from Libraries for the Future and the MetLife Foundation.

• Participating libraries include East Flagstaff Community Library, Glendale Public Library, Tempe Public Library. Health and Wellness Resource Center (http://www.peoriaaz.com/Library/library_databases_health.asp)

• Peoria Public Library's Health Information databases provide a variety of health sources online. Life Changes: The Future is Now.

• Parker Public Library's project includes computer training and consumer health classes that enable community members to independently access accurate and timely health information. Funded in part by LSTA grant.

• Operation Health Outreach

• Program developed by Glendale Public Library to raise public awareness and basic knowledge of critical health issues to minority groups. Includes free seminars, health fair, and resource collection.

- Turning Point (http://www.turningpointprogram.org)

- National Initiative to transform and strengthen the U.S. public health system; supports Public Health Information Center in libraries, health departments, and tribal centers.

- Training: Arizona Academy Without Walls trains frontline public health workers; Advocates for training in communities on health needs and participation in statewide public health planning.

And while the different groups that are served by Arizona Libraries are legion, it is important to mention that the needs of children and families are well targeted, for everyone's future depends on them. Arizona libraries provide leadership in school readiness by offering the following:

Access

○ to information about the vital role parents and childcare providers play in preparing children for school and

○ to the books that children need to have in their everyday lives.

Programs

○ that help parents and childcare providers understand their roles as children's first, most important teachers; and

○ that model best practices for parents and childcare providers through high-quality children's programming delivered by librarians knowledgeable in the pre-reading skills.

Resources for parents and childcare providers to use the strategies that they have learned to prepare their children to be successful in school.

Arizona State Library, Archives and Public Records provides the following:

- Funding from the Library Services and Technology Act administered by the Institute of Museum and Library Services.

- Training by offering workshops that help library staff members, volunteers, and their community partners develop their skills in early literacy.

- Consulting services through site visits and ongoing support by professionals knowledgeable in the areas of early literacy and library services to children and families.

Examples of the many projects being conducted throughout the state are highlighted below.

Building a New Generation of Readers (http://www.lib.az.us/extension/BuildingANewGeneration.pdf). A statewide early literacy project designed by the Arizona State Library, Building a New Generation of Readers provides public and school librarians with the tools and materials to teach parents and childcare providers strategies for preparing children to come to school ready to read.

The Arizona State Library supplies libraries with the Public Library Association's Every Child Ready to Read @ Your Library materials that are based on current federally funded research and have been evaluated and found to have significant influence on the early literacy behaviors of parents and childcare providers. Thirty-six libraries throughout the state are participating in the first year of this initiative.

Family Place (http://www.lff.org/programs/family.html)

Workshops facilitated by librarians in the 32 Arizona Family Place sites for children ages one to three and their parents and caregivers feature professionals from community agencies who provide information and answer questions informally while children and parents or caregivers interact with books and toys or work on an art project.

The Arizona State Library partners with Libraries for the Future in supporting this project. Flagstaff City-Coconino County Public Library's Literacy Begins at Home.

Workshops that included a family storytime presentation of literacy development and library services information, and the distribution of free books were held for the Early Head Start program, the Teenage Parenting program, the Mom-to-Mom Support Group, and the Healthy Families program.

Over 100 families attended workshops and an additional 119 families had literacy information and books distributed to their homes by Healthy Families family service workers. A total of over 1700 children's books of varying age and reading levels were distributed to families during the 2003-2004 grant period. La Paz County Libraries' Healthy Babies/Healthy Readers.

New parents, grandparents, and daycare providers who visited the La Paz County Health Department, WIC program, and Indian Health Services Hospital were given a goodie bag containing a baby picture frame magnet with library hours, a bookmark, and information about library services in La Paz County to encourage them to begin reading to the babies in their care.

During the 2003–2004 grant period, 500 parents, grandparents, or guardians, brought the coupon from their bag to a La Paz County library or its bookmobile to trade for a free board book. Tucson-Pima Public Library's Ready to Read.

Partnering with Child and Family Resources, the library trained 43 in-home childcare providers during 2003–2004 in early brain development as it relates to early literacy and pre-reading.

For the last class session, families attended. Storytimes were held, and information was given to parents.

Transformation of Libraries

Libraries not only are shifting from print to digital, but they are also moving from ownership to leasing the resources that they offer. As libraries change to serve the needs of a rapidly changing world society, we will perforce have to get "out from behind our desks" and "walk the beat" and know and be known by our diverse constituents, including our "resource allocators," to quote Bob Martin. As information technology evolves, we will have to assist our constituents to understand it, use it, and grow with it. We are the guides on the side!

While services such as coffee cafes, computer access, and collaborative environments often lead the list of new enticements offered by libraries, it is the library as "place," as "community," as "information haven" that keeps the "guests" returning.

Welcome to the new/old library!

Notes

1. Steve Jones, *The Internet Goes to College: How Students Are Living in the Future with Today's Technology* (Washington D.C.: Pew Internet & American Life Project, 2002). Available at www.pewinternet.org/reports/pdfs/PIP_College_Reprts.pdf.

2. E. J. Rodger, "Value & Vision." *American Libraries* 33, no.10 (November 2002): 50–52.

3. John Cotton Dana, *The New Museum: Selected Writings by John Cotton Dana,* edited by William A. Penniston (Newark, NJ: The Newark Museum Association; Washington, DC: American Association of Museums, 1999).

Index